WHO WAS JESUS?

WHO WAS JESUS?

A CRITIQUE OF THE NEW TESTAMENT RECORD

G. A. WELLS

Open  Court

La Salle, Illinois

OPEN COURT and the above logo are registered in the U.S. Patent and Trademark Office.

© 1989 by Open Court Publishing Company

First printing 1989

Printed and bound in the United States of America.

Library of Congress Cataloging-in-Publication Data

Wells, George Albert, 1926–
    Who was Jesus?: a critique of the New Testament record/G. A. Wells.
        p.   cm.
    Includes index.
    ISBN 0-8126-9095-8. – ISBN 0-8126-9096-6 (pbk.)
    1. Jesus Christ – Rationalistic interpretations.   2. Jesus Christ – Historicity.   3. Jesus Christ – History of doctrines – Early church, ca. 30-600.   4. Bible.   N.T. – Criticism, interpretation, etc.
    I. Title.
    BT304.95.W45   1989
    225.6′7 – dc20
                                                                    89-3285
                                                                    CIP

CONTENTS

A NOTE ON QUOTATIONS AND ABBREVIATIONS

Scripture quotations are (except where otherwise indicated) from the Revised Version (which I call RV), published 1881–85, of the Authorised Version or King James Bible of 1611 (which I call AV). Other English versions are referred to as follows:

NEB   *The New English Bible*, copyright of Oxford and Cambridge University Presses.

RSV   *The Revised Standard Version*, copyright of the Division of Christian Education, National Council of the Churches of Christ in the United States.

I use the terms Matthew, Mark, etc., sometimes to designate the author of the relevant gospel and sometimes to designate that gospel itself. Which meaning is intended will be clear from the context.

My three earlier books on Christian origins are designated as follows:

JEC   *The Jesus of the Early Christians*, London: Pemberton, 1971.

HEJ   *The Historical Evidence for Jesus*, Buffalo: Prometheus, 1982.

DJE   *Did Jesus Exist?*, 2nd edition, London: Pemberton, 1986.

The following abbreviations denote frequently-cited works:

Beare   Francis W. Beare, *The Gospel According to Matthew*, Oxford: Blackwell, 1981.

Brown   Raymond E. Brown, *The Birth of the Messiah. A Commentary on the Infancy Narratives in Matthew and Luke*, Image Books edition, Garden City, NY: Doubleday, 1979.

Burger   Christoph Burger, *Jesus als Davidssohn*, Göttingen: Vandenhoeck and Ruprecht, 1970.

Creed   John M. Creed, *The Gospel According to St. Luke*, London and New York: Macmillan, 1930 (many later reprints).

Elliott	J. K. Elliott, *Questioning Christian Origins*, London: SCM, 1982.
Evans	C. F. Evans, *Resurrection and the New Testament*, London: SCM, 1970.
Fitzmyer	Joseph A. Fitzmyer, *The Gospel According to Luke* (Anchor Bible Series), 2nd edition, Garden City, NY: Doubleday, 1986 (vol. 1 is quoted, unless vol. 2 is indicated).
Fuller	Reginald H. Fuller, *The Formation of the Resurrection Narratives*, London: SPCK, 1972.
Haenchen	Ernst Haenchen, *Der Weg Jesu. Eine Erklärung des Markus-Evangeliums und der kanonischen Parallelen*, 2nd edition, Berlin: De Gruyter, 1968.
Hooker	Morna Hooker, *The Message of Mark*, London: Epworth Press, 1983.
Lampe	*The Resurrection, A Dialogue Arising from Broadcasts by G. W. H. Lampe and D. M. Mackinnon*, ed. W. Purcell, London: Mowbray, 1966.
Nineham	D. E. Nineham, *The Gospel of St. Mark* (Pelican New Testament Commentaries), Harmondsworth: Penguin, 1963 or later reprint.
Schürer	Emil Schürer, *The History of the Jewish People in the Age of Jesus Christ*, New English version revised and edited by Geza Vermes and Fergus Millar, Edinburgh: T. & T. Clark. Volume 1 (1973) is quoted unless another volume is indicated. Volume 2 appeared in 1979, and volume 3 (in two parts, with continuous pagination) in 1986 and 1987.
Scobie	Charles H. H. Scobie, *John the Baptist*, London: SCM, 1964.

Von Campenhausen   Hans von Campenhausen, *The Virgin Birth in the Theology of the Ancient Church*, English translation from the German edition of 1962, London: SCM, 1964.

Wink   Walter Wink, *John the Baptist in the Gospel Tradition*, Cambridge University Press, 1968.

In each of my chapters, once details of a work have been given in a note, further references to it are given simply as page references in the text or notes of that chapter.

Introduction

Serious criticism of the New Testament began to be common in Protestant theological faculties of German Universities from the end of the eighteenth century, and there are good reasons for their remarkable candour. First, political disunity entailed many universities, all independent of any central authority, whereas in England at that time the only two universities were controlled by the established Church. Second, the arguments of these innovating theologians were tolerated so long as they remained learned discussions which did not reach the populace at large. And third, the theologians themselves were apt to claim that their criticism of events central to the traditional faith, such as the virgin birth and the Resurrection, did not impugn the religious value of these doctrines, which was to be defended on philosophical, not historical grounds. Hence it was with every justification that Schopenhauer characterized this period of German cultural history as one of "sceptical theologians and orthodox philosophers".[1]

Catholic theologians have been slow to follow the lead of their Protestant colleagues. Today they are allowed considerable freedom by the Roman Pontifical Biblical Commission, but this is a very recent development, and as Brown — himself a Catholic priest — has noted (p. 9) "historical criticism of the New Testament is relatively new on the Catholic scene". It seems that the scholarly elements in the Roman Church, fretting because the Papal condemnation of 'modernism' early this century restricted them to uncritical piety, have become powerful enough to effect their own unleashing.[2]

Catholics still insist on 'Biblical Inspiration', but allow that the inspired truth may in certain cases be not 'literal' but 'poetic', and may even vary with the literary form of the relevant canonical document. In this sense Fitzmyer speaks (p. 18) of "poetic truth, rhetorical truth, parabolic truth, epistolary truth". He adds that not every affirmation in the past tense in a Biblical narrative is necessarily meant to be "historical", but may to some extent be "metaphorical or symbolic".

Likewise, Brown says that "it is now clear in Roman Catholic thought that inspiration of the Scriptures does not guarantee historicity", and that there is no reason why a Catholic should not regard a gospel passage as a product of the evangelist's "creative imagination" so long as he or she does not deny the "theological truths" it contains (p. 245n.). The usefulness to apologists of this doctrine of different forms of truth derives from the fact that these are not required to be compatible: what is false as history or science may, it is held, be true as theology. In this sense Brown, although he demonstrates conclusively that the canonical narratives of Jesus's birth and infancy are not the literal truth for which they have been taught for hundreds of years, nonetheless insists that they are "worthy vehicles of the gospel message" (p. 8). One of his reviewers is quoted by his publisher as finding that he has redressed the error of a rationalism that was too blind to recognize their "theological significance". So now we know that, although they are factually untrue, they have an important theological message, and there must be no more of what Brown calls "rationalistic scoffing" (p. 25). As we shall see, both he and Fitzmyer, having thus assured themselves of this escape route, proceed to talk a great deal of sense about the New Testament. And for this we can be grateful.

There has, then, been what a theologian has recently termed "a certain necessary dismantling of the Christian edifice of the past".[3] (The metaphor is ill-chosen, as the actual buildings dedicated to Christianity have proved more durable than any Christian doctrine). But contemporaneous with such critical work from Christian scholars, there is today a resurgence of Fundamentalist and ultra-conservative belief, backed by scholarship of like kind. When I refer, as I frequently do, to 'conservative' apologists, I remain aware that any scholar may be conservative on some religious issues but not on others. The term is nevertheless a useful means of distinguishing commentators who are in general inclined to support doctrines enshrined in traditional Christian creeds from their more radical colleagues. Such conservatives have become alarmed at the gap which biblical criticism has created between many theologians and ordinary believers. Thus William Oddie, introducing a volume of essays entitled *After the Deluge* (London: SPCK, 1987) which aim at "desecularizing" the Church, complains that "many if not most of those charged with the leadership of Western Christendom are remote from the beliefs and assumptions of those who look to them for spiritual sustenance" (pp. 1, 24). "The authority of Scripture", he says, "has never been in any serious doubt until the present age" (p. 32). The standpoint he advocates is not that based on mere empirical facts but "the absolute judgement of a God-centred perspective" (p. 29). In his view, man's "unaided observation and reason" will not tell him the truths about himself and his place in the universe (p. 25). Of course, the doctrine that there are other sources of knowledge than honest investigation is about as old as human speculation, and still nearly universally believed. For Oddie, faith is to be seen, with Augustine, as inquiry's proper starting point (p. 9), and reason is to be made "subject to the authority of the Christian revelation" (p. 32). He strongly recommends Professor Wayne Hankey's essay in the volume, where "the tradition of the Fathers and mediaeval doctors" is said to be "an excellent place to start the recovery of a genuinely Christian biblical interpretation" (p. 82). Such authorities held that "the traditional doctrine of the Church" both derives from Scripture and itself makes Scripture intelligible; and according to both Oddie and Hankey, this reciprocity "is necessary if both Scripture and Church are the work of the Holy Spirit" (pp. 39, 49). Oddie's sugges-tion — breathtaking in its impudence — is that the critical scholarship of the past two hundred years in abandoning this standpoint has come to consist of inferences from questionable assumptions which are bigotedly accepted as "infallible" (p. 24). It is my purpose to show that the bigotry does not lie on that side of the fence.

I have taken up Jesus's story at its end in chapter 2 for the reason that Christianity, from its inception, has attached more importance to his Resurrection than to the events of his life. His nativity occupies me next as an example of how far fanciful imaginings could go even within traditions that came to be accepted as canonical. This third chapter is an updated version of the account I gave in JEC at a time when Catholic scholars were still committed to the historicity of the infancy narratives. There follow two chapers on Jesus's adult life, at the outset and at the end of his public ministry. The ministry itself, with its manifold miracles and controversies with persons of other persuasions, is frequently mentioned throughout the book, and I have not found it necessary to devote a chapter specifically to it. Its ethical teachings I have discussed elsewhere, and they have recently been searchingly criticized in a symposium entitled *Biblical v. Secular Ethics* (Buffalo: Prometheus, 1988), which includes contributions on 'The Moral Rhetoric of the Gospels' by one of the editors, R. J. Hoff-mann, and on slavery by Morton Smith. My final chapter gives a detailed account of the two Biblical apocalypses—the book of Daniel in the Old Testament and the book of Revelation in the New. These have worked more mischief among the Christian fringe over the ages than all the remaining Biblical books together.

After all this, we may ask, as so much of the New Testament evidence has proved both unreliable and inconsistent, whether we may reasonably doubt that Jesus is really any more than a legendary figure. My reader may find this a startling suggestion. What he is less likely to impugn is my evidence that, even in New Testament times, a welter of incompatible traditions were created and manipulated very differently by different Christian groups. This has long been clear to critical theologians, for whom Hartwig Thyen speaks, saying:

> There never was any such thing as a *single* primitive Christianity, *the* original confession, or *the* primitive Christology, on the basis of which we might be able to judge every development as either a justifiable or heretical elaboration of the *one* legitimate beginning . . . The single Credo of the church arises, not out of the deliberate elaboration of the one true origin, but out of the critical (and thus, of course, also tendentious) simplifying of the original diversity.[4]

Each of the four canonical evangelists has no hesitation in making Jesus say and do what is in fact representative of that evangelist's own theology, which is different again from early Christian theologies represented in the New Testament epistles. One may not unreasonably ask where all this leaves the historical Jesus.[5]

THE RELIABILITY OF THE GOSPELS

i. INTRODUCTION

It was what the Toronto theologian F. W. Beare calls "second-century guesses" that gave the four canonical gospels the names by which we now know them; for they were originally "anonymous documents" of whose authors "nothing is known".[1] Even as they now stand, there is nothing within them to indicate who their authors are, and to this the fourth gospel is, as we shall see, only apparently an exception. The earliest Fathers allude to and quote them without ascribing them to named authors. Justin Martyr, for instance, was, about AD 150, well acquainted with at any rate the first three of them, but does not name them. However, once Christian communities had come to acquire more than one gospel, it was natural that they should give them titles as a means of distinguishing them.[2] It was equally natural that these titles should not be colourless (such as 'document A' and 'document B') but ascriptions to persons believed to have been companions of Jesus, or at any rate of the earliest apostles. And so we find Irenaeus (bishop of Lyons about AD 180) naming all four as they are now named, and as the first to do so. R. T. France, who allows that "the headings 'According to Matthew', 'According to Mark' etc., are not part of the text of the gospels", adds that they "are generally believed to have been added early in the second century".[3] The evidence I have given hardly supports the word 'early'.

The earliest extant gospel is Mark's, used as a source by Matthew and Luke, each of whom was unacquainted with the other's work. Their two gospels are thus reworkings of a Greek gospel of a non-disciple. The fourth gospel, ascribed to John, is independent of the others, but clearly used sources which were in part identical with theirs. These statements oversimplify a complicated problem in that the exact relation of the gospels to each other defies final solution because of lack of evidence;[4] but what I have stated to be the case on the matter has justified itself by its utility as a hypothesis which has enabled commentators to make sense of the differences and similarities between the individual gospels.

That all four gospels were written between the commencement of the Jewish War with Rome in AD 66 and the end of the first century is what France calls "by far the majority view in twentieth-century scholarship" (p. 118). Many scholars, however, are prepared to allow a somewhat later dating for the fourth gospel, which Barrett calls a "quite credible product of any date between 90 and 140".[5] Luke obviously wrote some good time after AD 70, for he rewrote Mark's thirteenth chapter so as to give specific reference to the destruction of Jerusalem which occurred in that year, and also so as to avoid implying that it presaged the end of the world: Jerusalem is to remain in gentile hands "until the times of the gentiles be fulfilled" (Luke 21:24).[6] Fitzmyer concedes that "Luke has modifed his Marcan source in the light of what little he knew about the destruction of Jerusalem by the Romans" (p. 54). Matthew also alludes to this event in an insertion into the parable of the great supper (cf. HEJ, pp. 122–23) and, as Beare notes in his commentary (p. 7), a post-AD 70 date of composition for this gospel is generally agreed.

France is anxious to date all four gospels much earlier, so that they become (p. 124) "the earliest records of Jesus which have survived" (against the majority view that the Pauline, and also some other canonical epistles are of earlier date). He finds that the late J. A. T. Robinson has given a good lead in this direction, but that the prejudices of "most established scholars" prevent them from following it (pp. 120–21) — as if the majority of Christian theologians for some reason are obstinately determined to hold fast to ideas which have proved so subversive of Christian faith. France's fellow-theologian Kee has justly said that the proposals of Robinson and others to date the gospels before AD 50 "rest on a blend of wishful thinking and scholarly games".[7]

One reason for such 'wishful thinking' is that those of the canonical epistles which the majority of scholars date earlier than the gospels do not corroborate the gospels' portraits of Jesus. These epistles know him only as a supernatural personage who adopted human flesh to come to Earth in unspecified circumstances at an unspecified time in the past, who was crucified there in obscure circumstances and then was raised from the dead and returned to heaven. Paul, for instance, characteristically writes of

> Christ Jesus who, being in the form of God . . . emptied himself, taking the form of a servant, being made in the likeness of men; and being

found in fashion as a man, he humbled himself, becoming obedient even unto death, yea the death of the cross. Wherefore also God highly exalted him . . . . (Philippians 2:5–9).

Again, Paul elsewhere refers to Jesus as "the image of the invisible God, the firstborn of all creation; for in him were all things created, in the heavens and upon the earth . . . " (Colossians 1:15–16). Such a description does not suggest a familiar or recent historical personage.

The genuine Pauline letters do not include all the epistles bearing his name in the Bible, but only Romans, 1 and 2 Corinthians, Galatians, 1 Thessalonians and possibly also Colossians. These were certainly written before the Christian community at Jerusalem experienced the disruption and worse of AD 70, for their author was having sharp disagreements with the leaders of this community as to whether gentile Christians need to keep the Jewish law. By the time Mark's gospel, the earliest extant, was written, their freedom from this law was established and taken for granted. If, as seems likely, Mark wrote after AD 70, the destruction of Jerusalem will have made it almost impossible for him to have had, from his non-Palestinian and gentile orientation, accurate views of earlier events there. The community for which he wrote was certainly unacquainted with Jewish practices, for he has laboriously to explain them, or what he took for them (for example at 7:3–4).[8] And he himself betrays an ignorance of Palestinian geography hardly compatible with any real knowledge of that country.[9]

If Paul were the only pre-gospel Christian writer who failed to confirm the record of the gospels, one could perhaps dismiss him as an unhelpful mystic. But one finds that other early Christian documents write of Jesus in the same manner. These include the pseudo-Paulines 2 Thessalonians and Ephesians (ascribed to Paul, but actually written by another author at a later date), and also the letter to the Hebrews and 1 Peter. All these letters know Jesus only as someone crucified (and subsequently risen) in unspecified circumstances some time in the past, and they know Christians only as groups much given to quarrelling among themselves about their relation to Judaism and/or about the ontological status of Jesus (his relation to other supernatural powers, good and evil), but not as followers of a recently deceased teacher and wonder-worker.

ii. THE GOSPEL OF LUKE AND THE ACTS OF THE APOSTLES

The claim is frequently made that the gospels were written by eyewitnesses of the events described, or at any rate are based on eyewitness accounts, and the opening verses of Luke's gospel are often adduced in support. We read there that "the eyewitnesses and ministers of the word" (this latter phrase means 'preachers') reported "to us", i.e., to Christians (verse 2), the events which "have been accomplished among us" (verse 1), whereupon "many" (not alleged to have been eyewitnesses) undertook to record them in writing.[10] The original followers of Jesus thus wrote nothing down but merely preached. The author owns that he himself is writing even later than the 'many' who first made a written record, but he claims — I translate the Greek here literally — to have "followed all things accurately from the beginning". 'Followed' cannot be taken to mean 'participated in' (thus making the author a companion of Jesus), for one cannot participate in events 'accurately'. One can follow them accurately only in the sense of investigating them thoroughly, and the author is claiming no more than to have made a proper scrutiny of what his sources say about the relevant events from their inception onwards. Hence the RV renders the passage as: "Having traced the course of all things accurately from the first". As Fitzmyer concedes (p. 289), "Luke writes as a third-generation Christian". Only one of his sources is now extant, namely the gospel ascribed to Mark; and if Luke had really regarded it as reliably based he would not have contradicted it as freely as we shall see he in fact does.

It is universally agreed that the gospel of Luke and the Acts of the Apostles were written by the same author. Acts details the missionary travels of St. Paul and was long supposed to have been written by a companion of him. From this premiss, Sir William Ramsay began his book St. Paul the Traveller (1895) by declaring Luke to be as reliable a historian as Thucydides. That he was a companion of Paul has been argued because of references in Acts to 'we' or 'us', meaning Paul and his companions. Many theologians do not accept this interpretation of the 'we' passages,[11] and in any case a linkage between Paul and Luke is out of the question, as what is said of Paul in Acts is quite incompatible with what he himself says in his epistles in circumstances where he has no motive for dissembling (cf. HEJ, p. 9). As the theologian Vielhauer said in 1950, there are "crass contradictions" between these two sources which "concern both historical fact and theological doctrine".[12] I have gone into all this in chapter 7 of my HEJ, and although I am trying here to do more than merely appeal to authorities, I would note that Mattill concludes his survey of the relevant evidence by saying that the dominant view today, and the one which "has succeeded in putting the burden of proof on others", is that the historical Paul of the authentic epistles is quite different from "the legendary Paul of Acts".[13] On the Catholic side, Brown agrees that "the distance of Luke/Acts from Pauline thought makes it unlikely that a direct disciple of Paul wrote those works".[14]

Evangelical writers still argue that — I quote Miethe as typical of them — since Luke/Acts have been found to be "reliable historical accounts . . . about methods of travel, about the time it took to travel from place to place", it is quite unreasonable "immediately to rule them out when they talk about something 'spiritual' ".[15] So if I write a story in which a man travels from one place to another in a plausible number of hours and by a feasible method of transport, I am to be believed if I say that persons who, on the way, touched his handkerchief were cured of disease (Acts 19:11–12). Miethe also claimed that, according to "the testimony of scholars throughout the . . . world", Luke/Acts offers reliable information about "what was happening politically". In actual fact their author is in such complete confusion over the chronology of events that occurred in Palestine in the first half of the first century as to suggest that he was not close in time or place to them.

Let me give examples. In Acts 5, where the scene is Jerusalem about the mid-30s AD, Gamaliel reviews bygone Messianic risings and mentions that of Theudas. But we know from the Jewish historian Flavius Josephus (who lived in this first century AD) that Theudas's Messianic promises were made when Fadus was procurator (AD 44–46) and so could not have been known to Gamaliel at the time when he is represented as speaking. So conservative a Christian as F. F. Bruce does not think that Josephus had got the date wrong, but supposes instead that there was another Theudas, who did much the same as the one in Josephus, but a few decades earlier.[16] Gamaliel continues by saying that *after* Theudas there was a Messianic rising under Judas the Galilean at the time of the census. Luke knows of only one census, that under Quirinius (Luke 2:1–2) of AD 6 — forty years *before* Theudas. As we shall see, in his gospel Luke compounds the muddle by dating this census of AD 6 under Herod, who died in 4 BC. Fitzmyer concedes that such errors in the dating of Palestinian events of the first half of the first century show that "on many of these issues Luke's information was not the best" (p. 15).

iii. THE FOURTH GOSPEL

The gospel ascribed to John is the most disputed of the four, so obviously is it incompatible with the other three — "startlingly different" from them "in its presentation of Jesus", in Brown's formulation.[17] Of the 93 sections into which this gospel can be divided, only 25 have parallels in the other three, and many of these parallels are far from close. Exorcisms, so prominent in Mark, are entirely lacking. All John's healing stories are without clear parallel in Mark, and the only healing narrative John shares with other gospels is the story of the ruler's son (absent from Mark, but recorded at Matthew 8:5-13 and Luke 7:1-10). Whereas in Mark Jesus orders silence concerning his miracles, in John he demands belief in his august status on their account. They "manifest his glory" (John 2:11). His sayings are also very different in John: He does not proclaim the coming kingdom, but his own importance, and he speaks no parables.[18]

Brown distinguishes five stages in the composition of the fourth gospel. First, he says, there existed "a body of traditional material pertaining to the words and works of Jesus", similar to what has gone into the other three gospels but independent of it. (Hence the great divergence between John and them). This material was then developed in accordance with the theology of a particular Christian community (which for convenience can be called the Johannine community); then it was organized into a consecutive gospel, which the author later secondarily edited. The fifth and final stage was an "editing or redaction" by someone else which included the addition of chapter 21. John the son of Zebedee was "probably" the source of the material constituting stage 1: but as the gospel represents tradition that has gone through so much development, Brown allows that we cannot say for certain that any of it goes back to an eyewitness, although he is impressed by the testimony of second-century Fathers that this is the case, and by the gospel's own claim in two passages (John 19:35 and 21:24) to this effect. On his own showing, however, neither of these passages can carry much weight; for, as we saw, he endorses the (very widely accepted) view that the whole of chapter 21 is an addition to the gospel and belongs to the final redaction by

another hand; and 19:35 he regards as "a parenthesis, probably added in the editing of the Gospel".[19] Even so, he adds, the attribution of
the gospel tradition to an eyewitness disciple "would seem to represent the view prevalent in Johannine circles at the end of the first century". What was believed by Christians at that time about the origin
of the material is hardly conclusive evidence as to its true origin.

If Brown here in effect concedes that the evidence within the
gospel is indecisive, in a work of some ten years later he surrenders
the external evidence, the testimony of early Fathers, saying:

> Second-century information about the origins of the Gospels (often
> reflecting scholarly guesses of that period) has not held up well in
> modern scholarship . . . . There is a set tendency in the second-century
> information to oversimplify the directness of the connection between
> the evangelists and the eyewitnesses.

He adds that he no longer believes that anything in the fourth gospel
goes back to "one of the Twelve, John son of Zebedee", although he
holds to the view that the person called "the beloved disciple" in it
was "a companion of Jesus".[20]

Many scholars disagree with this estimate of the beloved disciple,
for the following reasons. The fourth gospel is anonymous up to the
end of its chapter 20, which is clearly meant as a solemn conclusion.
Only the appended chapter 21 identifies the author as "the beloved
disciple", and only the fourth gospel mentions such a person, making
him figure in three incidents in earlier chapters: the last supper, the
crucifixion, and the discovery of the empty tomb. The intention of
chapter 21 in ascribing the whole gospel to this allegedly close friend
of Jesus is to represent it as the writing of an eyewitness. But this suggestion carries no weight, not only because it occurs in an appended
chapter, but also because all three incidents where the beloved disciple figures in the fourth gospel have parallels in the other three where
he plays no part. The reasonable inference is that, at these points, the
fourth gospel drew on source material similar to that which underlies
the other three, but reworked it so as to introduce the beloved disciple.[21]

iv. THE GOSPEL OF MARK AND THE
MESSIANIC SECRET

What Brown has called the "set tendency" of second-century Christians to link the evangelists with eyewitnesses is very evident in the

case of Mark, the earliest surviving gospel, ascribed by the Fathers to a Mark who drew his information from the Peter who, according to all four gospels, had accompanied Jesus. For Brown this is again a "highly unlikely" hypothesis because of the attitude to Peter in this gospel.[22] The hypothesis seems to have resulted from uncritical harmonization. Once the gospel had come to be ascribed to someone named Mark—as Nineham notes, "the commonest Latin name in the Roman Empire"—readers of the first epistle of Peter, whose author introduces himself as "Peter, an apostle of Jesus Christ", would note the affectionate reference in it to "my son Mark" (5:13) and identify this person with the evangelist; for, as Nineham says, the early Church was "in the habit of assuming that all occurrences of a given name in the New Testament referred to a single individual" (p. 39). Today, however, most scholars agree with Kümmel that there are "decisive arguments" for regarding the epistle as "undoubtedly a pseudonymous writing" of about AD 90—barely within the possible life-span of the apostle Peter—showing no acquaintance with the substance of the gospel.[23]

Mark's gospel is not an account of Jesus's life such as a biographer (whether or not a personal acquaintance) would write. As Nineham says, it "consists of a number of unrelated paragraphs set down one after another with very little organic connexion, almost like a series of snapshots placed side by side in a photograph album". The evangelist has sometimes tried to link these paragraphs by composing a short phrase between them, "but essentially each one is an independent unit, complete in itself, undatable except by its contents, and usually devoid of any allusion to place" (pp. 27–28). Many theologians have come to realize that the reason for this is that Mark's material, as it reached him, was community tradition—fragments, oral and written, which had been used in the teaching and preaching of the church, handed on from preacher to preacher and consisting of stories about Jesus deemed of doctrinal importance. When these stories do include a reference to a specific time or place—to, for instance, the sabbath, the night, the mountain, the sea or the temple—it serves "a *practical* purpose", that is, "it is necessary for the full understanding of the contents of the paragraph" (p. 28n.). Nineham adds that all this is exemplified in Mark's third chapter, where "the successive paragraphs are so essentially separate that their order could easily be interchanged without doing any violence to the chapter as a whole".

The attempt to trace each gospel paragraph or 'pericope' (a Greek word meaning 'section') to one or other of the literary forms to which preachers would naturally resort (e.g. parables or miracle stories or stories inculcating some moral point) is known as *form-criticism*. If the tradition prior to Mark was formed in accordance with what Nineham calls "practical religious considerations", the same is true of the way all four evangelists handled it. What is called *redaction criticism* tries to ascertain what aims and presuppositions guided the redactor or editor who brought the individual units of tradition together to form a gospel, or who redacted a gospel compiled from such units by a predecessor. Each gospel, says Nineham, "was produced to meet some specific practical and religious needs in the church of its origin" (p. 29). This does not inspire confidence in its trustworthiness. The early preachers may well have shaped their material to fit their sermons — we have no information concerning their scrupulousness — and Mark may equally well have modified and embellished what he derived from them. Indeed, if he treated his predecessors as he himself was later to be treated by Matthew and Luke, this will certainly have happened.

Many Christians are glad to set aside, as Mark's own editorial interpretation, the statement he puts into Jesus's mouth that the purpose of his parables is to *conceal* the truth from the generality of people and so prevent all but an elect from being saved. In this sense he tells his disciples

> Unto you is given the mystery of the kingdom of God: but unto them that are without all things are done in parables: that seeing they may see and not perceive; and hearing they may hear and not understand: lest haply they should turn again, and it should be forgiven them (Mark 4:11–12).

This distinction is reiterated at 4:33–34, where we learn that he addressed the people exclusively in parables, "but privately to his own disciples he expounded all things." It has often been thought incredible that Mark could really have believed that the purpose of the parables was to conceal the truth and prevent repentance, but "other explanations of 4:12 are unconvincing" (Hooker, p. 27). The doctrine expressed there is the predestinarian one (familiar from Romans 9:18) that it is God's will to reveal saving knowledge to some but to hide it from others. This distinction is repeated in the ethically apparently so offensive passage "for he that hath, to him shall be given: and he that hath not, from him shall be taken away even that which he hath" (Mark 4:25). The meaning is that the elect are to be given progressively more insight, that all that is secret shall come to light, but only for those with ears to hear (verses 21–24).

That Mark has here accurately reported Jesus's teaching is very difficult to credit; for this parable-secret or teaching-secret is correlated with Jesus's repeated injunctions in the same gospel that his identity as Messiah, and his miracles which show him to be the Messiah, be kept secret. "The unclean spirits, whensoever they beheld him, fell down before him, and cried, saying, Thou art the Son of God. And he charged them much that they should not make him known" (3:11–12). We cannot readily believe that it is historically true that he encountered such evil spirits who, thanks to their supernatural knowledge, realised who he was; and if we abandon this position, we must also give up the authenticity of his commands to them to be silent about his status. Hooker concedes that "there is something artificial about these commands to secrecy" (p. 53). Some of his miracles are so public that his injunction to the witnesses not to tell of them could scarcely have kept them secret. Having, for instance, raised Jairus's daughter from the dead, "he charged them much that no man should know this" (5:43), even though her death had already become public knowledge (verses 35 and 39). The point Mark is nevertheless making is that the crowds, although amazed at Jesus's powers, do not realise that they show him to be the Messiah. Only supernatural beings and his closest disciples achieve this insight. Peter, for instance, roundly declares him to be "the Christ" (8:29), and Jesus tells both the disciples (8:30; 9:9) and the 'unclean spirits' not to pass such information on. That we are here dealing with a doctrinal factor governing the whole gospel, and not with eyewitness reportage, is strongly suggested by the absence of this 'Messianic secret' from the other gospels where onlookers frequently respond to miracles by bestowing exalted titles on the miracle-worker. As Watson notes, there is no such titular acclamation in the Marcan parallels to such passages, nor in any other Marcan miracle stories; and he adds that, unless these miracle stories are nevertheless intended by Mark to prove to his readers his claim that Jesus is the Christ and "the son of God" (1:1) — in the face of the apparent contradiction of this status posed by the crucifixion — it is hard to see why the evangelist has made so much of them; for they "form a higher proportion of Mark's material than the material of the other evangelists."[24]

Watson argues that the Messianic secret originated in the needs of the Christian community for which Mark wrote his gospel — a community which was experiencing, or at any rate, expecting persecution, and which required assurance that it was God's will that the majority of mankind should be as uncomprehending and as hostile towards Christianity as was in fact the case. The Marcan Jesus says that those who have abandoned everything "for my sake and for the gospel" must expect "persecutions" (10:29–30), and that his disciples "shall be hated of all men for my name's sake" (13:13); each of them must "take up his cross and follow me" and not repudiate him for the sake of escaping persecution (8:34–38), as some of them will nevertheless do (4:17). But these disciples are not, in the sequel, persecuted, and in stressing the theme of imitation of Jesus's sufferings, Mark is therefore not motivated by historical interest, but by the situation of the Christian community for which he wrote. In sum, "the doctrine of predestination expressed in Mark's secrecy theme . . . reinforces the community's sense of eliteness by attributing its separation from society to the saving activity of God", and "it explains the potentially threatening fact of the unbelief of the majority as being itself the result of divine activity. Mark sought by means of the secrecy theme to increase the confidence, cohesion and self-esteem of the group in the face of society's hostility" (p. 63).

V. THE QUESTION OF MIRACLES

The classic essay of T. H. Huxley amply illustrates that there are plenty of miracles in which no one now believes which are much better attested than those of Jesus. Huxley discusses the writings of Einhard (a historian of intelligence and character at the court of Charlemagne) who about AD 830 reported numerous miracles from either first- or second-hand knowledge: for instance, a demon had taken possession of a girl and speaking through her mouth in Latin to an exorcising priest, named himself "Wiggo". After the priest had cast him out, the girl could speak no more Latin, but only her own tongue. Huxley comments:

> If you do not believe in these miracles, recounted by a witness whose character and competency are firmly established, whose sincerity cannot be doubted, and who appeals to his sovereign and other contemporaries as witnesses of the truth of what he says, . . . why do you profess to believe in stories of a like character which are found in

documents of the dates and of the authorship of which nothing is certainly determined . . . ? If it be true that the four Gospels and Acts were written by Matthew, Mark, Luke and John, all that we know of these authors comes to nothing in comparison with our knowledge of Einhard . . . If, therefore, you refuse to believe that 'Wiggo' was cast out of the possessed girl on Einhard's authority, with what justice can you profess to believe that the legion of devils were cast out of a man among the tombs of the Gadarenes? [Mark 5:1–20 and parallel passages in Matthew and Luke] . . . . It cannot be pretended . . . that the Jews of the year 30 AD, or thereabouts, were less imbued with the belief in the supernatural than were the Franks of the year 800 AD. The same influences were at work in each case, and it is only reasonable to suppose that the results are the same.

And so, "where the miraculous is concerned, neither considerable intellectual ability, nor undoubted honesty, nor knowledge of the world, nor proved faithfulness as civil historians, nor profound piety, on the part of eyewitnesses and contemporaries, affords any guarantee of the objective truth of their statements when we know that a firm belief in the miraculous was ingrained in their minds and was the presupposition of their observations and reasoning".[25]

It is understandable that by the time the gospels were written, miracles had come to be attributed to Jesus. According to Jewish tradition, demonic power was to be crushed in the Messianic age, and Mark's miracle stories, where Jesus casts out demons from persons in whom they had lodged, were told—I quote the theologian Howard Kee—"in a community in which Jesus is regarded as an agent who has come in the end of time to defeat the powers of Satan".[26] Paul, however, the earliest Christian whose writings are extant, took a quite different view and held that Jesus had vanquished these powers not by standing up to them openly with miraculous displays of supernatural strength, but by submitting to a shameful death at their instigation, only to rise again in triumph over them (see HEJ, pp. 34–35).

As I have already intimated, if we wish to find out what the earliest Christians believed about Jesus, it is essential to study the extant documents in the order in which they were written, not in the order in which they are printed in Bibles, where the gospels are placed first. The earliest documents are those of the letters ascribed to Paul which were genuinely written by him, followed only a little later by four from other hands (all listed above, p. 7). The epistle of James and the three letters of John may also be as early as these. In none of these documents is there any suggestion that Jesus worked miracles, even though in some of them miracles are regarded as of great importance for the spread of the Christian message. Blomberg says, justly, that "the nineteenth-century liberal quest for a miracle-free layer of Christian tradition has been all but abandoned". But when he adds that "the positive consequences for historicity should be acknowledged just as readily",[27] he blurs the question at issue, namely whether *Jesus himself* worked miracles; for the fact that, in the earliest documents, Christian missionaries are said to have done so is no corroboration of the gospel record concerning his own behaviour. Quite the contrary: it looks as though what was from the first attributed to missionary preachers was only later attributed to him, as a result of a radical change in Christology, involving the abandonment of the Pauline view that Jesus had lived an obscure life of inconspicuous humiliation.

There is no mention of any miracle of Jesus even in the writings of the earliest Fathers (Clement of Rome, Ignatius of Antioch and Polycarp of Smyrna—known as the 'Apostolic Fathers' because they were believed to be the immediate successors of the apostles). Paul even comes close to actually denying that Jesus worked miracles when he insists that he can preach only "Christ crucified"—a Christ who submitted to a shameful death, not a Christ of signs and wonders (1 Corinthians 1:22–23). It is no answer to say that the purpose of the epistles was not to present history. Of course no writer can be expected to mention things that are irrelevant to what he has chosen to discuss. But if we believe the gospels, there was much both in Jesus's behaviour and in his teaching that would have been relevant to the situation of the epistle writers and which they would have been glad to mention, had they known of it. Furthermore, such a reply ignores the fact that epistles of later date than the gospels, although their purpose is not to 'present history', do nevertheless allude to much of what had by then come to be regarded as Jesus's 'history' in arguing their various concerns.

Mark includes a literary 'doublet' of a miracle story which well illustrates that his material reached him not as eyewitness testimony but as community tradition (as outlined above, p. 12). The doublet is also of interest because what Jesus is later in this gospel made to say about the incidents recorded in it shows how freely words were put into his mouth. The doublet consists of accounts of two miraculous feedings, of the 5,000 and of the 4,000. The sequence of events, and even the vocabulary, is in both cases remarkably similar. That two separate incidents are involved is hard to believe, since in the second the disciples—who are represented as having recently witnessed the first—have so completely forgotten it that they think it impossible for bread to be supplied to thousands in a desert place (Mark 8:4). Even quite conservative commentators agree that the doublet is best explained by assuming that a tradition of one such feeding existed, before Mark wrote, in two slightly different written forms, and that the evangelist who drew on these written sources incorporated both because he supposed them to refer to different incidents. Written and not oral sources are implied. Two oral traditions that are slightly discrepant can easily be combined in one story. But as soon as a tradition is fixed in writing discrepancies between it and a kindred tradition can result in both literary forms of the story being told.

Shortly after the account of the second feeding, Mark represents the disciples as in a boat on the Sea of Galilee: "and they forgot to take bread, and they had not in the boat with them more than one loaf" (8:14). This worries them, even though Jesus is with them and they have just witnessed his two stupendous miracles with bread. Jesus responds to this almost incredible obtuseness on their part by reminding them of *both* the feeding miracles (8:19–20). As Nineham observes (p. 214), if there was in fact only one feeding incident, these words of Jesus cannot be authentic. Whoever concocted them did not suspect that the stories of the two feedings developed from one original, and the words betray how readily 'words of the Lord' could be manufactured. This is the important fact which the pericope illustrates.

In the same context Jesus cautions the disciples to "beware of the leaven of the Pharisees and the leaven of Herod" (8:15). Mark seems to have been hard put to find a place for this isolated tradition, but as it is a figurative statement about bread, he has accommodated it in this discussion between Jesus and his disciples about real bread. What it means is far from clear, and Matthew tried to clarify it by adding the comment that 'leaven' here means 'teaching'. But Herod had no teaching, so Matthew makes Jesus warn his disciples "of the leaven of the Pharisees and Sadducees" (16:11–12)—a good example of how a canonical writer will adapt the work of a canonical predecessor and put new words into Jesus's mouth in the process.

The feeding of the 5,000 is the only miracle of Jesus's Galilean

ministry that is recorded in all four gospels, and it is the only miracle
story in the fourth gospel that is identical with those of the other
three. In the fourth gospel, however, the feeding has become a symbol of Jesus's true status: he does not merely supply bread to sustain
life, but is made to say that he is himself "the bread of life", in the
sense that "he that cometh to me shall not hunger, and he that
believeth on me shall never thirst" (John 6:35).

A well-known miracle story is Luke's narrative (7:11–17) of how
Jesus, happening to meet the funeral procession of the only son of a
widow, took compassion on her and restored him to life. No other
gospel gives the story, even though according to Luke (verse 17) the
report of the incident "went forth . . . in the whole of Judea and all
the region round about". It is an example of how traditions about
Jesus resulted from reflection on the Old Testament. Elijah had raised
a widow's only son from the dead (1 Kings 17:17–24) and Elisha had
performed a similar miracle (2 Kings 4:14–37). The evangelist is clearly anxious to show that the new prophet is in no way inferior to
them; hence the bystanders are represented as saying (verse 16): "A
great prophet is arisen among us".

The obvious comment on such a narrative is that if Jesus was a
mere man, he did not work miracles, while if he was 'the son of God',
he must have known that there were innumerable other cases of
widows losing their only sons under distressing circumstances. Why,
then, should he have had compassion only for the case brought before
his eyes? The same considerations are relevant to his various cures of
sickness, and there is an understandable reluctance among present-
day commentators who are not fundamentalists to see that any
miracle was involved, even though these cures are represented as in-
stantanious and complete. Typical is D. L. Edwards, who attributes
the phenomena to "the interaction of body and mind" – a borderland
little understood even today – and thinks that they "demonstrate the
power of religious faith over the physical symptoms of disease, particularly skin diseases then understood as 'leprosy' and other diseases
then understood as demon-possession".[28]

I have discussed the question of miracles in some detail in chapter
8 of my *Religious Postures* (La Salle, Illinois: Open Court, 1988). E.
R. Dodds has given a very informative account of the prevalence of
belief in them from the second to the fourth century, an "age of anxiety" occasioned by "barbarian invasions, bloody civil wars, recurrent
epidemics, galloping inflation and extreme personal insecurity". This

was a world where everyone believed in magic and where miracles were in consequence commonplace, with none of the contending parties prepared to assert positively that the miracles of the others were fictitious. Quadratus of Athens, for instance, argued around AD 125 that Jesus's miracles of healing were superior to the pagan ones not because they were more genuine, but because they were more lasting. Dodds wryly comments: "It would appear that the early Christians, like good physicians, followed up their cases". A very common belief (documented in the gospels, e.g. at Mark 3:22) was that miracles were worked by evil spirits. Hence, although "they might serve to impress the masses, . . . arguments based on them were inevitably two-edged".[29]

vi. NON-CHRISTIAN EVIDENCE

Non-Christian evidence is too late to give any independent support to the gospels. When Tacitus wrote (about AD 120) that "Christ" was executed under Pontius Pilate, he was merely repeating what Christians were by then saying (HEJ, pp. 16–17; France, pp. 21–23). The other pagan writer commonly adduced is Suetonius who wrote, also around AD 120, that Claudius (who reigned AD 41–54) expelled Jews from Rome because "they constantly made disturbances at the instigation of Chrestus". Many commentators think that, by 'Chrestus', Suetonius really meant 'Christus' (the Messiah); and Watson has convincingly argued that the disorders to which Suetonius here refers were caused by controversy between orthodox Jews and Jewish Christians at Rome about the truth or falsehood of Christianity.[30] No more about the 'historical' Jesus need have been included in this Christianity of Claudius's day than what extant Christian writers (Paul and others) were saying on the subject before the gospels became established much later in the first century; and that, as we saw (above, pp. 6f) does not confirm the gospels' portraits of Jesus. Suetonius also mentions Nero's persecution of Christians at Rome, but, as France notes, tells us nothing more than what we already know about this from Tacitus, and "nothing about Jesus himself" (p. 42). Pliny, as I have noted elsewhere (HEJ, p. 16), is equally unhelpful in the latter regard, as France (p. 43) agrees.

Rabbinic references to Jesus are entirely dependent on Christian claims, as both Christian and Jewish scholars have conceded. I quote Sandmel and Bornkamm, among others, to this effect in DJE, p. 12.

France, who gives no indication that this is the view of reputable scholars, regards what I say there as "dogmatic scepticism" (p. 39). Catchpole, however, in a thorough survey, gives the arguments of seven Jewish scholars who, between 1929 and 1963, totally dismissed, with varying degrees of firmness, the Talmudic evidence on Jesus.[31] I note in DJE (pp. 12, 16) that even Goldstein, who accepts as "authentic" five passages about Jesus in the "vast" rabbinic literature of the first two and a quarter centuries AD, admits that they do not conclusively establish even that he existed at all, as none of them can be shown to be sufficiently early.

Appeal is still commonly made to the Jewish historian Flavius Josephus, in whose *Antiquities of the Jews* it is suggested that Jesus was more than human, and where he is said to have been "the Christ", a "doer of marvellous deeds" condemned to crucifixion by Pilate "upon an indictment brought by the principal men among us". But a Pharisee such as Josephus would not have written so admiringly of him, nor have dropped the subject abruptly had he believed all this of him. The passage as it stands was obviously interpolated by a Christian writer — there are only three manuscripts of the chapter in which it occurs, none of them earlier than the eleventh century — and the only remaining question is whether the whole is an interpolation, or whether Josephus at this point made *some* mention of Jesus which was later reworked by a Christian hand. Conzelmann, in a standard religious encyclopaedia, says that the whole is an interpolation;[32] and Paul Winter, in the recent revision of Schürer's book (p. 433), names other "scholars of established reputation" who likewise consider the passage "a complete fabrication". Even if, as Winter himself and many others suppose, part of the passage was written by Josephus, its date (about AD 93) makes it too late to be of decisive importance, for the gospel account was already in written form by then, and Josephus could, like Tacitus, have taken his information from what Christians were by then saying.[33]

Winter allows that, even though the passage includes what he regards as "certain terms of speech, however fragmentary" that can be ascribed to Josephus, it is not possible to reconstruct what Josephus may originally have written at this point (pp. 434, 438). The Josephan 'terms of speech' may, as Herrmann holds, be there because the passage was added by someone who knew Josephus's style and made a pastiche from it.[34] France (p. 28) distorts the case I have made elsewhere for excising the whole passage when he says that my argument implies that all Josephus's stories about Pilate must occur together, in unbroken sequence, so that everything after the Jesus passage but in the same chapter will also have to go, as Josephus returns to Pilate only at the beginning of the next chapter. In fact my argument (in JEC, pp. 191–92 and DJE, p. 10) was that the Jesus passage occurs in a context which deals exclusively with the misfortunes of the Jews (only some of which are attributed to Pilate) and that Jesus's condemnation by Pilate at the behest of the Jewish leaders has no connection with such misfortunes except from the standpoint of a Christian, who would naturally regard this crime as the greatest misfortune ever to have befallen the Jews. If the whole passage is removed, there remains a coherent account of a series of their misfortunes—first, two instigated by Pilate, then (after the passage about Jesus) "another sad calamity which put the Jews into disorder", followed by yet another (4,000 Jews banished from Rome for the wickedness of four).[35]

Josephus's only other mention of Jesus occurs in a statement about the killing of James, "the brother of Jesus, him called Christ". This, if genuine and not a Christian interpolation, does nothing to confirm the gospel accounts of Jesus, and its late date makes it only marginally relevant to the question of his historicity. France, like many others, has pleaded (p. 27) that no Christian interpolator would have been content to designate Jesus as 'him called Christ'. In fact, however, Matthew, in a passage where he introduces Jesus to his readers, refers to him with these very words (1:16); and at John 4:25–26 Jesus claims to be the person who has just been referred to as "him called Christ", so that Christian use of the phrase is well attested. Indeed, it would be remarkable from an orthodox Jew such as Josephus, who might be expected to have qualified it with something like 'called Christ by some'. (Cf. Herrmann, pp. 101–02 for this and further evidence for interpolation). Also, Origen's comments on Josephus's mention of James do not really square with this passage (see JEC, pp. 193–94 and France's concession, p. 172 n.14). It is readily understood as a marginal gloss, from a Christian hand, incorporated innocently into the text by a later copyist (see DJE, p. 11).

The manner in which apologists exaggerate the significance of non-Christian evidence which they take as pertaining to the events recorded in the gospels is well illustrated by Habermas's statement that "within 100 to 150 years after the birth of Christ approximately eighteen non-Christian . . . sources from secular history mention . . .

almost every major detail of Jesus' life, including miracles, the Resurrection, and his claim to be deity".[36] It is all the more striking that so many of the earliest Christian documents do not do the same, but say nothing of any item in his biography except his crucifixion and resurrection (both in unspecified circumstances). And contrary to Habermas's suggestion, there is no early non-Christian evidence concerning the Resurrection. As the theologian Ulrich Wilckens has noted, "for the first century we are, without exception, forced to rely on the testimony of the Christians" on this matter: "There are no non-Christian witnesses of any sort who could give us information about the resurrection of Jesus and his appearances, or comment from a non-Christian aspect on the statements made about the resurrection by the early Christians".[37] As for Jesus's "claims to be deity", these are not merely absent from but even incompatible with the earliest Christian documents, where he figures as a supernatural personage higher in status than the angels, yet subordinate to the Father, to whom he will finally deliver up the kingdom (1 Corinthians 15:24 and 28), and himself then be merely the first-born among many brothers (Romans 8:29).[38]

One of Habermas's 18 secular sources on the life of Jesus is Thallus, who, he claims, mentioned "the darkness and the events surrounding the Crucifixion . . . about AD 52" (p. 106). Thallus's *History* has not survived, and only a few references to it in Christian writers are extant. Of these the one that Habermas has in mind is Julius Africanus's statement in the third century, apropos of the three-hour darkness from noon which covered the earth at Jesus's crucifixion (Mark 15:33): "Thallus says—wrongly it seems to me—that this darkness was an eclipse of the sun". Jacoby, who prints Africanus's quotation and who comments on it in a companion volume, notes that Thallus may in fact have made no mention at all of Jesus or Jewish history, but simply have recorded (as other chroniclers did) the eclipse in the reign of Tiberius for which astronomers have calculated the date 24 November AD 29.[39] It may have been Africanus who introduced Jesus in retorting that this was no eclipse but a supernatural event. If, however, Thallus did mention the death of Jesus, then his testimony would be important if it antedated the gospel traditions. But all we in fact know of him is that he wrote later than the eclipse he mentions and probably before Phlegon, the freedman of Hadrian (if Eusebius is right in asserting that Phlegon drew his information about the same eclipse from Thallus). Jacoby says that

Christian writers were drawn to Thallus's *History* because it "was the latest thing and appeared only in the second century". Thus if he mentioned the crucifixion at all, he probably derived his information from what Christians were already saying, and is therefore not an independent witness. Conzelmann's article on Jesus in a standard religious encyclopaedia notes curtly that "Thallus cannot be considered as witnessing" to events in the life of Jesus.[40]

The three-hour darkness at Jesus's death cannot, in the passover context in which it is set in the gospels, have been a solar eclipse, as the Passover is celebrated about the time of the full moon, and solar eclipses can occur only at the time of the new moon. The evangelists of course do not intend to represent the darkness as naturally caused, but as "a miraculous portent, no doubt signifying the judgment of heaven on what was taking place" (Nineham, p. 426). Nineham adds that similar portents are said to have marked the deaths of Julius Caesar and other pagan figures, and also of some of the great rabbis.

THE RESURRECTION

i. THE GOSPEL ACCOUNTS

According to Karl Barth, we "rightly turn up our nose" at the many inconsistencies "in the attempts of liberal theologians to explain belief in the resurrection naturalistically".[1] If inconsistencies are a ground for scornful rejection, then it will fare ill with the New Testament accounts of the Resurrection. A. E. Harvey notes in his *The New English Bible Companion to the New Testament* (Oxford and Cambridge University Presses, 1970, p. 297) — hardly a sceptical work — that "all the gospels, after having run closely together in their accounts of the trial and execution, diverge markedly when they come to the circumstances of the resurrection, and it is impossible to fit their accounts together into a single coherent scheme". Fuller gives a brief summary of what he calls the "palpable inconsistencies" (pp. 2–5), and early this century they were set out in detail by the Zürich theologian P. W. Schmiedel, who gives ample evidence that on this matter "the canonical gospels are at irreconcilable variance with each other" and that the non-canonical notices "serve to show how busily and in how reckless a manner the accounts of the resurrection of Jesus continued to be handed on".[2] Karl Barth's way out of all this is that we ought not to ask for evidence for the Resurrection, but should believe on faith alone; to which another theologian, Paul Badham, has appositely replied: "A faith which claims something which happened in the past is important cannot evade historical scrutiny of that claim."[3]

Strauss emphasized how glaring the contradictions are when he declared, of the Resurrection; "Rarely has an incredible fact been worse attested, and never has a badly attested one been intrinsically less credible".[4] Matthew makes Jesus's appearances to his disciples occur exclusively in Galilee, while Luke sites them exclusively 80 miles away at Jerusalem. (The final redactor of the fourth gospel tries to harmonize such discrepant traditions by appending a chapter of Galilean appearances, John 21, to a chapter of Jerusalem appearances.) I know that witnesses of an event can give discrepant accounts of it, but one would not expect the discrepancies to extend to essentials. If one witness of a street accident affirmed that it took place in London, we should not expect another to site it in Birmingham. If we were faced with such discrepant reports, and also had no other evidence that there had been any accident, we should dismiss the whole thing. But this is our position in regard to the Resurrection. As Elliott has said: "There is no independent witness to the Easter events outside the New Testament" (p. 84).

The documents make it clear that the Christophanies were not vouchsafed to enemies, only to those who either already believed or subsequently became believers. As Elliott puts it: "Jesus in his resurrected state is visible only to those who have faith" (p. 86); or, in the wording of the New Testament itself, only to "witnesses who were chosen before of God" (Acts 10:40–41). According to Acts, the appearances of the risen Jesus went on for 40 days. This feature contradicts even Luke (by the same author), which ends with Jesus leading his disciples on Easter day, after numerous appearances to them, from Jerusalem to the neighbouring locality of Bethany, where he solemnly blesses them with uplifted hands before "he parted from them and was carried up into heaven" — on that same day. Some manuscripts have only "he parted from them", but Fuller concedes, after discussing the manuscript evidence, that the words reporting the ascension are "textually Lucan and integral to the narrative" (p. 122). Evidently some copyists deleted them in order to represent the parting as only temporary and thus avoid contradicting Acts where the author seems to be drawing on a tradition not available when he wrote his gospel, and one on which he gladly seized because, while occasional appearances of the risen one might be dismissed by sceptics as hallucinations, a sojourn of forty days, during which he presented "many proofs" (Acts 1:3), was more substantial.

Conservative apologists admit what they call "apparent discrepancies" in the evidence for the Resurrection, but point out that certain cardinal facts are independent of them: all the accounts agree, for instance, that Jesus was crucified and subsequently raised. But this amount of agreement is frequently found in stories admittedly mythical. Historians agree that Wilhelm Tell is a legendary figure, but there are chronicles enough telling discrepant stories of how he founded the Swiss Confederation. Reverting to my example of a street accident, I would note that the conservative position implies that, although those who claim to be witnesses disagree even as to where it happened, and although there are no injured people, damaged vehicles or indeed any evidence apart from their discordant testimony, we are nevertheless to believe that an accident did occur. Scholars who today still defend Jesus's virgin birth as historical fact are obliged to resort to this manner of arguing: as we shall see, the event is documented only in the two nativity stories of Matthew and Luke (not elsewhere in the New Testament), and each of these stories is incompatible with the other, as well as being full of its own difficulties. But they agree in alleging that Jesus was virgin born. Such minimal agreement between narratives with no historical basis is, however, what one would expect if for some reason certain beliefs — about Jesus and about Tell — had come to be accepted and if believers then, independently of each other, tried to envisage historical circumstances which would justify these beliefs.

The discrepancies in the gospel accounts of the Resurrection events are not mere muddle but arise because one evangelist pursues theological purposes alien to another. For Luke, Jerusalem is of great theological importance,[5] and in order to place the appearances there he amends the Marcan narrative at two points. First he omits the record at Mark 14:28 of Jesus's prediction (during the walk to Gethsemane after the Last Supper) that after his Resurrection he would go before his disciples into Galilee. Then he rewords what Mark had recorded as the instruction to the women at the empty tomb. Mark has:

> Go, tell his disciples and Peter, *He goeth before you into Galilee*; there shall ye see him, as he said unto you (16:7).

In Luke this appears as:

> Remember how he spake unto you, *when he was yet in Galilee,* saying that the Son of man must be . . . crucified, and the third day rise again (24:6–7).

Having thus eliminated the instruction that the disciples should go to Galilee, Luke goes on to make the risen Jesus tell them to remain in Jerusalem "until ye be clothed with power from on high" (24:49), which he represents (at Acts 2:1–4) as happening at Pentecost, that is, some fifty days later.

Theologians speak in this connection of Luke's 'editing' of Mark; but we can hardly feel confidence in a writer whose theological purpose leads him to adapt a source so as to obliterate its plain meaning. As Evans has said, "it is not natural confusion but rather the lack of it, and the influence of rational reflection and apologetic" which have given rise to such contradictions (p. 129).

The best manuscripts of Mark end at 16:8. The remainder of chapter 16 is an appendix (distinguished as such in the RV, the RSV, and the NEB) which makes the risen Jesus promise (among other things) that believers will be able to handle snakes and drink deadly poison without coming to harm. Up to 16:8 there have been no appearances of the risen one. The women visitors to the tomb have discovered it to be empty, and have been instructed there by "a young man arrayed in a white robe" to tell the disciples to go to Galilee to experience an appearance. In Luke, the "young man" becomes "two men in dazzling apparel", and in Matthew he is called an "angel". Commentators point out that this is the meaning in all three gospels, as 'young man' sometimes designates an angel in ancient Jewish literature, and in the New Testament men in white and/or radiant clothes are always heavenly beings. In John (20:12) there are two angels. Commentators are apt to say that we have here various accounts, the exact details of which are not important. Of course the details are unimportant if the important fact is admitted that Jesus had risen from the dead and that real angels stood by his tomb and spoke to the women. If we accept all this, it does not matter whether there was one angel or two, whether they were outside the tomb or within.

Mark continues by representing the women as too afraid to deliver the young man's message to the disciples, so that "they said nothing to anyone". Fuller, like many others, thinks that the empty tomb story is no part of the early tradition, but "a later legend, introduced by Mark for the first time into the narrative" (p. 52). And it has often been suggested that Mark's motive for making the women keep silent was to account for the fact that, as he well knew, there was no already existing tradition about an empty tomb when he wrote. As Lampe says: 'The fact that the women do not pass the message on may suggest that the evangelist, or his source, knew that the story of the tomb and the angel was not part of the original Easter proclamation and had only developed at a relatively late stage in the tradition" (p. 48).

Whatever Mark's motive may have been, Luke reworded this

passage so as to make it lead in to the Jerusalem appearances he has added to Mark:

Mark 16:8

And they went out and fled from the tomb; for trembling and astonishment had come upon them: and they said nothing to anyone; for they were afraid.

Luke 24:9

And they returned from the tomb and told all these things to the eleven, and to all the rest.

I do not mean to suggest that Luke is here concocting a narrative he knew to be false. As he was convinced that it was "beginning from Jerusalem" that the Christian mission went forward to "all the nations" (Luke 24:47), he will naturally have supposed that his predecessor had got his facts a bit wrong, and so will have amended the Marcan narrative in perfectly good faith. One thing that this kind of 'editing' clearly indicates is that Mark's gospel was not regarded as authoritatively based on reliable eyewitness information.

If we turn from Luke to Matthew, we find similarly a narrative shaped by conscious purpose. Matthew has decided to have the sepulchre guarded by Jewish (or Roman) soldiers so as to prevent the Jews from alleging, when it is later seen to be empty, that disciples stole their master's body and merely pretended that he had risen from the dead (Matthew 27:62–66). In consequence, Matthew cannot accept Mark's statement that the women expected to enter the tomb (to anoint the body) and has to represent them as intending merely to visit it (28:1). Before they can look inside it, the guard has to be put out of action; hence the need for the "great earthquake" of the next verse — caused not by any natural seismic conditions, but by the descent from heaven of "an angel of the Lord" who both rolls away the stone sealing the tomb and petrifies the guards with fear. But why did not these soldiers, once they had recovered, tell of what they had seen and thus make it difficult for the Jews to deny the fact of the Resurrection? To provide a plausible answer to this question, Matthew has it that the chief priests persuaded the guards with bribes to pretend that they had slept on duty and thus given Jesus's disciples a chance to steal the body. The guards "took the money, and did as they were taught: and this saying was spread abroad among the Jews and continueth until this day" (28:15). This is psychologically quite incredible. "Whoever has seen an angel descending from heaven, with an appearance like lightning (28:3), is not going to say — even for a considerable sum of money — that he was asleep and saw nothing" (Haenchen, pp. 549–550). The phrase "until this day" betrays the whole narrative as late apologetic, accounting, to both Jews and Christians, for the silence of alleged Jewish witnesses. Lampe has noted that what he calls Matthew's "legend" of the guard has "no historical value", is "very much in the manner of the later apocryphal gospels", and reflects controversy with the Jews (p. 51).

C. H. Dodd refers to two passages in Matthew's account (28:8–10 and 16–20) which, he says, "represent the 'formed' tradition, stereotyped through relatively long transmission within a community", and express "the corporate oral tradition of the primitive Church".[6] In the first, the women have just been told at the tomb (as in Mark) that the risen one will appear in Galilee, whereupon (diverging from Mark's account) they run "to bring his disciples word", but are intercepted by the risen Jesus. Matthew may have added this detail because he feared that the testimony of the angel at the tomb, which is all that Mark offered, could be dismissed as hallucination. It is hard to see any other reason for this added episode, for in it Jesus effects no more than to repeat the angel's message that he will appear in Galilee. The women, however, introduce something novel in that at this point "they took hold of his feet and worshipped him". This kind of physical contact with the risen one is characteristic of the stage of tradition represented by the gospels, but excluded, as we shall see, by Paul, who also knows nothing of appearances to women. These, by the way, are also unknown to Luke. He records the women's visit to the tomb and their encounter there with "two men in dazzling apparel" (24:1–10), but says nothing of any appearance to the women, and goes on to imply at 24:22–24 that, up to that point, no one had seen Jesus.

In Dodd's second Matthaean passage the risen Jesus instructs the eleven on a Galilean mountain "to make disciples of all the nations". Such words could have been put into his mouth only when the fierce controversy about the gentile mission that dominates the earliest Christian literature was not only over and done with, but even barely remembered. The eleven are here further instructed to baptise all the nations "into the name of the Father and of the Son and of the Holy Ghost". This again can only be late, for there is no suggestion in the early literature — not even in Acts' account of the Church's early

history — that this formula was used. At Acts 2:38 Peter urges potential converts simply to "be baptised in the name of Jesus Christ".

Matthew's risen Lord also instructs the eleven to teach converts
"to observe all things whatsoever I commanded you". This represents a special theological interest of Matthew, who presents his
gospel, with its five carefully constructed Jesuine discourses, as the
new Torah; and 'all that I commanded you' is meant to refer back to
these (cf. Fuller, pp. 88–89). It is with such facts in mind that Evans
has said (p. 67) that, not only does the risen Lord not say the same
things in any two gospels, but also it is hardly the same Lord speaking: "In Matthew it is evidently a Matthaean Lord who speaks, in
Luke a Lukan Lord and in John a Johannine Lord." Each gospel was
written for a different Christian community, and — as Fuller puts it
(p. 172) — "the words spoken by the Risen One are not to be taken as
recordings of what was actually spoken by him, but as verbalizations
of the community's understanding of the import of the resurrection".

This second Matthaean passage also represents the risen Jesus as
declaring that "all authority hath been given unto me in heaven and
on earth". Dodd allows that the intention here is "clearly to introduce
the risen Christ as King of the World". He suggests that the passage
nevertheless has a ring of authenticity because it is "notably sober
and almost matter-of-fact in tone", entirely lacking "the conventional
symbolism of apocalypse" (pp. 116–17). He also hints that, apart
from these two passages in Matthew's chapter 28, even the remaining
accounts of the Resurrection events merit careful attention because
they lack the mythical tendencies of much ancient literature — this
when, in one of these remaining accounts, an angel is said to descend
from heaven, roll away the stone sealing the tomb and sit on it (Matthew 28:1–3). Although Dodd is certainly concerned to represent
these narratives in the best possible light, in his 1971 book on
Jesus — widely hailed on its appearance as the distillation of a lifetime of study — he concedes that whether "Jesus had in some way left
his tomb" is a question on which "the historian may properly suspend
judgment".[7] If we are to accept the miracle of the Resurrection, we
need grounds more positive than this.

If Jesus's tomb was empty, he did not leave his flesh and bones in
his grave; and so either they had been transformed into something
different, or else he rose in physical body. Paul (as we shall see) takes
the former view, and the gospels (other than Mark's, which gives no
evidence either way) the latter. They refer to the "flesh and bones" of

the risen Jesus (Luke 24:39), who "eats and drinks" with his disciples (Acts 10:41) and invites Thomas to touch him (John 20:27; cf. Luke 24:39 where he invites the eleven to "handle" him). It is on the basis of such evidence that the fourth of the Church of England's 39 articles affirms that he ascended into heaven (where he now "sitteth") with "flesh and bones". His risen body also has to be solid enough to support clothes, as no one supposes that the gospels would have us believe that he manifested himself naked. Yet, as the Bishops of the General Synod of the same Church of England have recently noted, this risen body must have been "of a very unusual kind"; for according to these same gospels, it enabled him to arrive within closed doors and vanish at will.[8] Badham has stressed what he calls the "internal incoherence" of the narratives here (p. 37): the body is represented as solid for some purposes but not for others.

ii. PAUL'S ACCOUNT

Paul's detailed statement on the Resurrection events is as follows (1 Corinthians 15:3-8):

(3) For I delivered unto you first of all that which also I received, how that Christ died for our sins according to the scriptures;

(4) and that he was buried; and that he hath been raised on the third day according to the scriptures;

(5) and that he appeared to Cephas; then to the twelve;

(6) then he appeared to above five hundred brethren at once, of whom the greater part remain until now, but some are fallen asleep;

(7) then he appeared to James; then to all the apostles;

(8) and last of all, as to one born out of due time, he appeared to me also.

The passage does not locate the crucifixion in time. It places the Resurrection three days after the death, but does not say when the death occurred. The appearances are said to have been vouchsafed to Paul and to his contemporaries, but it is not said how near in time they are to the death and the Resurrection. Someone who claims to see a ghost does not necessarily suppose that it is the wraith of a recently deceased person. The reference to Jesus's burial (verse 4) need not be taken to imply knowledge of a tomb, still less of a post-

Resurrection empty tomb. Paul may simply be emphasizing the reality of Jesus's death, as when we say someone is 'dead and buried' (cf. Evans, p. 75 and note). That he was actually buried is important theologically for Paul, who regarded the death, burial, and Resurrection as reflected symbolically in Christian baptism of total immersion: into the water constitutes death; under the water, burial; and out of the water, resurrection (Romans 6:3–4 and Colossians 2:12 where references to Jesus's burial are explicit).

As we have seen, in the gospels Jesus's tomb is said to be empty because he rose in physical body. Paul, however, has a quite different view of rising from the dead and roundly declares — in the same chapter of the epistle where he writes of Jesus's Resurrection and subsequent appearances — that "flesh and blood cannot inherit the kingdom of God" (1 Corinthians 15:50). It is "clear enough", says Bishop Carnley, that in verses 3–8, Paul understands Jesus's Resurrection as "a truly representative sample of the resurrection of all believers", to which he makes reference in this later verse.[9] In the same context (verse 43) he writes of the dead being raised "in glory"; and at Philippians 3:21 he argues directly from the Resurrection body of Christ to the future resurrection body of believers: Christ "will change our lowly body to be like his glorious body". As Fuller has noted (p. 20), if Paul believed that Christ's physical body had been transformed he could not have accepted any tradition that Jesus rose in physical body and ate and drank.

Of course, if Jesus rose, he will have left his tomb empty even if his body had been transformed into something quite different. But whether Paul had any actual knowledge of an empty tomb is another matter. In 1 Corinthians he is writing to men who were denying that there was a resurrection of the dead, and had he known of an empty tomb, he would surely have been glad to adduce this as evidence of resurrection, instead of merely saying, as he does, that Jesus was buried and then raised. As Conzelmann notes in a standard religious encyclopaedia, Paul seems to suppose that Jesus ascended to heaven at once on being resurrected, and with a body of heavenly radiance, so that his subsequent appearances were made from heaven.[10] So much is implied even in Acts' version of Jesus's appearance to Paul, who sees "a light out of heaven" (Acts 9:3ff) and hears a voice, which his companions also hear, although they see no one. Later, at Acts 22:9, his companions are said to have seen the light, but not to have heard the voice. The implication of both passages may be that all saw the light, but only Paul saw the figure of Jesus in it. However construed, all this is quite different from the physical appearances recorded in the gospels.

Paul would surely have rejected as blasphemous any claim to have eaten and drunk with the exalted one. Luke's story of the risen Jesus consuming broiled fish (Luke 24:41–43) represents later apologetic, relevant to a situation where Christians were replying to Jewish and gentile incredulity with a narrative which established the physical reality of his Resurrection, but which today can only strike many readers as more than slightly ridiculous.[11]

One important factor which helps to account for Paul's testimony is that, when he wrote, Christian leaders established their authority by claiming to have seen the risen Lord.[12] For Paul, an 'apostle' was precisely a person who had had such a vision and been called to the Lord's service in consequence of it, for it is on this basis that he declares himself to be as much an apostle as were rival Christian teachers: "Am I not an apostle? Have I not seen Jesus our Lord?" (1 Corinthians 9:1). The psychological predisposition to such visions can hardly have been absent if there was such a strong motive for claiming them.[13] One reason why this is not known to the general reader is that the word 'apostle' puts him in mind of the 'twelve apostles' and so makes him think that only someone who had been a close disciple of Jesus during his lifetime could be an apostle. In fact the first author who uses the term fairly consistently in this sense is Luke (both in his gospel and in Acts), his purpose being thereby to resist heresy by limiting true doctrine to what had allegedly been pro-claimed by men who had kept Jesus's company from his baptism to his ascension. For earlier Christian writers, and for those of about the same date as Luke but ignorant of the gospel traditions, the term had no such implication. For instance, at Revelation 2:2 the Church of Ephesus is congratulated for having tested "them which call themselves apostles and . . . are not". If 'apostles' here meant (twelve) companions of Jesus, they could have been identified without being put to the test and "found false".[14]

As, according to Paul, Jesus sometimes appeared to more than one person on a given occasion, some apologists hold that there real-ly must have been some external reality to be perceived. It still would not follow that what was there was interpreted correctly. There are examples enough of collective perception of what were taken for ghosts.[15] The evidence offered by sworn eyewitnesses at witchcraft trials likewise suggests that what people observe depends at least as much on their habits of thought as on what is actually there. A firm belief in the miraculous and in the ceaseless efforts of the Devil was presupposed in the observations and reasonings of witnesses and judges alike at these trials, and, as Huxley noted (see above, p. 16), the number of witnesses counts for very little when all are affected by the same underlying beliefs. More recently, at the battle of Mons (1914), angels, "varying in number from two to a platoon" were widely believed to have fought on the British side.[16] The virgin Mary is alleged to have been seen by two children at La Salette (France) in 1846 and by three children at Fatima (Portugal) in 1917, complaining in both cases of neglect of sacred rites. A standard religious encyclopaedia regards these as instances of the type of popular piety that in Romance-speaking areas was linked with nineteenth-century revivalist movements.[17] At Fatima the initial appearances were followed by "an awed crowd of 30,000" seeing "first Our Lady of Sorrows, followed by Our Lady of Carmel, then Saint Joseph holding the Holy Child in his arms, and lastly the Lord Jesus". A "solar prodigy" on the same occasion (13 October, 1917) was "witnessed by thousands of people within a twenty-five mile radius": the sun spun three times, then "moved away from its natural axis, and falling from side to side plunged down towards the earth at tremendous speed, zigzagging wildly as it came".[18]

It is of course true that hallucinations, even when induced by some common physical means, will not be the same for different people, since they depend not only on the present physiological state but on the stock of memories in the mind of each individual. But inasmuch as the appearances of Jesus were vouchsafed to groups such as the 500 and more of 1 Corinthians 15:6, who may, like Paul, never have known Jesus personally, the agreement between what each person experienced could have been minimal yet sufficient for all to say that they had seen a vaguely-conceived risen Jesus. Furthermore, the nonconformist is mistrusted, and so every individual, whatever he may inwardly feel and believe, may try to give the impression that he believes what those around him seem to believe – a phenomenon made familiar by Hans Andersen's story of the emperor's new clothes. These conditions prevail not only in crowds – where every member is ready to sink his private view in deference to what he takes to be the general opinion, as soon as he thinks he has ascertained it – but wherever people feel that their actions may be subjected to public scrutiny. And with early Christianity we are dealing with a social phenomenon where unbelief is a cardinal crime (John 3:18 and 36) for which whole communities are to be most frightfully punished (Matthew 10:14–15). "He that doubteth is like the surge of the sea driven by the wind and tossed" (James 1:6).

What is striking about the whole passage I have quoted from 1 Corinthians 15 is, as Elliott says (p. 83), that "Paul does no more than provide a list. There are no details of how, where or when the Easter encounters took place or what happened". And the items in his list correlate very poorly with the record of appearances in the gospels. Beare even says that Paul's account of the appearances "has no relationship with any of the accounts in the gospels" and is not reflected in them "in any shape or form" (pp. 541–42). Let us study the details.

The gospels know nothing of the appearance to above 500 simultaneously. Again, Paul places an appearance to Peter (alias Cephas, verse 5) as the first in time of all those which he records, whereas in the gospels Peter plays only a very minor role in the appearances. They contain no *account* of an appearance to him. At Mark 16:7 an appearance to "the disciples and Peter" is promised by the angel in the empty tomb; and Luke 24:34 mentions, in a surprisingly casual manner, that an appearance to Peter had occurred without making it clear whether this was the first the risen Jesus made. The eleven disciples and others with them in Jerusalem are there reported as saying: "The Lord is risen indeed and hath appeared to Simon". This, says Eduard Schweizer, "sounds like a set formula and shows by its brevity that this is all Luke knew about an appearance to Peter".[19] The other two gospels are completely silent on the subject of an appearance specifically to Peter.

Paul also records in verse 5 an appearance to "the twelve". Critical theologians have given weighty reasons for doubting whether this means the twelve who, according to the gospels, accompanied Jesus throughout his ministry. One of their arguments is that it is universally agreed that Paul's words here are not his own composition, but that he is quoting an already existing creed about the Resurrection events, for the passage is full of un-Pauline words and phrases.[20] He never mentions 'the twelve' elsewhere — only in this one passage which, for him, was a quotation — but could hardly have avoided doing so had he known them as the companions of Jesus's ministry. He knows nothing of 'twelve' as leaders of Jerusalem Christians, whom he names as Cephas, James and John.[21] For him, then, the twelve could only have been personages named in a creed which specified witnesses of the appearances. And the Christian community which formulated this pre-Pauline creed would have known these twelve not as companions of Jesus, but as a group of enthusiasts who, having heard of the appearance to Peter, thought that it presaged a general resurrection of the dead (cf. below, pp. 40f). In the exalted state of mind which went with such expectation, the group would have become convinced that Jesus had appeared also to them, but have fallen apart when the hope that had led to its inception was not fulfilled. If it had persisted as an important group, Paul would surely have mentioned it again, and not merely named it once in a creed he quoted. Such considerations convinced Schneemelcher that "the twelve are a phenomenon of the post-Easter community, which indeed soon disappeared again"; and he refers his readers to Vielhauer's "conclusive proof" of this.[22] That Paul's mention of the group he calls 'the twelve' is not dependent on knowledge of the traditions which were later recorded in the gospels is also apparent from the fact that, according to the evangelists, the risen Jesus did not appear to his twelve disciples, but to eleven of them, Judas (whom Paul never mentions) having defected. Mark 16:14 and Matthew 28:16 are quite specific on the matter, and record appearances not to 'the disciples' but to 'the eleven'.

As already noted, the gospels themselves completely contradict each other on where the appearances to the disciples occurred. There was, then, little uniformity in the traditions concerning a matter of the greatest importance to Christianity. It looks as though there was initially simply a belief that the risen one had appeared, and that, as this lacked any true historical basis, discrepant accounts of the relevant localities came in time to be composed.

The apologists' case is not helped by the fact that Paul, in his statement about the appearances, is reciting an early Christian creed. That the earliest extant mention of the Resurrection occurs in a formula handed down from even earlier Christians is readily explicable if the event is in fact unhistorical. The earliest Christians will simply have asserted that Christ died and was raised, and will have embodied these convictions in the kind of preaching formula that Paul here quotes. The next stage in the development will have been to offer supporting evidence by listing recipients of appearances, and this stage is represented in the Pauline passage. Such visions are quite in accordance with religious psychology,[23] and Paul himself records that he and others were prone to supernatural visions (Colossians 2:18; 2 Corinthians 12:1–4). The next stage in the developing tradition was to give actual descriptions (not mere listings) of the appearances, as in the canonical gospels. Finally, in the apocryphal Gospel of Peter, there is a description of the Resurrection itself. These stages are summarized by Fuller (pp. 28–29, 66–67) who shows that, in the course of the development, the claims about the Resurrection become different sorts of claims. The theologian John Hick admits that the earliest references to the Resurrection simply allege Jesus to be risen, and that the gospels elaborate this message into a catena of incompatible stories characterized by "progressive degeneration from history to legend", so that we cannot tell whether he did actually emerge from his grave, or whether this was merely an idea based on "a series of visions" of him "as a glorified figure of exalted majesty".[24] In other words, the stories of the appearances (the stage represented in the gospels) do not record events on which the Resurrection faith was based, but are clumsy attempts to justify this faith by allegations of underlying events. That such divergent accounts could be written by authors who had already come to believe (for reasons that need to be investigated) that Jesus rose from the dead is perfectly plausible: that their narratives provide any basis for such belief is not.

iii. THE ORIGIN OF THE RESURRECTION FAITH

Defenders of the miracle of the Resurrection take comfort, with Pannenberg, in the thought that "the legends created by excessive criticism have been less credible than the biblical reports themselves".[25] He is here alluding to the theory that Jesus did not die but merely "swooned" on the cross, recovered consciousness in the cool tomb, crept out unnoticed when the earthquake rolled the stone away, and showed himself from time to time to his followers. Such nonsense is not the result of 'excessive criticism', but of yielding up only some of the traditional assumptions while clinging obstinately to others. In this example, belief in miracles has been surrendered, but the view that the gospels are based on eyewitness reports is retained, so that the miracle of Resurrection is construed as a misunderstanding on the part of Jesus's entourage.

It is equally unsatisfactory to trace the gospel Resurrection narratives to deliberate lies by eyewitnesses of the crucifixion who concocted Resurrection stories they knew to be false. Schmiedel shows how such stories as the sepulchre guard (unique to Matthew) and the empty tomb could have arisen in stages in perfectly good faith.[26] He imagines a Christian confronted with the charge that the disciples had stolen the body. The obvious retort would be: "The Jews, we may be quite certain, saw to the watching of the sepulchre; they could very well have known that Jesus had predicted his rising again on the third day". Another Christian, hearing this, might take it not for conjecture, but for a statement of fact, and pass it on as such. But if Roman soldiers guarded the tomb they must have witnessed the Resurrection. What, then, did they see of it? The attempt to answer this would give rise to the story of the angel coming down from heaven and rolling away the stone. This again might well have originated as conjecture, but have been passed on as fact. And in order to explain why the soldiers did not tell of their experiences, it would be said that the Jewish authorities bribed them to suppress the truth and circulate instead the rumour that the disciples had stolen the body. A similar series of processes could have led to the story of the empty tomb. If Jesus was risen, his grave must have been empty. "Therefore no hesitation was felt in declaring that, according to all reasonable conjecture, the women who had witnessed Jesus's death had wished to anoint his body and thus had come to know of the emptiness of the grave". But why should not the disciples have gone to the sepulchre? Schmiedel answers: "The earlier narratives represent them as fleeing and deserting Jesus at Gethsemane (Mark 14:50, Matthew 26:56), and remaining in concealment while they were in Jerusalem". Luke's narrative changes this by very significantly omitting Mark's statement that they dispersed at Jesus's arrest, and by saying that "certain disciples" (24:24) did in fact go to the sepulchre. John expands this, naming the visitors as Peter and the beloved disciple, and reporting on their rivalry. It is clear that if, for some reason, the belief that Jesus was risen was once established, all these other traditions could have arisen in the way indicated.

What, then, occasioned this belief in the first place? Our psychologists are not very successful in explaining even ordinary mental phenomena, so one must not expect too much by way of explanation of apparitions. Furthermore, it is almost universally believed that Jesus was crucified ca. AD 30, and that the gospel account that persons who became convinced of his Resurrection included some who had known him before his death is not to be challenged. I do not myself believe that the earliest (pre-gospel) Christian literature supports either of these premises. I have argued elsewhere that the earliest Christians regarded Jesus as a supernatural personage who had come down to Earth in human form long (one or two centuries) ago, had lived quite obscurely, been crucified in circumstances about which nothing was any longer known, and had risen from the dead. However, I do not wish to make my account here dependent on these views; so I shall try first to specify what might account for the appearances whether or not Paul or the other early 'apostles' had known Jesus personally, and second to inquire how belief in these appearances might have arisen among disciples who had so known him.

Every careful reader of the New Testament must notice how its authors twist and torture the most unpromising passages from the Jewish Scriptures into meaning something about Jesus. But "the resurrection seems to have baffled them, and no adequate Old Testament quotation is ever produced" (Elliott, p. 82). Nevertheless, the Jewish Wisdom literature does seem to have influenced the earliest Christian thinking on the Resurrection. Proverbs 3:19 and 8:22–36 represent Wisdom as a supernatural personage, created by God before he created Heaven and Earth, mediating in this creation and leading man into the path of truth. In the Wisdom of Solomon (from the Old Testament Apocrypha) Wisdom is the sustainer and governor of the universe who comes to dwell among men and bestows her gifts on them, although most of them reject her. 1 Enoch tells that, after being humiliated on Earth, Wisdom returned to Heaven. It is thus obvious that the humiliation on Earth and exaltation to Heaven of a supernatural personage, as preached by Paul and other early Christian writers, was well represented in the Jewish background. And it is not just that such ideas could have influenced Paul; they obviously did, for statements made about Wisdom in Jewish literature are made of Jesus in the Pauline letters. 1 Corinthians 1:23–25 comes very near to expressly calling the supernatural personage that had become man in Jesus 'Wisdom'.

There is another factor. Paul uses the phrase "first fruits" apropos of Christ's Resurrection (1 Corinthians 15:20) and also of the gift of the spirit to the Christian community (Romans 8:23). Both Jews and early Christians expected the end of the world to come quickly, and thought it would be presaged by a general resurrection and by the gift of the spirit. In these circumstances it is hardly surprising that some persons should, as Paul records, come forward with 'gifts of the spirit' and make ecstatic utterances. But if the presence of the spirit was a sign that the first fruits of the harvest of the end-time had already been gathered, then the resurrection must also be nigh. It may have been partly on this basis that early Christians came to believe that Christ was risen, that resurrection had, to this extent, already begun; and that a pledge had thus been given that a general resurrection of mankind would shortly follow.

In this connection I may mention Goguel's discussion of Talmudic evidence for the belief that the general resurrection will occur three days after the end of the world. Early Christians affirmed a close and direct relation between the Resurrection of Jesus and this general resurrection, and so, he says, "it is natural that the resurrection of the Christ was placed in a chronological rapport with his death similar to that which was thought would occur between the end of the world and the general resurrection".[27] Fuller notes that this implies that Paul's reference to Jesus's Resurrection 'on the third day' "is not a chronological datum, but a dogmatic assertion: Christ's resurrection marked the dawn of the end-time, the beginning of the cosmic eschatological process of resurrection" (p. 27).

It is in any case clear that the earliest Christian thinking on the Resurrection occurred within the context of Jewish apocalyptic thought: soon the end would come, the dead would be resurrected and judged, the righteous would then enjoy eternal blessedness, and the wicked would be punished. As the theologian J. L. Houlden says, "in its origins the resurrection faith was part and parcel of a conviction that the last days, as foreseen in apocalyptic, were in process of realization and soon to be consummated. In its totality that conviction was not borne out by events."[28] Elliott suggests how this apocalyptic framework facilitated belief in Jesus's Resurrection among disciples who, after his death, felt that he was still guiding them:

> Resurrection was the natural first-century Jewish way of describing this continuing influence . . . . Some people thought that John the Baptist had been raised from the dead (Mark 6:14ff), and that Elijah's spirit lived on in Elisha (2 Kings 2:15) and legends exist in the New Testament telling of people who were raised from the dead by Jesus and, later, by Peter and Paul. All these provide the environment in which belief in Jesus' resurrection took shape and flourished. These Jewish ideas would and did find favour in the Hellenistic world outside, where stories of dying and rising gods were part of the native folk myths. Thus to talk of the resurrection of Jesus would not have seemed so strange. (p. 90)

Elliott adds that the earliest impression of Jesus's abiding power after his death may well have been felt at his disciples' communal meals. "It is significant how many of the Easter Narratives have a eucharistic setting". Many theologians understandably find this kind of explanation more acceptable than believing the muddled evidence for a supernatural event.

Let us now turn to the gospels and their clear statement that the persons who saw Jesus risen had known him before his death. That they experienced mere subjective visions is often said to be excluded by the fact that they regarded his execution as the end of all their hopes. At his arrest they deserted him and fled (Mark 14:50). Peter, in this gospel the only one with courage enough to follow him as he was led a prisoner to the high priest's house, did so only to deny him in the courtyard there. In Mark this is the last we hear of the disciples until the women at the empty tomb are told to announce Jesus's Resurrection to them. Now if they really despaired at his arrest and execution, then it is not possible to believe that, on three separate occasions, he had predicted his own Resurrection, "telling" or "teaching" them (Mark 8:31, 9:31 and 10:32–34) that "the Son of man" must be killed and "after three days rise again". Morna Hooker says, justly, that it is "impossible to believe that the disciples were incapable of understanding the plain meaning of these words" (p. 92). Pannenberg (p. 132) takes the same view, and notes that most scholars share this scepticism concerning the authenticity of these predictions. Perhaps one reason for this is that, if authentic, they would put Jesus's attitude to his own death in a somewhat questionable light; for "can facing death be the same if one *knows* that three days later one is going to be raised up to share the glory of the Father?"[29] If, then, we set them aside as unhistorical, we are left with disciples despondent at Jesus's death. How could such despondency have been replaced by belief in his triumph over death? Carnley notes in this connection:

> Most of those who have argued for the subjective nature of the visions contend that psychological disturbance induced by the guilt of having deserted Jesus sufficiently accounts for them. The presence of the guilt is hinted at in the New Testament traditions at least in the case of Peter, whose denial of Jesus (Mark 14:66–72) may have had psychological repercussions, and Paul, whose persecution of Christians may have been a contributing factor to his experiences (Acts 26:9–11). The fact of the temporal dispersion of the experiences might count against the

possibility of the visions being caused by brief mass hysteria following close upon Jesus' death, but not if, in the passage of time, nagging guilt was a basic contributing factor. (p. 71)

He notes too that this "subjective vision hypothesis" is by no means implausible, and that today "even a relatively conservative scholar such as James Dunn admits that it is a possibility given the evidence we have" (p. 244). The late J. A. T. Robinson (author of *Honest to God*) tentatively held it in 1973 when he hinted that the disciples experienced hallucinations which made them love one another.[30]

ix. CONCLUSION

I have to agree with Bishop Carnley's remark that:

One of the most conclusive results of contemporary redactional studies of the New Testament traditions of the appearances, no less than of the empty tomb, is that an original nucleus of tradition has been developed during the course of its transmissions and that the resulting diversity can be explained by reference to apologetic motives and concerns along the way; the modification of the tradition is an inevitable by-product of the attempt to communicate and defend resurrection belief in different contexts to different people with different preconceptions and concerns. All this conditions what is said. The diversity of the resulting traditions cannot just be added together to form one synthetic account of what is supposed to have happened at the first Easter. (pp. 67–68)

He also finds that "fundamentalist writers and ultra-conservative popularizers of the Easter faith do the Church no lasting service by nervously seeking to defend a superficial harmony of the gospel narratives" (p. 27). Bishop Carnley's account of the New Testament evidence, and of what theologians since the end of the eighteenth century have made of it, is both full and fair, and his book, like many of those to which I have made reference, shows how much students outside the faith can learn from the work of serious Christian scholars. Nevertheless, his conviction that "our present experience of the spirit of Christ convinces us that the stories of the empty tomb and appearances are substantially true" (p. 249n.) supplies no adequate basis for such convictions. He states his position more fully as follows:

> The tradition of the 'heavenly visions' of the raised Christ did not stand alone in the experience of the first Christians . . . They had access to a second empirical anchor of their resurrection belief and eschatological hope, [namely] the continuing presence of a reality in the life of the Christian community which is identified as the 'presence of Christ' . . . . This additional datum is one to which we have direct access in the present, so that it grounds our continuing Easter faith no less than theirs. (p. 248)

I have suggested (above, p. 40) that in fact the early Christian emphasis on experience of the spirit of Christ was a potent source of erroneous belief; and Graham Shaw (until recently Chaplain of Exeter College, Oxford) has found, contrary to Carnley, that precisely this early Christian emphasis destroys "the most widespread basis for belief both in the resurrection of Jesus and in our own life after death".[31] So let us look more closely at the role of the spirit in early Christian communities.

Paul says that a man is no Christian if he does not possess the spirit of Christ (Romans 8:9), and that "in the spirit" a man can "speak mysteries" (1 Corinthians 14:2). In this latter context he goes on (verses 26ff) to note that, at Christian worship, some make spirit-inspired utterances, not understanding what they are saying, and others supply an interpretation. This procedure — interpretation of unintelligible utterances — could readily lead to the establishment of all manner of ill-founded doctrines. Moreover, at these meetings for worship, those who considered themselves "prophets" (and that included all present, verse 31) could pronounce some "revelation" (cf. below, pp. 85, 129f, 185, 192). Shaw points out that this kind of thing has been characteristic of many religions and has "a social rather than a supernatural origin". The way in which such spirit-inspired pronouncements could make the Resurrection of Jesus plausible to early believers is evidenced in chapter 8 of the epistle to the Romans, which is entirely about the role of the spirit in their lives and the associated promise of resurrection: "Jesus' Spirit speaking in their midst was a sign both of Jesus' continuing life, and also of their inclusion in that life" (p. 166). And "the corollary of this position is that the validity of much of Paul's gospel is dependent on the authenticity of the charismatic phenomena to which he appealed in the experience of his hearers" (p. 167). Paul's evidence for the Resurrection is a series of immediate revelations, to others and finally to himself, which puts him in the same position as the charismatics to whom he refers.

My survey in this chapter reinforces Shaw's statement that, when "with increasing urgency Christians asked what historical events could vindicate the metaphysical uniqueness of Christ, tending to place ever greater weight on the resurrection, the result was that the poverty of the factual basis for such claims only became more obvious" (pp. 273–74).

Quite apart from doubts resulting from historical inquiry, it is disconcerting to find Paul putting his arguments for Jesus's Resurrection in the very implausible context of an alleged link between sin and death, with death figuring as God's punishment for sin: "For as in Adam all die, so also in Christ shall all be made alive"—all, that is, who "belong to Christ" (1 Corinthians 15:22–23). At Romans 5:12, 15, and 17, death is expressly said to be a consequence of sin. But this is ridiculous. I again quote Shaw:

> Physical death is an integral part of organic life, and long predates the appearance of man. Man did not introduce death into an uncorrupted world; he evolved in an environment in which death was a necessary part of its organic processes. The assertion of a link, therefore, between human sin and actual death cannot be true; and Paul's theology of cross and resurrection, the conquest of sin and death, is thus deprived of any coherence (p. 280).

A further weakness is that part of Paul's argument for resurrection of the dead depends on spurious analogies. He holds that the seed develops into the plant only if it is first dead (1 Corinthians 15:36). In fact the seed that does so develop is not dead at all. He then introduces the contrast between seedtime and harvest: a dead and perishable body is "sown" (by being buried), but is then "raised" as imperishable; sown "in dishonour, it is raised in glory"; sown "in weakness, it is raised in power"; sown "a natural body, it is raised a spiritual body" (verses 42–44). The reader is meant to suppose that the phenomena of seedtime and harvest justify these stark contrasts, whereas, as Shaw says, "the use of harvest language itself is nowhere justified" (p. 98). Then, inevitably, Paul has recourse to the Old Testament, saying (verse 45): "So also it is written. The first man Adam became a living soul, the last Adam became a life-giving spirit". Genesis 2:7, which is here alluded to, says only that Adam "became a living soul" and nothing about 'the last Adam'.

Shaw allows that it is quite probable that Paul "had a convulsive experience" which he interpreted as a manifestation of the risen Jesus "in the light of claims he had already heard". Nevertheless, "that Christ was raised to life anywhere other than in Paul's imagination is unlikely" (p. 96). One can understand Shaw's statement that, if the intention of his book was not to "recognize the truth" but "to defend the articles of the creed", then "its implications would be devastating" (pp. xi, 182). If the earliest witness to Jesus's Resurrection has been shown to make out such a poor case, one can have little confidence in the very different and discrepant cases made out by later hands.

EPILOGUE TO CHAPTER TWO
A RESURRECTION DEBATE

In 1987 the New York firm Harper and Row published, as a book entitled *Did Jesus Rise from the Dead?*, the record of a 1985 debate between Professors Antony Flew and Gary Habermas at Liberty University (Lynchburg, Virginia), an institution known also as the Baptist College of the American evangelist Jerry Falwell. Habermas teaches theology there; Flew is emeritus Professor of Philosophy at Reading and known particularly well as an authority on the Scottish Enlightenment philosopher David Hume. The book includes a discussion following the debate in which Habermas is backed by two Christians as committed as himself (David Beck and the editor of the book, Terry L. Miethe). Of a panel of five philosophers, appointed to judge the content of the debate, four declared Habermas the winner and the fifth voted for a draw. A second panel of five professional judges of debates adjudicated on the argumentation technique of the two contestants and voted three to two in favour of Habermas.

The book also prints comments on the debate by a religious philosopher (Charles Hartshorne) and two theologians—Wolfhart Pannenberg and James I. Packer. Pannenberg is well-known as a commentator who, as we shall see, admits some mythical elements in the gospel Resurrection narratives. Packer is described as "one of the best-known evangelical theologians of our time" (p. xv). That these three scholars are only very mildly critical of Habermas shows how seriously his ultra-conservative position is taken, and that it is therefore worth detailed dissection. As the acknowledged winner of the debate, Habermas concludes the book with a response to their comments.

The speakers in a debate, after their initial prepared statements, have to rely on what comes to mind on the spur of the moment, and this leads almost inevitably to muddle. We may, for instance, meaningfully discuss what time gap there is between the dates of events alleged in a document and the date when the original of this document was written. We may equally meaningfully discuss what interval there is between this latter date and the date of the oldest extant copies. What is not meaningful is confusion of these two topics, as when Habermas declares (p. 67) that, as we feel no unease because our oldest copies of Plato are a good thousand years later than the originals (topic 2), we have no reason to jib at the accuracy of the creed outlining the death, burial, Resurrection and subsequent appearances of Jesus which is quoted by Paul only decades after these were supposed to have occurred (topic 1). (Whether in fact *all* these events – in particular Jesus's crucifixion and Resurrection, as against his subsequent appearances – were regarded as recent by Paul and his Christian contemporaries is something that I have questioned; cf. above, p. 32.)

The discussion after the debate is somewhat repetitive, each side pressing home points already made. Flew, as the solitary atheist, adumbrated some good points throughout, but did not have all the New Testament evidence and its problems immediately to mind. And he was up against opponents whose speciality lies in that very field. To those well-informed on these matters, who can supplement his suggestions from their own knowledge, his case will appear more persuasive than it did to an audience relying exclusively on what they heard. When one finds one of the philosopher judges deciding at the end that it was time he "began to take the resurrection seriously" (p. xiv), it is obvious that educated people are still susceptible to theological blandishments, which therefore need to be exposed *in extenso*.

On one matter the agreement of both sides in this debate is to be welcomed: namely that the kind of theological writing on the Resurrection which abandons its historicity yet affirms its significance is "nonsense", and that "there is no meaning if there is no event" (p. ix). This is directed against theologians such as Rudolf Bultmann, who maintained, on the one hand that the Resurrection of Christ is "the eschatological event *par excellence*", that "cross and resurrection form a single, indivisible cosmic event which brings judgment to the world and opens up for men the possibility of authentic life" (by which is meant "life based on unseen, intangible realities"); and on the other hand that "the resurrection is not an event of past history", and that "if the event of Easter Day is in any sense an historical event additional to the event of the cross, it is nothing else than the rise of faith in the risen Lord, since it was this faith which led to the apostolic preaching".[1]

Although we may agree to deplore such doublethink, what inspired it — and this is something that Habermas never indicates — was the conviction that vindicating the Resurrection as a historical fact on the basis of the New Testament evidence was a well-nigh hopeless task. Habermas does, however, allude to the difficulty of such an undertaking when he says: "Perhaps" — only perhaps! — "even a majority of the German theologians" (notably more sceptical than the British)" . . . believe that Jesus was raised from the dead" (p. 62). So we are to understand that at any rate a minority of Christian theologians find such a position no longer tenable.

Both sides in the debate seem to think (pp. ix, 3) that the Resurrection, if a fact, would prove Jesus to be God. This was certainly not the view of Paul, nor of other early Christian writers (cf. above, p. 23). Also, I find it irritating that both sides repeatedly say that the risen Jesus met Paul "on the road to Damascus". The encounter may well have taken place in that city, for Paul says elsewhere that he *returned* there after spending the first period of his Christian life in Arabia (Galatians 1:15–17). But the Damascus road is specified only in Acts' romantic version, and only a minority of scholars suppose that the author of Acts had more than sketchy knowledge of Paul, filled out with conjectures.

Habermas expresses great confidence in the general reliability of the gospels and the Acts of the Apostles (pp. 43, 58). He does not argue such matters, but names scholars who take this view. Altogether, he follows a technique which may fairly be called intimidation through numbers: "Craig lists forty-four critical scholars who argue for the empty tomb" (p. 71). As we have seen, it would be equally easy to enumerate Christian scholars who think otherwise, both on the trustworthiness of the gospels and on the empty tomb. If one were to trust in their authority, instead of in that of their more conservative colleagues, one would at least have the justification that Christians would be unlikely to make such concessions unless there were compelling evidence for them.

As a further appeal to authority, Habermas sternly tells Flew that, if he denies that there is eyewitness testimony in the gospels, he is "going to have to argue with eminent scholars such as Raymond Brown", whose major commentary on the fourth gospel "concludes that the Apostle John is the chief contributor to the historical tradition behind it" (p. 55). Habermas's implication is that, if eyewitness testimony is conceded in the case of the fourth gospel — "perhaps" (he repeatedly uses this adverb to avoid conceding or claiming too much) "the most disputed of the four" — it can hardly be denied the other three. It would be truer to say that, if John has got the record right, the others must have got it badly wrong.

Since Habermas believes (p. 40) that the New Testament narratives of Jesus's birth and infancy are defensible as history, he himself is 'going to have to argue' with Brown, who has given a very full demonstration that they are legendary. Brown, a Catholic priest, is a very undogmatic scholar, and what he says about the fourth gospel (cf. above, pp. 10f) is much more guarded than Habermas suggests. He also makes it clear that he does not believe that the first three gospels were written by eyewitnesses of Jesus's ministry.

Habermas introduces his account of the textual evidence with an allusion to the tools of "form and redaction criticism" (p. 19), implying that they had strengthened the case for orthodoxy.[2] Fuller, who applies these tools throughout his book, reaches the conclusion that "they have altered our whole understanding of the gospel narratives", which "can no longer be read as direct accounts of what happened, but rather as vehicles for proclamation . . . . The Christian cannot be required to believe that the Risen One literally walked on earth in an earthly form, as in the Emmaus story [Luke 24:13–32], or that he physically ate fish as in the Lucan appearance to the disciples at Jerusalem, or that he invited physical touch as in the Thomas story" (pp. 172–73).

Habermas proceeds to name (on a single page) 16 theologians (even though many of them were sceptical about the Resurrection) because some of them "refuted each other's theories, leaving no viable naturalistic hypotheses" (p. 20), so that the Resurrection must be accepted as a supernatural event. (One of the second panel of judges very appositely commented (p. xv) that Habermas's "citations of so many scholars kept him from spending more time on the content of his argument"). The obvious 'naturalistic' hypothesis is that the whole thing is a legend, but one way in which he disposes of this view is by saying that Otto Pfleiderer (a radical enough theologian) "was critical" of it and "even admitted that it did not explain Jesus' Resurrection" (p. 21). Habermas is not always to be trusted in the use he makes of the numerous authorities he mentions. In the pages of Pfleiderer to which he refers, the Resurrection is expressly called a "Christian myth", and all that is conceded is that it is not *totally* explicable in terms of parallels with dying and rising pagan gods, but "had its most direct source in the historical fact of the death of Jesus and the following visions seen by his disciples".[3]

The whole argument of Habermas and his supporters depends on harmonizing the epistles with the gospels and Acts and thereby eliminating the significance of the gap in time and circumstances between them. When, for instance, Flew pointed out that the gospels know nothing of the appearance of the risen one to above 500 simultaneously (alleged by Paul), Habermas replied that Matthew "does say that Jesus appeared on a hillside" and "more may have been there than just the eleven disciples". But no other audience is mentioned, and it is the eleven alone that Jesus here addresses and instructs (Matthew 28:16–20). On the basis of Habermas's harmonization, Miethe can suppose that "the claims of seeing Jesus' resurrected body are close enough in time to the original event that we have dozens, dozens of eyewitnesses running around, the church is causing all this havoc, the Roman empire is being affected, so much so that Caesar's household is involved, and Christians are being persecuted" (p. 102). He can then triumphantly ask why, if such claims were untrue, someone did not put a stop to them by disproving them. When Flew countered by asking why such epoch-making events were not remarked upon at all by writers of the time, he was told that he was in error, that they were indeed noticed — by Thallus (pp. 106–07; cf. above, p. 23).

Habermas sets out his harmonization as follows: Paul quotes an already existing Christian creed which lists Jesus's appearances; and Luke, who knew Paul personally (p. 58), wrote a gospel which described these appearances, he, like other evangelists, being an eyewitness to such events or at any rate having access to eyewitness reports. Furthermore, as Paul admits to having visited Peter and James in Jerusalem, he in all likelihood obtained the creed he quotes from them, and they, according to the gospels, had known Jesus personally. So unless the appearances were hallucinations we could hardly have stronger evidence for the Resurrection: a creed based on statements by men who had known both the historical and the risen Jesus, and promulgated by men who were prepared to die for their beliefs (p. 59).

This final point carries little weight as, apart from the fact that we are today familiar enough with religious and political fanatics prepared to die for their various faiths, Christianity originated in a Jewish environment where martyrdom was highly prized. Beagley has recently endorsed Bousset's description of the Jewish religion as "a religion of martyrdom . . . , born of the martyrdom and suffering of the pious ones of the Maccabean time".[4] 1 Maccabees, written probably about 100 BC, records (1:62–63) that in 167 BC many Jews chose to die rather than eat what the Mosaic law stipulates to be unclean food. 2 Maccabees, written about 50 BC, tells of Jews who died rather than eat, or even pretend to eat, swine's flesh (6:18–31; 7:1–42), and indicates that some of these died in the hope of resurrection — a factor also of importance as part of the background to earliest Christianity. In any case, Habermas exaggerates the extent of martyrdom in early Christianity. That many suffered the death penalty is not borne out even by the Church's own account of its early history in Acts, where, for instance, most of the twelve quickly disappear from the narrative. His statement that "most of the apostles" died for their Resurrection message (p. 154) far outruns the evidence.

I have commented earlier on Luke as an eyewitness. That he was a companion of Paul is, for Habermas, indicated "by such signs as" references in Acts to 'we' or 'us', meaning Paul and his companions. (Note the characteristic suggestion that there is far more evidence than this particular "sign" and that 'we could, an if we would'). We saw that many theologians do not accept this interpretation of the 'we' passages, and also regard the Paul of Acts as quite incompatible with the Paul of the epistles. As for the suggestion that Paul "took great care to interview the apostles personally in order to ascertain the nature of the Gospel, which includes the Resurrection (Gal. 1:18–20; 2:1–10)" (p. 56), we may note that, whatever Paul's purpose was in visiting the apostles, it was certainly not to ascertain the nature of the gospel; for in the very epistle here adduced he stresses that his gospel is dependent on no human authority, but came to him through a direct revelation: "For I make known to you, brethren, as touching the gospel which was preached by me, that it is not after man. For neither did I receive it from man, nor was I taught it, but it came to me through revelation of Jesus Christ" (Galatians 1:11–12; cf. the opening verse of this epistle).

In the course of the discussion Flew's opponents make much of the fact that the Greek of 1 Corinthians 15:5–8 translated as 'he appeared to' is, in more literal rendering, 'he was seen by', the verb being *horaō* (I see). David Beck, for instance, holds that this rules out the possibility that Paul was "referring to some kind of vision". He "is using ordinary observation terms" and is thus "referring to a physical body" (p. 97). But at Colossians 2:18 Paul denigrates some rival who made too much of his 'visions'—in more literal translation, 'of the things he had seen'—using the same Greek verb where the reference is clearly to fanciful imaginings. Fuller notes that, in the Septuagint (the Greek translation of the Old Testament that has greatly influenced the New), this same verb is used of appearances of angels and of God, and that the question whether what appears is seen "with the physical eye or with the eye of the mind or the spirit is left entirely undetermined" (p. 30). Habermas, *after* the debate, the discussion and the voting, allowed that "*horaō* does not specify either bodily or visionary sight" (p. 165).

Flew pointed repeatedly to marked differences between the Pauline and the gospel accounts of the appearances, and Pannenberg takes his side on this issue, agreeing that:

> the Gospels, especially Luke, present the reality of the Risen One in a much more earthly fashion than the report in Acts on Paul's conversion by the light and the voice coming to him from heaven . . . . The Easter narratives in the Gospels, however, represent a much later stage of the tradition than Paul's own remark (Galatians 1:15), which fits with the story in Acts (p. 131).

He adds that it is "not possible to deny legendary elements" in the Resurrection narratives, and so he cannot "consider the Gospels in every respect as historically reliable sources, as Professor Habermas says they are" (p. 132).

The Virgin Birth

1. INTRODUCTION

It is now generally accepted that many of the canonical epistles were written before the gospels, and that the earliest extant gospel is Mark's, used as a source by Matthew and Luke, each of whom was unacquainted with the other's work. The fourth gospel, ascribed to John, is independent of the others, but clearly used sources which were in part identical with theirs.

The virgin birth of Jesus is recorded in only two of the 27 books of the New Testament, namely the gospels of Matthew and Luke. None of the epistles nor the book of Revelation make any mention of it. All that Paul says about Jesus's birth is that he was "born of a woman" (Galatians 4:4). He believed that Jesus existed as a supernatural being before the world was created, and he is here arguing that he humbled himself by being born as an ordinary Jew "under the law". Anything but a quite ordinary birth would go against this argument which is concerned to stress Jesus's extreme self-abasement in adopting human existence.

Of the four gospels, the earliest (Mark's) shows no knowledge of Jesus's origins, and does not even mention Joseph's name. It introduces Jesus as an adult "from Nazareth of Galilee", coming to be baptized in the Jordan by John the Baptist. The fourth gospel does not name his mother as Mary and has nothing to say about his birth. It begins with a metaphysical prologue which states that, to those who believe in him, Jesus gave the power to become children of God, "which were born not of blood, nor of the will of the flesh, nor of the will of man, but of God" (John 1:13). To see any allegation of virgin birth here would mean ascribing such a birth to all believers. A few late manuscripts have tried to introduce a reference to Jesus by changing the 'which' and the 'were born' into the corresponding Greek singulars. What the evangelist is really saying is that true Christians do not owe their becoming such to their natural origin, nor to any earthly conditions.[1]

After this prologue, the fourth gospel introduces Jesus as an adult, called "the lamb of God" by John the Baptist; whereupon

Philip describes him as "Jesus of Nazareth, the son of Joseph" (1:36, 45). In continuing his presentation the evangelist never disavows these statements that Jesus was naturally born and hails from Nazareth, not from Bethlehem. He even represents the Jews as rejecting his Messianic claims on the ground that he was not born in Bethlehem (7:42). In this gospel his brothers seem not to regard him as of supernatural origin, for "even they did not believe on him" (7:5).

The fourth gospel is not an early work, and its author may have known traditions that Jesus was virgin born and deliberately rejected them. However, that the doctrine is also absent both from the epistles and from the earliest of the four gospels does suggest that it entered Christian tradition only at a relatively late stage. This is confirmed by non-canonical evidence, in that the earliest Christian writer outside the canon to mention the doctrine is Ignatius of Antioch, writing probably about AD 110. (What he says on the subject shows that he was dependent on the same kind of traditions as Matthew had drawn on.[2]) It is confirmed even more strikingly by the only two canonical gospels which do treat of the birth and infancy; for in both of them, the accounts of Jesus's ministry (his adult preaching and wonder-working) which follow the infancy narratives were clearly drawn from traditions which knew nothing of the infancy material. Let me illustrate.

According to Matthew's infancy narrative, Herod and all Jerusalem knew of the birth in Bethlehem of "him that is born King of the Jews" (2:2–3), and Herod proceeded to slaughter all the male children of Bethlehem in order to eliminate him (2:16); yet when the adult Jesus comes to his "own country" and preaches there, he is regarded by the inhabitants as a familiar but totally undistinguished citizen, whose "wisdom" and "mighty works" take them completely by surprise. They say of him:

> Is not this the carpenter's son? Is not his mother called Mary? And his brethren, James, and Joseph and Simon and Judas? And his sisters, are they not all with us? Whence then hath this man all these things (i.e. this wisdom and these mighty works)? (13:54–56).

It is, then, precisely the "indisputable ordinariness" (Von Campenhausen, pp. 12–13) of Jesus's home, occupation, and family relationships that is alleged to have stood in his way. Even Herod's son has no inkling of his origins (14:1–2). The foremost Catholic exegete of the nativity stories, Raymond E. Brown, has said that it is obvious from these and other discrepancies that "the stories of the ministry were shaped in Christian tradition without a knowledge of the infancy material", and Matthew "never really smoothed out all the narrative rough spots left by the joining of two bodies of once-independent material" (p. 32). Brown adds that "if the first two chapters had been lost and the Matthaean Gospel came down to us beginning with 3:1, no one would ever have suspected the existence of the missing chapters" (p. 49). He shows that Luke's gospel displays exactly the same discrepancy between infancy narrative and main body: "If John the Baptist was a relative of Jesus who recognized him even before his birth (Luke 1:41, 44), why does John the Baptist give no indication during the ministry of a previous knowledge of Jesus and indeed seem to be puzzled by him (7:19)?" (p. 32).

Such residual discrepancies are the more striking because Matthew and Luke have obviously 'edited' the material about the ministry that reached them from Mark's gospel so as to eliminate any suggestion that Jesus was misunderstood by his own family who — if the birth narratives record historical facts — must have been well aware of his supernatural origin. Mark 3:21 has it that "the ones from beside him" (or "those alongside him") went out to seize him, thinking he had lost his senses. Some older English versions translate the Greek here as though the reference were to 'his friends'. However, the meaning in this context is 'his family', for when they reach him in verse 31, they are identified as his mother and brothers. Matthew and Luke simply omit this story. Again, at Mark 6:4 Jesus says: "A prophet is not without honour, save in his own country, and among his own kin, and in his own house". Matthew cuts out the words "and among his own kin", and Luke makes Jesus say merely that "no prophet is acceptable in his own country".

The New Testament epistles (and not only the Pauline ones) make it obvious that the earliest Christian preaching concentrated almost exclusively on the crucifixion and Resurrection. At this early stage these events were simply alleged to have happened and not given any historical context. I have given the evidence concerning the Resurrection in this regard in the previous chapter, but it may surprise readers to learn that the crucifixion is also, in the earliest documents, invariably mentioned with no specification of time, place or attendant circumstances. It is merely said again and again that it took place "in due season" (Romans 5:6), "for us", "for our sins". Not until the gospels is the event set in a definite historical context, and I have argued elsewhere that this discrepancy strongly suggests that, for earlier writers, the crucifixion was not something that had occurred recently in known circumstances, but was believed to have happened in unknown circumstances one or two centuries previously. Be that as it may, the distinction between what is said about it in the two layers of tradition is a real one that is constantly blurred by apologists. Typical is A. E. Harvey, who claims that the crucifixion "under Pontius Pilate" is "not ony described in considerable detail in all four canonical gospels", but is "referred to on countless occasions in the other New Testament writings";[3] whereas in fact these 'countless' other references are not to a crucifixion under Pilate, but to one in completely unspecified circumstances.

However one interprets this earlier evidence, it is clear that, by the time the earliest gospel was written, Christian interest in the crucifixion had led to the formation of a detailed passion narrative. And it is understandable that, by then, interest had extended further to what Jesus had done and taught in his lifetime, so that this narrative is preceded by an account of his ministry. But only the yet later gospels of Matthew and Luke represent a stage where curiosity had reached out to his origins; and their accounts are so full of difficulties in themselves and so discrepant with each other as to suggest that there was no reliable information on the subject, that all that tradition provided was an allegation of virgin birth at Bethlehem in the days of Herod the Great which speculation had free rein to develop—as free as we have seen to have been the case with the Resurrection appearances.

ii. THE BIRTH AT BETHLEHEM

a. Matthew's Account

Unlike Luke, who introduces Joseph and Mary as residents of Nazareth from the first, Matthew implies that their home was in "Bethlehem of Judea"; for he begins his second chapter by recording Jesus's birth there, and he represents the holy couple as wishing to return there after their flight from Herod into Egypt. They failed to do so only because Joseph was warned in a dream that Herod's son Archelaus (who by this time had succeeded his father and reigned over the southern part of the kingdom) was an equal danger to them;

and so they went instead to live in Nazareth in Galilee (2:21–23). Here, in the north, another of Herod's sons, Antipas, was ruler.[4]

Matthew represents the change of abode from Bethlehem to Nazareth not only as unexpected but also as fulfilment of prophecy; and he says the same of Herod's slaughter of the Innocents in Bethlehem. This massacre is not mentioned by Luke, nor by any ancient historian. It is in particular unmentioned by the Jewish historian Flavius Josephus, who in the first century AD recorded the history of Herod and his family, and even stressed its horrors. This particular horror would in any case have constituted a quite unnecessary action on Herod's part. Exotic magi from the east with royal gifts would have made a great impression in a small place like Bethlehem, and it would have been no great task for Herod's intelligence system to discover which child they had visited and then kill him. This would have been more to Herod's purpose than the hit-or-miss method of killing all the male children under two years in the place (cf. Brown, pp. 188–89). Apologists have nevertheless argued that Herod was ferocious enough to have done something of this kind, particularly in the final years of his life, and that Matthew's account therefore rings true in respect of this detail. The answer must be made that Matthew himself may well have had the same idea; that he knew enough about the reign of Herod to realize that ferocious acts could plausibly be attributed to him, and to anticipate that readers who also knew something (if not much) of him would find such a story believable.

Brown makes this point, and adds (pp. 227–28) that an Old Testament parallel to Matthew's story was ready at hand, namely the Pharaoh's massacre of the Hebrew male children of Egypt (Exodus 1:22), from which the infant Moses nevertheless escaped. It has long been recognized that Matthew is much concerned to portray Jesus as a second — and greater — Moses. "The experiences of the leader of the Exodus are, as it were, recapitulated in the great Redeemer who will bring about the final deliverance of the people of God" (Beare, p. 72).

Altogether there is much in Matthew's infancy narrative which although "quite implausible" as history, is perfectly intelligible as "rewritings of Old Testament scenes or themes" (Brown, p. 36). For instance, the Joseph of the infancy narrative dreams dreams (he is thrice advised in a dream, and on two of these occasions the advice is said to come from an angel). He also goes down into Egypt, the only man in the New Testament to do so. Precisely these two activities are associated with the patriarch Joseph, the hero of Genesis 37–50. Matthew's story of the magi, the "wise men from the east" (2:1) and their guiding star seems to owe something to the story of Balaam in Numbers 22–24, where this soothsayer from the east is represented as foretelling the destruction of Moab and Edom at the hands of a future ruler of Israel, symbolized by a rising star:

> There shall come forth a star out of Jacob,
> And a sceptre shall rise out of Israel,
> And shall smite through the corners of Moab,
> And break down all the sons of tumult.
> And Edom shall be a possession. (Numbers 24:17–18)

The commentator in the old *Century Bible* notes that "it is difficult to believe that the author of these lines had in view any other than King David, who first reduced Moab to subjection (2 Samuel 8:2)".[5] The lines (like the whole of the Pentateuch) date from long after David, and so the 'prophecy' was written with hindsight. The early Church came to regard it as referring not to David, but to the Messiah, and so for Matthew it seemed appropriate that a star should point to the Messianic child.

Matthew's magi are not said to be kings nor to be three in number. (This latter idea arose probably because they present three gifts, gold, frankincense and myrrh to the newborn child.) Their story is firmly set in a context of astrological belief. They observed the star "at its rising" (Matthew 2:2, cf. NEB, not "in the east", as older versions have it. When Matthew means the relevant Greek noun to mean 'the east', he uses it in its plural form, as in the previous verse). "The moment of a star's appearance above the horizon was of prime importance in astrology. Probably it is assumed that the star appeared at the precise moment of the Saviour's birth or conception" (Beare, p. 77).

On reaching Jerusalem the star turned south to Bethlehem — miraculously, as the apparent movement of all stars in the sky is from east to west. It seems an unnecessary miracle, as Herod has instructed the magi to seek the child at Bethlehem (2:8), and no star is needed to guide them across the five miles from Jerusalem to this known destination. The star is, however, made to perform a useful function by the further miracle of hovering "over where the young child was", i.e., as the sequel makes clear, above the very house where he lay (2:9–11). A star which not merely turned south but also came to rest so as to point out a particular house would have "constituted a celestial phenomenon unparalleled in astronomical history: yet it received no notice in the records of the times" (Brown, p. 188). Noteworthy in this connection is that there is no suggestion in Matthew, as there is in Luke, that Jesus was laid in a manger because Joseph and Mary could not find accommodation in an inn. "When the astrologers find him, he and his mother are in a house, and the reader would naturally assume that it is their own house" (Beare, p. 76).

Apologists have tried hard to find some astronomical occurrence which might have been interpreted as the star of the magi. Halley's comet (visible every 77 years) appeared 12–11 BC; there was a rare conjunction of the planets Jupiter and Saturn in 7 BC, and Mars passed by early in the following year. None of this makes Matthew's story into plausible history, for, as with his account of Herod's slaughter of the Innocents, he may have been drawing on some remembered phenomenon and linking it, with considerable distortion and embellishment, with Jesus's birth. Matthew wrote after AD 70, and what legends had then come to be told of astronomical occurrences of two or three generations earlier, "in the days of Herod the king", might have prompted his story. Such a story was not unusual in that Mediterranean world, which had "many a star, many a planet to herald important births".[6]

If, as we have seen, the traditions of Jesus's ministry knew nothing of those embodied in the infancy narratives, the latter themselves, as they stand in the two relevant gospels, are composite and comprise elements of different provenance. For instance, Matthew's first chapter records the virgin birth, but does not name any place of birth. His second chapter seems to mark the beginning of another, originally independent, birth story, which locates the event in Bethlehem, but knows nothing of a *virgin* birth. Nothing in it presupposes information from chapter 1. This second chapter itself combines originally independent stories. Joseph, prominent in 2:13–23, is totally absent from 2:1–12, and this is quite intelligible if the substance of 2:1–12 came from another tradition in which he had no major part. At the beginning of this chapter, the wise men are guided by the star to Herod at Jerusalem, and their question "where is he that is born King of the Jews?" leads, by means of an investigation of the Scriptures, to the answer: in Bethlehem. But this place is in the sequel pointed out to them by the star, thus making the scriptural investigation unnecessary. On all this, Brown comments:

> Why does the star, which eventually leads the magi to the house where Jesus is, not lead them directly to Bethlehem from the East, so that a stop at Jerusalem would not be necessary? We seem to have two different stories pointing to Bethlehem, one through investigation of the Scriptures, the other through the star. Herod's failure to find the child at Bethlehem would be perfectly intelligible in a story in which there were no magi who came from the East and where he had only general scriptural knowledge about Bethlehem to guide him. It becomes ludicrous when the way to the house has been pointed out by a star which came to rest over it, and when the path to the door of the house in a small village has been blazed by exotic foreigners (p. 191).

b. Luke's Account

Although the infancy narratives of Matthew and Luke are quite independent, neither evangelist having read the account of the other, both were clearly acquainted with traditions which located Jesus's birth in Bethlehem during the reign of Herod the Great, and both knew from Mark's gospel that he spent his adult life in and around Nazareth and in Galilee generally. But on these bases they build very differently. Matthew, we saw, makes Bethlehem the home of his parents, and solves the problem of the family's later departure from that place with his stories of persecutions and angelic warnings, which are unknown to Luke. Luke however makes the parents resident in Nazareth, so his problem is to get them to Bethlehem for the birth. His solution is to make Joseph and Mary go there because Augustus had ordered a census of the whole Roman Empire: "Now it came to pass in those days there went out a decree from Caesar Augustus, that all the world should be enrolled" (2:1). By enrolment is meant the registration of names and property as a basis for taxation.

There is in fact no evidence for a census of the whole Empire under Augustus. Obvious authorities, such as the *Monumentum Ancyranum*, Dio Cassius, and Suetonius are silent on the matter, and the only witnesses who speak of such a thing are Christians, from the sixth century onwards, which creates "a very strong suspicion that they simply drew their information from Luke" (Schürer, p. 409). The census thus seems to be "a purely literary device used by Luke to associate Mary and Joseph, residents of Nazareth, with Bethlehem" (Fitzmyer, p. 393).

By the expression "in those days" (2:1) Luke means "in the days of Herod, king of Judea" (1:5) — a verse which introduces the story of Mary's kinswoman Elisabeth. She, having in her old age become pregnant with John the Baptist, "hid herself five months" (1:24). A month later, the angel Gabriel visits Mary, informs her of her kinswoman's condition, and tells her that she herself will conceive Jesus miraculously; whereupon Mary "arose in these days", went to Elisabeth and stayed three months with her (1:39–40, 56). On her arrival, Elisabeth addresses her as "the mother of my Lord" and says "blessed is the fruit of thy womb" (1:42–43), clearly indicating that Mary herself is also pregnant. Chapter 2 takes up Mary's story when she is about to give birth to her child. This will be six months later, and it was "in those days" that Augustus decreed the census (2:1). Thus Luke's initial "in the days of Herod" (1:5) is followed by the phrase "in these days" (1:39) and "in those days" (2:1), with no suggestion of any gap in time, and with intervening events which in no way imply any such gap. Hence, "for all its vagueness", this phrase "dates the birth of Jesus in 'the days of Herod' " (Fitzmyer, p. 399).

Now a Roman census in Palestine in Herod's time was out of the question. Although then under Roman influence, it was not made part of the Empire until AD 6, ten years after Herod's death, when Augustus deposed Herod's son Archelaus and incorporated his territory into the province of Syria. Herod was a client king, holding his title and authority from Caesar and the Senate; he had to defend the imperial frontier and was not allowed to make treaties or wage war at pleasure, but was permitted freedom in his management of Palestine's internal affairs. If the Romans had — contrary to their known policy — carried out a valuation census on his territory, this would have been extremely unpopular, would have "offended the people to the quick", as Schürer says; in which case we should expect it to be recorded by Josephus, for "on no other period is Josephus so well informed, on none is he so thorough, as on that of Herod's last years" (p. 418). But he makes no mention of it.

Luke not only alleges a Roman census on Herod's territory in his lifetime, but also says: "this was the first registration, and it was made when Quirinius was governor of Syria" (2:2).[7] Herod died in 4 BC, but Quirinius became governor of Syria only in AD 6 (Schürer, p. 420). His career "is fairly well known and defies all attempts either to attribute to him two censuses in Judea or to date the start of his legateship of Syria to any other period than AD 6–7" (Fitzmyer, p. 402).[8]

Josephus mentions a census under Quirinius in the year AD 6. This was quite in order, for Judea had just been converted into a Roman province, and the imperial legate needed to make a list of the inhabitants and a reckoning of their landed property for the purpose of apportioning the taxation. Josephus says that this census was the first and that it was altogether novel for the Romans to raise a tax in Judea. (The passages are quoted by Schürer, p. 419.) He also says that it caused the Jews to revolt, under the leadership of Judas the Gaulonite of Gamala. The Acts of the Apostles, written by the author of the third gospel, refers (5:37) to "Judas of Galilee in the days of the enrolment" (*apographē*, as at Luke 2:2). He would not have referred to this census of AD 6 as *the* enrolment if he had known of an earlier one. Hence we must infer that in his gospel he had in mind the census of AD 6, but antedated it and supposed it to have occurred in Herod's lifetime.

It is not hard to see how this error could have happened. The death of Herod in 4 BC and the Roman annexation of Judea in AD 6 were both "striking events in Palestinian history which would leave their mark in the minds of men" and "serve for approximate dating in a society not given to exact documentation".[9] It would be all the easier to confuse the two, as each was followed by an uprising. According to Josephus, Varus, then legate of Syria, had to intervene in 4 BC with the whole of his army. But the uprising of AD 6 was the more sharply remembered because it was then that Roman rule and taxation were imposed.

A further objection to Luke's account is that even the census of AD 6 would not have affected Galilee, where Mary and Joseph were living. When Herod died, the southern part of his kingdom (Idumea, Judea, and Samaria) was given to Archelaus, but Galilee in the north was put under another of his sons, Antipas. Archelaus was deposed in AD 6 and his territory annexed to the Empire, but Antipas remained in office and ruled Galilee until AD 39. Luke implies that the inhabitants of Galilee were affected by a Roman census that in fact applied only to more southern provinces. Again we see that he is not concerned with accuracy of historical detail. His purpose is to get Mary from Nazareth to Bethlehem in time for the birth of her child. In obedience to the imperial decree:

All went up to enrol themselves, every one to his own city. And Joseph also went up from Galilee, out of the city of Nazareth, into Judea, to the city of David, which is called Bethlehem, because he was of the house and family of David: to enrol himself with Mary, who was betrothed to him, being great with child (2:3-5).

We are thus required to believe that the 'own city' to which everyone was required to go was the place where his family originated; and that Joseph therefore went to Bethlehem, 85 miles away, because a thousand years earlier his ancestor David had been born there. But the practical Romans had no such cumbersome custom. "In a Roman census, landed property had to be registered for taxation in the locality within which it was situated", and "the person to be taxed had to register in the place where he lived or in the chief town of his taxation district" (Schürer, p. 411). It would have been ridiculous to make a man give his returns miles away from his home, where the authorities would be unable to check the entries he made. In any case, Schürer adds, "it is very doubtful whether a registration according to tribes and genealogies was possible; many were no longer able to establish that they belonged to this or that family". Nor would Mary have needed to accompany Joseph, for the particulars needed for a Roman census "could be supplied by the father of the family".

From all these considerations we can hardly avoid the inference that Luke has invented the journey of Mary and Joseph across some 80 miles of difficult country in order to have Jesus born in the place which, he stresses, is "David's city" (2:11), as he thought was expected of the Messiah.

We can see already by now that the infancy narratives of the two evangelists cannot be harmonized. In Matthew an angel announces the virgin birth to Joseph in Bethlehem in a dream. In Luke the angel, named as Gabriel, comes to Mary in Nazareth, and not in a dream but in person. The exalted status of the child is attested in Luke by an angel's words to shepherds and the song of the heavenly host (neither of which is mentioned in Matthew), but in Matthew by the appearance of the star (not mentioned in Luke). The child receives his first adoration in Luke from the shepherds who go unmentioned in Matthew, and in Matthew from the magi (unmentioned in Luke). In Matthew the holy family lived originally at Bethlehem, but in Luke they go there only because of a census of the people (not mentioned by Matthew). After the birth they went, according to Luke, first to

Jerusalem, where the child was presented in the temple, and where the pious and aged Simeon hailed him as "a light to lighten the gentiles", and the prophetess Anna gave thanks to God for his birth. Then the holy family went straight back to Nazareth (2:39), where by the grace of God the child's early years were passed in uninterrupted growth (2:40). None of this is known to Matthew, who represents these early years as disturbed by perils and changes of abode. Matthew implies (2:16) that the child was a little under two years old when the family fled from Bethlehem to Egypt, and obviously older, perhaps years older, when they left Egypt to settle in Nazareth. As Brown notes, their flight into Egypt "is quite irreconcilable with Luke's account of an orderly and uneventful return from Bethlehem to Nazareth shortly after the birth of the child" (p. 225).

iii. LUKE'S PARALLEL BETWEEN JOHN THE BAPTIST AND JESUS

Luke's narrative begins with the story of the priest Zacharias, visited in the temple by the angel Gabriel who tells him that his aged wife Elisabeth "shall bear thee a son, and thou shalt call his name John" (1:13). Old Testament material has obviously been remodelled here. Luke is "reviving the pattern of the births of Old Testament promise-bearers and saviours — Isaac, Samson and Samuel — who are likewise miraculously born to old and barren women through the unexpected intervention of God" (Von Campenhausen, p. 27). And Luke's description of Zacharias and Elisabeth "is taken, at times almost verbatim, from the Old Testament description of Abraham and Sarah" (Brown, p. 36).

Zacharias is struck temporarily dumb as a punishment for questioning Gabriel's announcement; and Elisabeth, on becoming pregnant, hides herself for five months (1:20 and 24). Both these events are dictated by what Creed calls "the necessities of the narrative" (p. 12); for when Gabriel subsequently visits Mary and promises her a child he needs a sign with which to dispel her incredulity, and this sign consists in his assurance to her: "Behold, Elisabeth thy kinswoman, she also hath conceived a son in her old age; and this is the sixth month of her that was called barren. For no word from God shall be void of power" (1:36–37). Obviously, but for Zacharias's dumbness and Elisabeth's seclusion, Mary would have come to know of her kinswoman's pregnancy, which thus would not have been available as a trump card to Gabriel.

If the conception of John the Baptist required a miracle, that of Jesus requires an even greater one, a virginal conception. The parallelism between John and Jesus in this chapter is what Fitzmyer calls a "step-parallelism", i.e. "a parallelism with one-upmanship. The Jesus-side always comes off better" (p. 315).

Gabriel comes to Mary in Nazareth and tells her: "thou shalt conceive in thy womb" (1:31). She takes this as implying a natural conception, for she replies: "How shall this be, seeing I know not a man?" — a question which can only mean: 'I have no such acquaintance with any man as might lead to the fulfilment of this prophecy'. But the exact opposite of this is involved in the actual situation. She is betrothed to Joseph (1:27) and must necessarily have looked to the fulfilment of the prophecy through her marriage with him. Mary's question is thus not how a woman in her situation would have reacted to the angel's announcement, but is perfectly intelligible from the needs of Luke's narrative. The real purpose of her question is "to advance the dialogue" (Fitzmyer, p. 350), "to give the writer an opening for the angel's prophecy as to how the conception is to come to pass" (Creed, p. 19). And so the angel is able to answer by telling her that "the Holy Ghost shall come upon thee" so that she shall give birth to "the Son of God" (1:35).

Luke's second chapter may well have been drawn from a different tradition — one which knew nothing of a virgin birth; for at 2:7 and 48 it is implied that Jesus is the first-born son of Mary and Joseph. Chapter 2 itself combines three incidents which may have been originally independent stories: the homage of the shepherds, Simeon's recognition of Jesus as the saviour, and the temple-teaching of the twelve-year-old. Each of these stories — they are all found only in Luke — shows when Jesus's true significance was recognized, and Luke has simply combined them into a sequence.

The story that the twelve-year-old amazed the learned doctors in the temple records also Mary's lack of comprehension at the behaviour of her child (2:48–50). This blank failure to understand that the child was abnormal is not what one would expect from a mother who had been visited by an angel and told that he would be born of "the Holy Ghost", be "great" and be given the throne of David to "reign over the house of Jacob for ever; and of his kingdom there shall be no end" (1:32–35). Mary's entire oblivion in the temple of all these stupendous circumstances does seem to imply that the temple story comes from some pre-Lucan source which knew nothing of the traditions represented in the annunciation. Fitzmyer observes that it may belong to "a tradition which grew up about the childhood of Jesus and that continued to manifest itself in the apocryphal gospels, such as the *Infancy Story of Thomas*, which tells what Jesus did or said at the ages of five, six, eight and twelve" (pp. 435–36).

Returning to chapter 1 we note that it contains the Benedictus or joyful song of Zacharias at the birth of his son (1:67–79) and the Magnificat which Mary is represented as speaking in exaltation at her own pregnancy when she visits the pregnant Elisabeth (1:46–55). Since these two songs are only loosely connected with their context and are full of Jewish ideas (they mention Israel, David, "our Fathers" and God's covenant with Abraham), there is general agreement that they are Jewish or Jewish-Christian hymns which Luke has incorporated into his narrative (with perhaps a few verses of his own composition to adapt them to this context). If the Magnificat were omitted, the account of Mary's visit to Elisabeth (1:39–45) would terminate naturally with 1:56 ("And Mary abode with her about three months and returned unto her house"). Likewise, if the Benedictus were omitted, 1:57–66 (the birth of John and his naming as John, with the final statement that "the hand of the Lord was with him") would terminate naturally at 1:80 ("And the child grew and waxed strong in spirit and was in the deserts till the day of his showing unto Israel"). Much of the substance of both hymns has little relevance to the situation of the persons Luke represents as speaking them. That Mary has conceived a child gives her no ground for the martial tone of the Magnificat (the proud have been scattered and the mighty put down). Brown thinks that we have here "a hymn that describes Israel, specifically the poor and oppressed remnant" (p. 340). Similarly, most of the Benedictus has little relevance to John the Baptist. It is a Messianic hymn, rejoicing in the horn of salvation that has been raised up in the house of David, to the discomfort of the Jews' enemies; whereas John is not of Davidic descent at all, but of the priestly line.

It is doubtful whether the evangelist even meant the Magnificat to be spoken by Mary; for although all Greek manuscripts introduce it with "and Mary said", some old Latin manuscripts have here, instead, "and Elisabeth said", and this may well be the original reading (unless, as the NEB suggests, "the original may have had no name" and have simply been "and she said"). For, first, it is hard to see why a copyist should change 'Mary' to 'Elisabeth', while the opposite change is quite intelligible as prompted by increasing Mariolatry. Second, Elisabeth's position as an aged and barren woman resembles that of the long-childless Hannah (mother of Samuel), whose song of 1 Samuel 2 the Magnificat to some extent follows. Elisabeth, not Mary, is the one who, like Hannah, has been raised from the humiliation of childlessness. Third, the words immediately following the Magnificat at Luke 1:56 are "more natural and grammatically better if Elisabeth is the author of the hymn" (Elliott, p. 12). This verse reads: "And Mary abode with her about three months." If Elisabeth had hitherto been the speaker, it makes good sense that Mary is actually named here, as the subject of the verb, and that Elisabeth is referred to with the pronoun 'her'. But if Mary had been the speaker up to verse 55, it is most unnatural that Elisabeth should then be called 'her' (cf. Creed, p. 22). If, then, the Magnificat is Elisabeth's song of thanksgiving, the evangelist meant it to apply to John the Baptist, not to Jesus, and it then becomes a true parallel to the Benedictus, which is the thanksgiving song of Elisabeth's husband for the birth of John.[10]

In the present chapter I am concerned only with the relation between Jesus and John as it appears in Luke's infancy narrative. What dealings the two men are supposed to have had as adults will occupy us in the next chapter, and we shall see that this is a matter that is handled very differently in the different gospels.

iv. THE NATIVITY AS FULFILMENT OF PROPHECY

Matthew represents five details in his infancy narrative as fulfilment of 'prophecies', but in fact the relevant Old Testament passages bear no relation to the events which he describes as fulfilling them. Let us study the details.

(a) When the angel has told Joseph that Mary will bring forth Jesus "of the Holy Ghost", the evangelist adds:

All this is come to pass, that it might be fulfilled which was spoken by the Lord through the prophet, saying, Behold the virgin shall be with child, and shall bring forth a son. And they shall call his name Immanuel; which is, being interpreted, God with us (1:22–23).

The reference is to Isaiah 7:14, where the prophet is addressing Ahaz (King of Judah about 735–715 BC) in Jerusalem. At this time, the united kingdom of David and Solomon had been divided into Israel in the north, ruled over by Pekah, and Judah in the south. Pekah had allied himself with Rezin, king of Damascus (Syria), intending a revolt against Assyria, the super-power of the day, and wanted Ahaz to join them. When he refused, they attacked him in Jerusalem, "but could not prevail against it" (Isaiah 7:1). Isaiah assured him that he really had had nothing to fear from these two adversaries, and that, before a child shortly to be born to a "young woman" will be old enough to tell good from evil, "the land whose two kings thou abhorrest shall be forsaken" (7:16). As early as the child's birth, the political and military situation will be so much improved that his mother will give him a name of good omen, Immanuel (verse 14).

The AV and the RV render Isaiah 7:14 as "a virgin shall conceive and bear a son". But the Hebrew text makes no reference to a virgin and uses the word 'almah', meaning 'young woman', which is the rendering given in recent scholarly English versions such as the RSV and the NEB. (American fundamentalists burned copies of the RSV because of this change). It is the Septuagint (an influential Greek version of the Old Testament) that uses the word meaning virgin, and renders the passage: "the virgin shall be with child and thou [the husband] shall call his name Immanuel". Brown notes that both the standard Hebrew (Massoretic) text and the Septuagint, and of course Matthew, use the definite article (*the* young woman or *the* virgin, not *a* young woman), so that it is "likely that Isaiah was referring to someone definite whose identity was known to him and to King Ahaz, perhaps someone whom the king had recently married and brought into the harem" (pp. 147–48). Even in the Septuagint version, nothing supernatural is asserted. Isaiah is simply saying to Ahaz that a woman who is *now* a virgn will (by natural means, once she is united with her husband) conceive the child.

Isaiah, then, did not suppose that this child would be the Messiah, to be born about 700 years later. In any case, Messianism as we know it from later Jewish history did not exist in his day. Messiah simply means 'anointed' and was used to designate kings and high priests who were always anointed with oil. Saul, the first Israelite king, is called "the Lord's anointed" (1 Samuel 24:6). The term at this stage did not indicate a future redeemer. But when the Babylonian Exile of 587–539 BC brought the monarchy to an end, expectations that the anointed kings of the House of David would deliver the Jews from their enemies or from catastrophe were transferred to an anointed king of the indefinite future; "and thus hope was born in *the* Messiah, the supreme anointed one who would deliver Israel" (Brown, p. 67n.). When such expectations developed, many Old Testament passages were reinterpreted as references to this coming Messiah. But even then, Isaiah 7:14 was not understood in this way in Jewish usage.

In sum, Isaiah's oracle "does not predict a miraculous birth from a virgin, nor does it bear upon the birth of a Messiah still more than seven centuries in the future. It is an assurance to King Ahaz, terrified as he is by the threat of an invasion from the north, that the danger is negligible". And the name Immanuel "is to be given by way of a thankful acknowledgement that God has made his presence known among his people by removing the danger that has threatened" (Beare, pp. 71–72).

(b) Herod is troubled to learn from the wise men that a "King of the Jews" has been born. He "gathers together all the chief priests and scribes of the people" to inquire from them the relevant locality. (The author obviously knew nothing of "the bitter opposition that existed between Herod and the priests, nor of the fact that the Sanhedrin was not at his beck and call": Brown, p. 188). They tell him:

> In Bethlehem of Judea: for thus it is written by the prophet,
> And thou, Bethlehem, land of Judah,
> Art in no wise least among the princes of Judah:
> For out of thee shall come forth a governor,
> Which shall be shepherd of my people Israel (2:5–6).

The first three lines of the citation are drawn from a textual tradition of Micah 5:2 that is identical neither with the Massoretic text nor the Septuagint. This indicates the multiplicity of texts available in Matthew's day — "variant Hebrew wordings, Aramaic targums and a number of Greek translations" (Brown, p. 103). The final line has been added from 2 Samuel 5:2, where David is reminded that "the Lord said to thee, Thou shalt feed my people Israel". This, of course, *pace* Matthew, cannot belong to what was said by "the prophet" Micah, but it does serve to associate Jesus with David, which was doubtless the evangelist's intention. He was clearly also very much concerned to insist that the credentials of the Messiah include birth in Bethlehem rather than in some other city such as Jerusalem; but the passage in Micah says only that from the insignificant clan of Ephrathah, which included Bethlehem — the text reads "Bethlehem Ephrathah", little "among the thousands (clans) of Judah" — a ruler of Israel shall come forth. A few verses later there is mention of deliverance from an impending Assyrian invasion, and the writer seems to have had in mind not a Messiah of the remote future, but a leader who would deliver Judah from the Assyrian. Also, he does not say that Bethlehem will be his birthplace, only that he will come forth as leader from it. The Old Testament makes David a native of Bethlehem, but does not suggest that he was there as king; in Jewish tradition up to Matthew's time, Jerusalem, not Bethlehem, was the city of David. Micah's prophecy of a ruler emerging from Bethlehem does not seem to have been understood by pre-Christian Jews as referring to the Messiah, for it is interpreted messianically only in the Targum of Micah (about AD 300) and not, for instance, at Qumran, even though Micah was used there. Hence, as Burger notes (p. 24), the location of the Messiah's birth at Bethlehem was not common Jewish tradition ready and waiting for Christians to assimilate. However, both Matthew and Luke, in their wholly independent infancy narratives, make Jesus be born there, and so this must have been a widespread tradition among the early Christians, perhaps inspired by "the tendency to imagine that the Messiah Son of David must recapitulate the experience of his famous ancestor" (Beare, p. 79).

(c) Joseph, warned in a dream by an angel to flee from Herod into Egypt, remained there with Mary and the child until Herod's death, "that it might be fulfilled which was spoken by the Lord through the prophet, saying, Out of Egypt did I call my son" (2:13-15). This is cited from Hosea 11:1, where the prophet is reminding the people of Yahweh's loyalty to them in the past when he delivered them from Egyptian captivity: "when Israel was a child, then I loved him, and called my son out of Egypt". Here, 'my son' means the nation, not the Messiah, and the reference is to a past deliverance (the Exodus), not to a future one. Matthew's use of the passage well illustrates his complete lack of concern with historical interpretation of the Scriptures.

(d) When Herod saw himself foiled, he had all the male children of Bethlehem and its environs killed. "Then was fulfilled that which was spoken by Jeremiah the prophet, saying,

A voice was heard in Ramah,
Weeping and great mourning,
Rachel weeping for her children;
And she would not be comforted,
because they are not." (2:17–18)

Rachel was Jacob's second wife, mother of Joseph and Benjamin, and according to one tradition she was buried at Ramah (near Jerusalem). Commentators explain that Jeremiah envisages her weeping in her tomb (31:15) "as she watches the columns of captives ('her children') marching along the road into exile, under the guard of the victorious Assyrians after the fall of the (northern) Kingdom of Israel (2 Kings 17:6)" (Beare, pp. 82–83; cf Brown, pp. 205–06). For Matthew she has come to represent the mothers of Bethlehem weeping for their murdered children, and the historical context of the passage in Jeremiah has been wholly lost.

(e) Joseph is warned in a dream to avoid Herod's son Archelaus, ruler of Judea, and so "withdrew into the parts of Galilee, and came and dwelt in a city called Nazareth: that it might be fulfilled which was spoken by the prophets, that he should be called a Nazarene" (2:22–23). No such passage exists in the Old Testament, and Matthew's ascription of it to "the prophets", rather than to a particular prophet, may indicate that he did not have in mind any passage that would exactly bear him out. There are, however, a number which, with some manipulation, can be made to yield the meaning desired. One suggestion, favoured by Howard C. Kee, is that Matthew, who will have known from Mark of Jesus's connection with Nazareth, produced a prophecy about Jesus's coming from that obscure hamlet by taking the consonants of the Hebrew text of Isaiah 11:1, which promises a 'shoot' (n-tz-r in Hebrew), later interpreted as the Messiah, and providing it with different vowels, which can be done readily in Semitic languages.[11]

In sum, Matthew is clearly much concerned to prove from the Jewish Scriptures that Jesus really is, according to his origin and home, the expected Messiah. That the passages he adduces for this purpose are not to the point typifies the use of the Old Testament made by the authors of the New. The latter "tear passages out of context, use allegory or typology to give old stories new meanings, contradict the plain meaning of the text, find references to Christ in passages where the original authors never intended any, and adapt or even alter the wording in order to make it yield the meaning they require."[12] This is the verdict not of some rationalist 'scoffer', but of the Lady Margaret's Professor of Divinity in the University of Cambridge. The argument that the Old Testament can be read as prophecy of Jesus has lost all force.

V. THE GENEALOGIES

Both Matthew and Luke give genealogies which purport to show that Jesus is descended from David. Some Old Testament passages which had come to be regarded as prophecies concerning the distant future were interpreted to mean that the Messiah will come from the line of David, and so anyone who had come to be regarded as the Messiah might well be held to belong to it. Jesus can be descended from David only through Joseph, for while Matthew is silent about Mary's ancestry, Luke states that she is kindred to Elisabeth, who is "of the daughters of Aaron" (1:5), i.e. of the tribe of Levi, not of Judah, as was David. It is in fact Joseph's ancestry that is traced in both genealogies, not Mary's. Luke's table (3:23ff) does not even mention her, and Matthew names her only as the partner of Joseph, the descendant of David. But according to these same evangelists, Jesus is not born of Joseph at all, but of the Holy Ghost, and so the whole genealogical apparatus which aims at showing his descent from David fails to do this because the virgin birth story has been grafted onto it. Von Campenhausen says:

> Both the Lucan and the Matthean genealogical trees show that they originated in communities that as yet knew nothing of the virgin birth and regarded Jesus as Joseph's child . . . . Only in the last link of the chain have the evangelists attempted an artificial twist by way of correction, so as to accommodate it to the virgin birth. (p. 11)

Thus Matthew, having said that "Abraham begat Isaac", and so on down to the father of Joseph, finishes by saying, not 'Joseph begat Jesus', but that Joseph was "the husband of Mary, of whom was born Jesus, who is called Christ" (1:16). And Luke, who begins his table with Jesus and works back to Abraham and beyond, says Jesus was "the son (as was supposed) of Joseph, the son of Heli, the son of Matthat", and so on (3:23–24). Von Campenhausen adds that the manuscript variations of these passages show how little the text satisfied its readers, even in very early times.

The reply has often been made that, to the Jewish way of thinking, legal paternity completely took the place of natural paternity, so that Jesus can be regarded as Son of David even though Joseph was only his legal father. Beare takes this position (pp. 61, 67), but von Campenhausen dismisses it as "a makeshift for which there is no adequate basis" (p. 11). It certainly fails to account for the insistence of Paul — the earliest extant Christian writer, who of course knows nothing of the virgin birth — that Jesus was "born of the seed of David according to the flesh" (Romans 1:3). And the fourth gospel represents some Jews as saying that "the scripture said that the Christ cometh of the seed of David" (John 7:42). This seems to have been the Jewish expectation, and mere legal paternity could hardly have fulfilled it.

Be that as it may, the genealogical trees given by Matthew and Luke are irreconcilable with each other. They agree quite well from Abraham to David, as one would expect, for the ancestry of David was available from the Old Testament (1 Chronicles 1 and 2, and Ruth 4:18–22).[13] However, from David to Joseph each table has its own names, the only ones common to both being Shealtiel and Zerubbabel his son, both well known from traditions concerning the Babylonian captivity. This section of Luke's table, apart from containing different names from those given in Matthew, also has about twice as many as are recorded there. As early as 1835 D. F. Strauss inferred from this that the genealogies are unhistorical, that Jesus's lineage was in fact utterly unknown, and that tradition, under these conflicting forms, attempted to prove his Davidic descent because it had come to be supposed that he was the Messiah, who was expected to be so descended.

That Matthew's list begins with Abraham betrays its artificiality, for, as Beare has noted, "no ancient society kept records which extended unbroken over so long a period as extends from Abraham to Christ" (p. 62). Further artificiality is apparent when the evangelist divides the list into three series, each of 14 names, pointing out that the end of each series coincides with an important historical event — the reign of David, the Babylonian captivity, and the birth of Jesus. Here are his series, together with other information they contain:

Abraham	Solomon (whose mother was "her that had been the wife of Uriah", i.e. Bathsheba)	Jechoniah
Isaac	Rehoboam	Shealtiel
Jacob	Abijah	Zerubbabel
Judah	Asa	Abiud
Perez (whose mother was Tamar)	Jehoshaphat	Eliakim
Hezron	Joram	Azor
Ram	Uzziah	Sadoc
Amminadab	Jotham	Achim
Nahshon	Ahaz	Eliud
Salmon	Hezekiah	Eleazar
Boaz (whose mother was Rahab)	Manasseh	Matthan
Obed (whose mother was Ruth)	Amon	Jacob
Jesse	Josiah	Joseph, "the husband of Mary, of whom was born Jesus, who is called Christ"
David the King	Jechoniah "at the time of the carrying away to Babylon"	

The second series consists of 14 names only because four kings have been omitted from the list given in the Old Testament. This could well have been an error made in good faith: for although I have spelled the names in all three series as they are given in the R.V., manuscripts make it clear that Matthew took them from Septuagint.

(Even in the R.V., the third name in the first series is given as 'Jacob', as in the Septuagint of 1 Chronicles 1:34, whereas the standard Hebrew (Massoretic) text gives it as 'Israel'). The Greek forms of some of the royal names are similar and are also followed by names which have identical initial letters, so that the evangelist's eye could readily have glided from one name to another further on in the list, just as modern typists or compositors sometimes omit material occurring between two identical words in a passage.[14]

Matthew then begins his third series by repeating the name Jechoniah. This too—although it spoils his neat scheme of 3×14—could have been prompted by his reading of the Old Testament; for the Septuagint of 1 Chronicles 3:16–17 states that Jechoniah had a son, Zedekiah, but, then, instead of naming his descendants, reverts to Jechoniah, naming his son as Shealtiel. As Burger says (p. 97), Matthew thus accurately reproduces the intention of the Chronicler in making the post-exilic line issue from Jechoniah.

With Zerubbabel, the son of Shealtiel and the last descendant of David of historical importance, Matthew leaves the guidance of the Old Testament, even though 1 Chronicles could have supplied him with eleven more generations. The next nine names in this final series of 14 (up to but not including Joseph) are otherwise unknown and are far too few for the long period thus covered. Zerubbabel was born about 570 BC, so that there are only twelve names (including his) from this time to that of Jesus, which makes each generation as long as 50 years, instead of the normal 25–30 years. (There were, for instance, 18 generations of kings in Judah in the 400 years between David and the Babylonian exile). It seems clear that Matthew is here forcing his list into agreement with the overall scheme of 3×14 for which he has settled (1:17). As Brown observes, "even God did not arrange things so nicely that exactly fourteen biological generations separated such crucial moments in salvation history as the call of Abraham, the accession of David, the Babylonian Exile, and the coming of the Messiah" (p. 74)—apart from the fact that there were not, in history, 14 generations in the second series and that the third achieves 14 only by repeating the final name of the second. Beare notes that Matthew probably saw a mystical meaning in the number fourteen, which is "the sum of the numerical values of the three letters that make up the name of David in Hebrew . . . . In his mind, this number reflects the thought that in Jesus the promises of God to

Israel are brought to fulfilment, and that the appointed channel of fulfilment is the Davidic monarchy in the person of the 'son of David' who will be acknowledged also to be the Son of God". Beare adds that this kind of number symbolism was "not unusual in the world in which Matthew lived" (p. 63).

My table above (p. 74) shows that Matthew includes four Old Testament women (Tamar, Rahab, Ruth, and Bathsheba) in his genealogy — quite unnecessarily, as Jesus's descent is traced through the male line. All four were aliens and three of them guilty of some kind of unchastity. Tamar was a Canaanite widow who disguised herself as a prostitute and offered herself to her widower father-in-law Judah, as a result of which she gave birth to Perez (Genesis 38). Rahab was a harlot of Jericho who sheltered Israelite spies (Joshua 2). There is no support in the Old Testament for Matthew's statement that she was partnered by Salmon or in any way connected with the Davidic line, but in two Talmudic passages a section of the genealogy of Judah (as given in 1 Chronicles 4:21–23) is applied to her by a play on words.[15] Ruth was a Moabitess who, as the wife of Boaz, became the grandmother of Jesse. Bathsheba was the wife of Uriah the Hittite and David's mistress. She became his wife and bore him Solomon after he had callously contrived her husband's death. All four women, then, contributed to the advancement of Israelite interests, and so bear comparison with Mary, who brought the Messianic hope to fulfilment. Whether this was Matthew's motive for including them can only be guessed. In spite of the irregularity in the lives of three of them, all four, according to Brown, "came off quite well in the Jewish piety of Jesus's time", so that there is "little likelihood that Matthew's readers would have understood them as sinners" (p. 72). Johnson has given evidence that, in pre-Christian Judaism, the four women "had come to occupy a traditional place in the ancestry of the Davidic Messiah", and that Matthew, who believed firmly in a Davidic Messiah, included them in his genealogy for this reason.[16]

Luke traces Jesus's ancestry not merely to Abraham, but right back to Adam, "the son of God". His tree does not emphasize numerical features as Matthew's does, and the sum total of ancestors may not even be a multiple of seven (eleven times seven), as there is considerable manuscript variation. The many unknown persons listed will have invited scribal tampering, so that the total varies from 72 to 78. My diagram on the following page shows that, while Matthew makes his table run from David to Solomon and then through the line of kings, Luke selects Nathan from among the sons of David, and so traces Jesus's descent through a line not royal. He nevertheless rejoins the royal line after the fall of the monarchy by listing Shealtiel and Zerubbabel; and against 1 Chronicles 3:17, he makes Shealtiel the son of an otherwise unknown Neri, instead of the son of the last king, Jechoniah. His motive in avoiding the royal line until the Exile was probably theological: it would have led him to Jechoniah (given, as we saw, a prominent place in Matthew's table). Jeremiah had passed judgement on this wretched king, saying "no man of his seed shall prosper, sitting upon the throne of David" (22:30; cf 36:30–31). As Luke expressly says that God will give Jesus "the throne of his father David" (1:32), he thus had reason to avoid making Jesus a descendant of this king.

THE TWO GENEALOGIES, FROM DAVID TO JOSEPH

Matthew 1	Names common to Matthew and Luke	Luke 3
	David	
Solomon		Nathan
Eleven others		Seventeen others (none identical with Matthew's line, and all otherwise unknown. Some anachronistically with patriarchal names). *
Josiah		Melchi (otherwise unknown)
Jechoniah		Neri (otherwise unknown)
	Shealtiel	
	Zerubbabel	
Eight others (otherwise unknown)		Seventeen others (none identical with Matthew's line, and all otherwise unknown)
Jacob		Heli
	Joseph	

*"The custom of naming children after the patriarchs did not develop until after the Exile" (Brown, p. 92).

My diagram shows that the two evangelists diverge already in their naming of Jesus's grandfather. Some twenty years ago I discussed (in JEC, pp. 35–36) attempts to explain the discrepancies away. Now even a Catholic scholar admits that such attempts "solve nothing", that the two genealogies "resist all harmonization", and that "most commentators realize today that we have in them neither official public records nor treasured family lists" (Fitzmyer, pp. 496–97).

vi. THE ORIGIN OF THE VIRGIN BIRTH TRADITIONS

Nothing in the Jewish Scriptures suggests that anyone was or was to be born of a virgin, but in the Graeco-Roman world in which Christianity originated such an idea was not uncommon and was derived from much older cults. Particularly the saviour-gods of paganism were often reputed to be virgin born, and as Gilbert Murray noted, the underlying idea is that the father-god supplied the human race with a saviour without being actuated by lust.[17] Some of the goddesses who gave birth without carnal intercourse were not virgins, but were called so by way of adoring flattery, just as "nearly all male gods were at times termed beneficent, whatever might be the cruelty of their supposed deeds".[18] Enslin finds little difference between Matthew's story that Mary was found pregnant of the Holy Ghost (1:18) and the Egyptian belief, reported by Plutarch, that "it may be possible for a divine spirit so to apply itself to the nature of a woman as to imbreed in her the first beginnings of generation".[19]

By the beginning of our era, the idea of divine impregnation, continually obtruded on the Jews by their pagan neighbours, had begun to affect their own outlook, with the result that some Old Testament worthies came to be regarded as born in this manner. Thus Philo, the Alexandrian Jew born about 20 BC, tells that "the Lord begat Isaac", who is "to be thought not the result of generation, but the shaping of the unbegotten". He records similar views about Leah, whose husband is "the unnoticed", Zipporah, found "pregnant but by no mortal", and Samuel, whose mother "received divine seed".[20] Christian apologists claim that such stories of birth without male concourse do not imply birth from a *virgin* mother. If in fact this was a detail added in the Christian legend, the reason for such an addition is not hard to discern: for the idea that birth from a virgin enabled Jesus to be born without any suggestion of "the lust of the flesh" is expressly stated in an apocryphal Christian work known as the *Epistula Apostolorum*, which purports to be a letter from the eleven disciples after the Resurrection to Christians of the four regions of the earth, and may date from the mid-second century.[21] Boslooper typifies the apologists who insist that only the Christian legend tells of "divine conception and human birth without anthropomorphism, sensuality or suggestions of moral irregularity". For him, the story inculcates the sanctity of sex, premarital chastity, heterosexuality, and the necessity of monogamy and fidelity in marriage; and it had to consist of a mythical narrative "since it was only in this form that primitive peoples could grasp these truths".[22]

The traditional date of Jesus's birth is entirely without scriptural warrant. The primitive Church was far more interested in his death and Resurrection than in his incarnation, and felt no need to celebrate his coming down to Earth at all. In the pagan world, 25 December, the day of the winter solstice in the Julian calendar, was regarded as the sun-god's birthday, since the days begin to lengthen and the power of the sun increases from this turning point in the year. The emperor Constantine the Great "pursued the deliberate policy of uniting the worship of the sun with that of Christ", for he favoured Christianity because "its organization made it best able to unite the Empire".[23]

vii. CONCLUSION

It will be obvious from all this that the accounts given in Matthew and Luke of the birth and infancy of Jesus are, in the wording of the old *Encyclopaedia Biblica*, "irreconcilable and mutually exclusive".[24] Protestant scholars long ago admitted this, but Catholics have only recently begun to make such concessions. In the *Bibellexikon* of the Catholic New Testament scholar Hermann Haag (published at Zürich in 1956) the virgin birth was still stoutly defended, and I had to come to terms with his detailed arguments in my 1971 book on Jesus. Today, however, the Catholic exegete R. E. Brown allows that it is "quite impossible" to harmonize the two canonical infancy narratives (p. 497) and that we have "no reliable information" about the source of either (p. 7). He is unimpressed by the standard defence (which we have met already apropos of the Bible stories of Jesus's Resurrection appearances) that they are sober in tone (in spite of their many miraculous elements) compared with what we find on the subject in apocryphal gospels; and he asks, appositely: "Is this a difference of kind (history vs. fiction) or a difference of degree?" One might, he adds, "argue that both canonical and non-canonical narratives result from the attempts of Christian imagination to fill in the Messiah's origins, and that in the case of the apocryphal narratives the imagination had a freer and further exercise" (p. 33n.).

The purpose of the infancy narratives is clearly to show that all the titles deriving from the post-resurrection experience of early Christians—Messiah, Lord, Saviour, Son of God—applied to Jesus not merely in virtue of his Resurrection, but pertained to him from his very conception. The earliest gospel, Mark's, suggests that he was chosen to be the receptacle of the spirit at his baptism (1:10), but even this was, for later tradition, not enough, and "it was necessary to have him literally begotten of God, by whom his mother had become pregnant."[25] The Fourth gospel outdoes even this in a prologue which asserts that he existed before his birth on Earth and before the creation of "all things", when he was with God as the "word" (logos) responsible for this creation. The evangelist thus has no need to establish his exalted status by means of a miraculous birth, and is able simply to say that he "became flesh" and then introduce him as a grown man.[26]

It is perhaps surprising that, after his very thorough demolition of the credibility of the gospel birth and infancy narratives, Brown declares that Jesus may nevertheless historically have been conceived without a human father, and that it is "easier to explain the New Testament evidence by positing historical basis than by positing pure theological creation" (pp. 527–28). Another Catholic scholar, James P. Mackey, suggests that this is too conservative a position, as "Brown is as adamant as anyone that the principal point of the nativity stories is to establish the presence of the divine spirit at the very conception of Jesus and the corresponding confession that he was Son of God". For Mackey, there is nothing about his arrival on the human scene that would enable us to use that title of him, for his origins "were obscure in the extreme . . . . He was a most ordinary man".[27]

Traditions concerning Jesus's virgin birth, prefaced as they were to those which detailed his adult life, left the faithful wondering how he spent the intervening years, and, as Metzger notes, "when people are curious, they usually take steps to satisfy their curiosity. So we should not be surprised that members of the early Church drew up accounts of what they supposed must have taken place".[28] Hence a number of apocryphal gospels refer to the early years of Jesus's life. If the canonical ones do at least include one incident within this period (Luke 2:41–51), they are totally silent as to what Jesus accomplished between death and Resurrection; and so other apocryphal gospels tell of his descent into the underworld. Metzger adds that "popular yearning" for such additional information has not subsided even to-day, "as is witnessed by the continuing production of still other 'new' gospels" (p. 169n.).[29] I have tried to show that the canonical stories concerning the virgin birth and the Resurrection owe a good deal to imaginative reconstruction of what was 'supposed must have taken place'; and we shall be seeing elements in the passion narratives which may well have originated in the same way.

THE PRELUDE TO THE PUBLIC MINISTRY

i. JESUS AND JOHN THE BAPTIST

Theologians who concede that the infancy narratives and the accounts of the Resurrection appearances are largely, if not wholly mythical, hold that the gospel records of Jesus's adult life bring us onto more solid ground. Let us therefore investigate the incidents concerning John the Baptist which in the gospels prelude Jesus's public ministry.

First, however, let us recall that both the narrative material and the speeches in Mark have been put together from fragments of tradition which reached the evangelist from a great variety of sources, oral and written, after having been used in the teaching and preaching of the Church (cf. above, p. 12). The sequence of the events of Jesus's life prior to the Passion is no part of this primary material, but a creation of Mark, whose order of events is, on the whole, preserved by Matthew and Luke (whereas the fourth evangelist follows independent traditions which lead him both to some different events and to a different sequence in the events he shares with the other gospels). As for the speeches in Mark, their composite nature is well illustrated at 9:35–50, where the individual items are linked only by what theologians call 'catchword connections' — a word or phrase in one seems to have reminded the evangelist of a similar word in another, independent saying, and this led him to put them together as successive utterances in a single speech. It is, says Stanton, an "assured result" of New Testament studies that "the gospel traditions in Mark are like pearls on a string".[1]

Next, it is necessary to take cognizance of a hitherto unmentioned element in the relation of the gospels of Matthew and Luke to each other. As I have said, it is very widely agreed that neither of these two evangelists knew the work of the other. Hitherto, we have been concerned only with those sections of their gospels which are com-

pletely divergent from each other (e.g. the infancy narratives) or
where each evangelist, independently of the other, has adapted the
account of Mark. There are, however, about 230 verses common
(verbatim or nearly so) to Matthew and Luke that are not found in
Mark; and although most of them are inserted into Matthew's Marcan material at a different spot from where they are inserted in
Luke's, the inserted material manifests a general underlying sequence
that is the same in both gospels. The only obvious explanation of all
this is that both evangelists were here drawing on a common non-
Marcan Greek source, not now extant. It is known as Q (German
'Quelle'=source), and may be earlier or later than Mark, of which it
is independent.[2] Some of its material has been slightly differently
adapted by Matthew on the one hand and by Luke on the other, giving verbal differences between the parallel passages which, although
slight, indicate differences in the theology of the two evangelists. A
good example is the following passage, where Luke (unlike Matthew)
has adapted his source so as to make Jesus mention the Holy Spirit,
the importance of which for salvation Luke stresses in a manner
almost unique in the New Testament:

Matthew 7:11	Luke 11:13
If ye, then, being evil, know how to give good gifts unto your children, how much more shall your Father which is in heaven give good things to them that ask him?	If ye then, being evil, know how to give good gifts unto your children, how much more shall your heavenly Father give the Holy Spirit to them that ask him?

Q consists mainly of sayings of Jesus, and unlike the Pauline and
many other epistles it sets his life in first-century Palestine by
associating him with John the Baptist. But it makes no mention of
Pilate, nor of Jesus's Passion and crucifixion. The evidence for this is
that such additions as one finds in Matthew and in Luke to the Marcan
passion narrative are quite different from each other, and are followed by a return to the Marcan order and substance. Furthermore,
in Mark Jesus repeatedly predicts his Passion; but in Matthew and
Luke such predictions are either taken over from Mark, or are
peculiar to the one or the other gospel and hence form no part of Q.

　　The Christian community for which Q was written regarded Jesus
as an apocalyptic preacher who sent out his disciples as itinerant
preachers, predicted martyrdom for them and promised a judgment

shortly to come when God will intervene, condemn the wicked and vindicate the faithful. A typical passage is Luke 10:12–16 (paralleled in Matthew 10) where Jesus sends out his disciples "as lambs in the midst of wolves". In their travels they are to be dependent for food and lodging on those to whom they preach. They are to heal the sick and declare "the kingdom of God is come nigh unto you". Any city that refuses to listen will suffer a frightful fate in the judgment, as rejecting them is said to imply rejecting Jesus, and God who has sent him. Whether there was a historical Jesus who spoke on these lines is another matter, but the Q document was written for a community which believed he had acted in this way. Some of the predictions in Q are stylized in form, and may well have been put into his mouth by prophets in the early Church who felt that they were carrying on what they believed to have been his work and speaking with his authority.

Kee observes that "the closest historical analogy we have for the itinerant charismatic preachers pictured in Q is that of the prophetic-revolutionary leaders whom Josephus describes as raising the people in the years just before the Jewish revolt of AD 66–70", although there is no nationalism in the message of Q.[3] Q seems to represent the standpoint of a Christian community conscious of the failure of the Jesus movement among their fellow Jews, and explaining this failure in terms of Old Testament traditions that Israel had always rejected God's prophets: "Blessed are ye when men shall hate you . . . for in the same manner did their fathers unto the prophets" (Luke 6:22–23; Matthew 5:11–12). Jesus is made to complain that "this generation" rejected first the ascetic John the Baptist, saying that he was possessed by a demon, and then himself, the opposite of an ascetic, because they regarded him as "a wine-bibber, a friend of publicans and sinners" (Luke 7:31–34; Matthew 11:16–19). The Q community presumably understood the death of Jesus as the rejection of God's final messenger and believed that he would return shortly as eschatological judge. What were held to be his remembered words, and sayings uttered by prophets inspired by him, were valued as guidance for living in the interim.

Q represents Jesus as suffering in so far as he is rejected by mankind, but his suffering has no atoning power. The suffering stressed in Q has no redemptory effect, but consists in the tribulation which is to befall men in the last days. We saw earlier (p. 16) that Jesus was expected to defeat powerful evil spirits. These would not give up their hold over the world without a struggle, and this was to bring great suffering to mankind and convulsions in nature during the days leading up to their final defeat.

There appears to be no reference to the Resurrection in Q. Cross and Resurrection are both absent probably because Q is concerned to represent Jesus as an authoritative teacher, and as God's agent who will soon be confirmed in this capacity when the world is brought to its end. Kee notes that "the main thrust of the Jesus tradition in Q is to point forward to the future kingdom of God rather than to depict the historical life of Jesus" (pp. 117–18).

It may seem surprising that a Christian document about Jesus which was important enough to be later incorporated into two canonical gospels should record what purports to be his teaching but make no reference to his Passion or Resurrection. But just such a document came to light in 1945, and was even in antiquity called a 'gospel', as we know from patristic references to it. I refer to the apocryphal Gospel of Thomas, discovered at Nag Hammadi in Upper Egypt. It is written in Coptic, a late form of Egyptian used by Christians in Egypt, and is very probably a translation of a Greek original. It "relates no episodes in the life of Christ and lacks all narrative and personal information about him".[4] It consists of 114 of his sayings with no indication of where or under what circumstances they were pronounced. In this document he is valued only as the speaker of words of salvation. He does not die to atone for our sins, but his words will save us if we can understand them and implement their teaching. Scholars still argue as to whether this work is dependent on canonical gospels (some of its sayings are very similar to those which in them appear in a definite situation), or whether it represents an independent tradition dating from about AD 140.

The relevance of all this to the present chapter is that a gospel passage about the Baptist, whether in Mark or from Q, may be composite: it may consist of manifold traditions which are of different provenance, or of material which has been supplemented or even altered so as to accommodate it to an overall view of the nature and importance of Jesus. If analysis succeeds in reconstructing an earlier form of the material, this may then be found to have different implications from those it appears to have in the gospels. Elliott rightly notes that four layers must be distinguished. "First there is the historic John; secondly, the traditions about John as put out by John's disciples; thirdly, these traditions as reinterpreted by Jesus's followers; and fourthly the use made of these traditions by the individual gospel writers" (p. 18; cf. p. 30). Each rewriting, he adds, probably introduced some distortion.

The historical Baptist was a preacher with a following of his own which persisted in some areas into the second century, as is evidenced by Christian polemics against it (Scobie, pp. 201–02). He is unmentioned in the Talmud, probably because, like the Essenes (also not mentioned there), he was on the very fringe of orthodox Judaism. However, the Jewish historian Josephus mentions him as "a pious man" who exhorted the Jews "to come together for baptism" which was to "purify the body when the soul had previously been cleansed by righteous conduct". When "everybody turned to him", the tetrarch feared that his "so extensive influence over the people might lead to an uprising", and had him put to death.[5] This passage is almost certainly genuine. It is true that elsewhere Christian scribes have retouched Josephus's text. But if this passage had been interpolated by a scribe familiar with the gospels — the only other early source of information about the Baptist — then its account of the motives for John's imprisonment and execution would not be (as they in fact are) entirely different from those specified in the gospel version of these events (Schürer, p. 346n).

This is Josephus's only mention of the Baptist, whom he does not in any way link with Jesus. Nor are the two men linked in the first-century Christian epistles. Paul, who makes it clear that Christianity was a baptist sect, never mentions John. In fact in none of the New Testament epistles, which refer so often to Jesus's suffering and death, is there so much as a passing reference either to the mission of John or to Jesus's Galilean ministry. It is the gospels which bring the two men together, and they do so for theological reasons. In what follows I shall first give Mark's account of each relevant incident and then discuss alternative or additional accounts in the other gospels.

Mark 1:1–3 represents John the Baptist as "the beginning of the gospel [or 'good news'] of Jesus Christ" by running together two passages, one from Malachi, altered to serve the evangelist's purpose, and one slightly adapted from the Septuagint of Isaiah, as the Hebrew text does not give the meaning required.

(i) At Malachi 3:1, Yahweh speaks of a "messenger" — perhaps an angel is meant — who will "prepare the way before me", i.e., who will be the herald of God who is about to come in judgment. ("The Lord

whom ye seek shall suddenly come to his temple".) This final book of
the Old Testament, dated about 460 BC when Judah was a Persian province, complains of laxity in ritual observances (priests, for instance,
allow blemished and inferior animals to be sacrificed) and of im-
morality and unbelief among the people: men divorce their wives and
marry foreign women, and evil-doers prosper to such an extent that
doubts have come to be expressed about God's justice. But Malachi
gives an assurance in this passage that Yahweh will appear suddenly,
both to purify unworthy priests and to purge the land of sinners.
This judgment is regarded as imminent, as a threat to the existing
generation. Mark, however, identifies the 'messenger' as John the
Baptist, and makes him herald, not God but Jesus by changing
Yahweh's statement that "he shall prepare the way before *me*" to "he
shall prepare *thy* way", where the pronoun refers to "Jesus Christ the
Son of God" in the preceding verse (Mark 1:1-2).

(ii) The other passage quoted here by Mark is from the second
division of the book of Isaiah. What is genuinely Isaianic in its first
division is set in Jerusalem in the Assyrian period (eighth century BC)
and frequently mentions Isaiah by name. The second division (from
chapter 39) does not once refer to him, is set in Babylon two centuries
later, and promises the Jews prompt release from captivity there
because of the rising power of Persia. An instruction is given to
prepare a way for God through the wilderness for the return of the
exiles to Jerusalem:

> Comfort ye, comfort ye my people, saith your God . . . . the voice of
> one that crieth, Prepare ye in the wilderness the way of the Lord, make
> straight in the desert a high way for our God (40:1-3).

Here the crier is not in the wilderness and is not preaching, but the
Septuagint places him there ("the voice of one crying in the
wilderness, prepare ye the way of the Lord"), thus enabling Mark to
make the passage into a prophecy of the Baptist's preaching in the
desert. 'The Lord' renders the divine name Yahweh, but for Mark it is
a path for Jesus that is to be prepared; and so instead of continuing
with Isaiah's "make straight . . . a high way for our God", Mark writes
"make his paths straight", where 'his' refers back to 'Lord', taken to
mean Jesus. The composite quotation (the whole of which Mark, er-
roneously, attributes to Isaiah), thus reads:

Behold I send my messenger before thy face,
Who shall prepare thy way;
The voice of one crying in the wilderness,
Make ye ready the way of the Lord,
Make his paths straight.

The original meaning has been completely disregarded, and a wilderness preacher sent to prepare the way for Jesus extracted from it. The Qumran sectaries, who survived until the Romans destroyed their settlement in AD 68, followed the Hebrew text of the Isaiah passage and took it, equally arbitrarily, to mean their own retreat into the desert from a Jerusalem given over to wickedness: "Prepare in the desert Yahweh's way."[6]

Mark's siting of the Baptist's activities in "the wilderness' is theologically significant. The wilderness is the traditional haunt of evil spirits, and in New Testament times it was believed that it was the place of encounter between opposing heavenly and infernal powers.[7] It is also the place where some of the Jews of this time expected the Messiah to appear. The idea was that the age of salvation would correspond to the early history of Israel, and a number of Messianic fanatics felt that they were called as the second Moses or Joshua to bring things to a head in the wilderness (cf. Schürer, pp. 463–64). The association of wilderness and Messiah is alluded to when Jesus warns against "false Christs" and against their supporters who say: "Lo, here is the Christ . . . . Behold, he is in the wilderness" (Matthew 24:23–26). The Baptist, then, is located in the wilderness because he combats evil and heralds the Messiah.

Matthew follows Mark in quoting "Isaiah the prophet" on the voice in the wilderness calling for the way of the Lord to be prepared (3:3). Luke significantly quotes not only this but the two verses in Isaiah that follow it as representing a prophecy of John's preaching; for these two verses include the statement that "all flesh shall see the salvation of God" (Luke 3:6; cf. Isaiah 40:5, "And the glory of the Lord shall be revealed and all flesh shall see it together"). Whereas in many passages in Matthew salvation is said to be the prerogative of the Jews, Luke consistently emphasizes its universality and so found this reference to 'all flesh' very much to his point.

Mark continues, saying "even as" Isaiah prophesied, "John came, who baptized in the wilderness and preached the baptism of repentance unto remission of sins" (1:2, 4). Forgiveness of sins is no mean function, and at 2:5–7 it is implied that, in the Jewish view, God alone can forgive them, and that it is blasphemous of Jesus to claim to do so. Mark, then, although clearly anxious to subordinate John (as Jesus's forerunner), nevertheless assigns to him a function which even in Jesus is considered excessive. This suggests that the expression "baptism of repentance unto remission of sins" is not Mark's own construction—he would have given John a more subordinate role—but reached him from earlier tradition about John's baptism.

Matthew was obviously not prepared to credit the Baptist with such powers, and assigned to Jesus the function of "saving his people from their sins" (1:21) by the sacrificial shedding of his blood in death. And so he studiously deleted the phrase 'unto remission of sins' from the Marcan account of the Baptist's activities—he mentions (3:6 and 11) the 'repentance' specified by Mark, but not the forgiveness—and inserted it into the report of Jesus's words at the Last Supper. In Mark 14:24 this reads: "This is my blood of the covenant, which is shed for many". To this Matthew 26:28 adds "unto remission of sins". Once again, we see how one evangelist 'edits' the work of another in the interests of his own theology.

Mark next notes that "John was clothed with camel's hair and had a leathern girdle about his loins" (1:6). Zechariah 13:4 reveals that a "hairy mantle" was the conventional garb of a prophet, and John's clothing is clearly modelled on that of the prophet Elijah (described at 2 Kings 1:8 and margin as "a man with a garment of hair" and "girt with a girdle of leather about his loins"). The final verses of the book of Malachi (added to it later) interpret the 'messenger' of 3:1 as Elijah who will return to earth: "Behold I will send you Elijah the prophet before the great and terrible day of the Lord come" (4:5). By New Testament times the returning Elijah had come to be regarded as the forerunner of the Messiah: "The scribes say that Elijah must first come" (Mark 9:11). Mark, who makes the Baptist this forerunner, does not actually say that he is Elijah, but merely implies it. After the Baptist's death, Mark's Jesus says (9:13) that Elijah has already come, but again does not expressly say that the Baptist was he. This reticence seems to be occasioned by one of the artificial features which Mark has imposed on his material, namely the so-called 'Messianic secret', in accordance with which Jesus's true status is not understood by people who come into contact with him.[8] If Mark's Jesus had proclaimed that John was Elijah, forerunner of the

Messiah, then his own status as Messiah would have been disclosed. Matthew dispenses with the Messianic secret, and so is able to adapt Mark 9:13 so as to make the identification of the Baptist with Elijah explicit: he represents Jesus's audience as understanding that "he spake unto them of John the Baptist" (17:13); and at 11:14 Matthew makes Jesus declare, with an explicitness unique in the New Testament, that John *is* Elijah.

Mark next devotes two sentences to the substance of the Baptist's preaching. I quote them together with the parallel passage in Matthew, which derives from Q. (The agreements here of Matthew and Luke against Mark are too numerous and substantial for the passage to be independent reworking, by those two evangelists, of Marcan material):

Mark: 1:7–8	*Matthew 3:11 (cf. Luke 3:16)*
There cometh after me he that is mightier than I, the latchet of whose shoes I am not worthy to stoop down and unloose. I baptized you with water: but he shall baptize you with the Holy Ghost.	I indeed baptize you with water unto repentance: but he that cometh after me is mightier than I, whose shoes I am not worthy to bear: he shall baptize you with the Holy Ghost and with fire.

The idea that the spirit of Yahweh will be poured out immediately before the end of the world and the final judgment is stated in Joel (2:28–31):

> And it shall come to pass afterward that I will pour out my spirit upon all flesh . . . The sun shall be turned into darkness, and the moon into blood, before the great and terrible day of the Lord come.

The addition in Matthew and in Luke, from the Q source, of the words "and with fire" to Mark's account make it quite clear that the coming one is to effect this final judgment. He will pour a river of fire onto the wicked, but God's spirit, and all the blessings that go with it, onto God's people. The context in Q in which this is set shows that these events were expected to happen soon:

> Even now is the axe laid unto the root of the trees: every tree therefore that bringeth not forth good fruit is hewn down and cast into the fire . . . The fan [of the coming one] is in his hand, and he will thoroughly

cleanse his threshing-floor; and he will gather his wheat into the garner, but the chaff he will burn up with unquenchable fire (Matthew 3:10–12; Luke 3:9,17).

It is clear, then, that for Q, if not for Mark, the coming one will simply judge, not give any further opportunity for repentance and salvation. John's call is the last opportunity, and only those who submit, with proper contrition, to his 'baptism of repentance' will belong to the 'wheat' soon to be gathered into the heavenly barn. Hence this baptism must not be allowed to unworthy persons, who would thereby be saved from the wrath to come. Here it is of interest to see how the Q material is manipulated differently by Matthew and by Luke. In Luke it is "the multitude" who are turned away as unworthy, as an "offspring of vipers" (Luke 3:7). Matthew, however, makes John's audience consist of "Pharisees and Sadducees" (3:7), obviously thinking that they, rather than an indiscriminate multitude, deserve such strong abuse. Matthew can see no good in Pharisees and later (in an extended passage, peculiar to his gospel, of his chapter 23) makes Jesus denounce them as "hypocrites" and "serpents", even though they are his neighbours, neighbours being people who, according to his own teaching in this same gospel, are to be loved (5:43; 19:19).

The reason for Matthew's polemic is not that the historical Pharisees were in fact wicked, but that he was writing in a post-AD 70 situation where they were the dominant party in Judaism, and Christian propagandists were competing with them in trying to attract followers. Thus he makes Jesus complain (23:13) that the Pharisees prevent Jews from turning Christian: "ye shut the kingdom of heaven against men; for ye enter not in yourselves, neither suffer ye them that are entering in to enter". *Odium theologicum* is always more violent against rivals than against outsiders. I object to your making proselytes only if in so doing you divert potential proselytes from me. The Antichrist for Luther is not Mohammed, Buddha, Confucius or Aristotle, but the Pope.

Who, then, is this mightier, coming one, so superior to John, who will effect the final judgment? Yahweh himself may be meant, although his superiority to any mortal, even to a prophet such as John, was so obvious to any Jew that it could have seemed blasphemous for John to stress that he was unworthy to carry God's shoes. The evangelists (and Q) wish us to think that Jesus is meant, but it is far from certain that this was the original implication of the traditions they were reworking. If John's call to repentance was the last opportunity, there is no room for a subsequent ministry by Jesus. Hence some commentators suppose that in a pre-Q stage of the tradition, the mightier coming one meant, if not God, then at least some supernatural personage who would shortly bring the world to an end. If this is so, it confirms the impression given by Josephus that the historical Baptist had no connection with Jesus.

After Mark's very brief account of the Baptist's preaching, Jesus is introduced: he "came from Nazareth of Galilee and was baptized of John in the Jordan" (1:9). We have seen that Matthew was not prepared to allow John to forgive sins and reserved this power for Jesus: and so we are not surprised to find this evangelist — in contrast to Mark — making John so conscious of Jesus's superiority that he hesitates to baptize him (3:13–14); but Jesus, overruling this modesty, instructs him to proceed (verse 15). Luke changes Mark's account even further, and "avoids saying that Jesus submitted to John's baptism by using a passive verb: 'During a general baptism of the people, when Jesus too *had been baptized*' (3:21). Thus he does not need to say by whom! And just in case readers might assume John was responsible, Luke precedes this story by telling us that John the Baptist was already in prison by this time" (Elliott, p. 24).

What happened at Jesus's baptism also depends on which gospel one reads. Mark has it that as he came out of the water, "he saw the heavens rent asunder and the Spirit as a dove descending upon him: and a voice came out of the heavens, Thou art my beloved Son, in thee I am well pleased" (1:10–11). Matthew changes the voice so as to make it an announcement not just to Jesus, but to the public: "This is my beloved Son", etc. (3:17). In the fourth gospel, this revelation is directed neither to Jesus as in Mark, nor to all witnesses as in Matthew, but to John, who twice confesses that prior to it, he did not know who Jesus was. So in this gospel, Jesus is baptized merely for John's sake — to enable him to recognize him as the Lamb of God. The event has also occurred before the narrative begins — note in this connection the past tense in the following quotation of the relevant passage (John 1:29–34) — so that the evangelist (going in this respect even further than Luke) is able to omit the actual baptism scene:

(29) On the morrow he seeth Jesus coming unto him, and saith, Behold the Lamb of God, which taketh away the sin of the world! (30) This is

he of whom I said, After me cometh a man which is become before me: for he was before me. (31) And I knew him not: but that he should be made manifest to Israel, for this cause came I baptizing with water. (32) And John bare witness, saying, I have beheld the Spirit descending as a dove out of heaven; and it abode upon him. (33) And I knew him not: but he that sent me to baptize with water, he said unto me, Upon whomsoever thou shalt see the Spirit descending, and abiding upon him, the same is he that baptizeth with the Holy Spirit. (34) And I have seen, and have borne witness that this is the Son of God.

The Christological title 'Lamb of God' (verse 29) is absent from the other three gospels. Here, in the fourth, the Baptist is represented (verse 30) as knowing even Jesus's pre-existence (i.e. that he existed as a supernatural being before he was born on Earth). This doctrine of pre-existence is not baldly stated in the other gospels (and certainly not even hinted at by the Baptist there), and commentators agree that it is even quite foreign to Luke (Fitzmyer, p. 197). The fourth evangelist, however, takes a different view and represents Jesus (at 17:5) as reminding God of the splendour they had experienced together before the world was created. Such material reflects the theology of the Johannine community, not any authentic historical traditions about Jesus.

The first three gospels agree in affirming that, immediately after his baptism, Jesus went into the wilderness, where he was tempted by the Devil, that he and John never met again, and that by the time he began his ministry John had been imprisoned. The fourth gospel contradicts this and represents the two men as both at work baptizing people before John's imprisonment (3:22–24). Here, then, Jesus baptizes (although the first three gospels give no hint that he ever did so), and John continues to baptize, even though the sole purpose of his baptism, namely to manifest Jesus to Israel (1:31) is already accomplished. The point of all this is that it enables the evangelist to bring out Jesus's superiority: "Jesus was making and baptizing more disciples than John" (4:1). It is what Fitzmyer, in another connection, has called parallelism involving one-upmanship (see above, p. 65).

We saw earlier that already Matthew took exception to John's baptism being "for remission of sins". If, as in the fourth gospel, Jesus is "the Lamb of God which taketh away the sin of the world", then John's baptism can have but a modest function, and he is accordingly completely self-effacing, his final statement being that Jesus must increase and he himself decrease (3:30). After this we hear no more of him. "His death is not even mentioned [as it is in the other gospels], so unimportant is his person" (Wink, p. 95). His sole function is to be a 'witness' to Jesus's Messiahship. He not only repudiates any claim to be himself the Christ (and even calls upon his own disciples to take cognizance of this denial, 3:28), but declares too that he is neither Elijah, nor even the prophet, but merely the voice in the wilderness (1:19–23), "sent before the Christ" (3:28), but certainly not in order to proclaim him as judge at the end of the world; for one of the most striking differences between the fourth gospel and the other three is that it is practically devoid of apocalyptic ideas. Its Jesus does not preach an immediate and catastrophic end of the world.[9]

Luke was likewise writing in a situation where the final judgment had failed to materialize, in spite of the predictions in Mark and Matthew that it was imminent. And therefore in some passages he adapts Marcan material so as to delete any implication of a prompt end to the present dispensation. Thus Jesus's proclamation at Mark 1:15 ("the time is fulfilled and the kingdom of God is at hand: repent ye and believe in the gospel") becomes in the Lucan parallel (4:15) what Fitzmyer calls "a bland narrative statement about Jesus's preaching in synagogues and being praised by all the people" (p. 232). Luke also makes Jesus tell the parable of the pounds, inherited from Q, for the purpose of correcting any idea that "the kingdom of God was immediately to appear" (Luke 19:11, unrepresented in the parallel account of Matthew 25:14ff). And he sometimes rephrases words of Jesus so as to make them guides to everyday living, rather than pointers to some catastrophe. The best-known example is Luke 9:23: "If any man would come after me, let him deny himself, and take up his cross daily, and follow me", where 'daily' has been added to the Marcan material (Mark 8:34).

This concern to avoid implication of immediate catastrophe influences what Luke has to say about the Baptist, whose declaration at Matthew 3:2 ("The kingdom of heaven is at hand") has no equivalent in Luke. In a passage with no canonical parallel, Luke makes the Baptist give moral advice (tax collectors are not to demand more money than is due, soldiers are to be content with their pay) which suggests that ordinary everyday life will continue and not shortly be brought to a catastrophic close (Luke 3:10–14). Even more significantly, Luke has retained nothing of the Baptist's role as Elijah and suppresses Mark's hints on this matter. Mark 9:9–13, where Elijah is said to have come, and Mark 1:6, where John is represented as dressed as Elijah was, are absent from Luke. Strangely enough, however, he retains some Q passages which predict a prompt end and, as we saw in this connection, he allows the Baptist to preach about the axe which already lies at the root of the trees and to declare that the winnowing fan of judgment has already been taken up (see above, pp. 91f). Perhaps, then, Luke had not completely abandoned the expectation of an early end, although he was obviously less confident about it than previous Christian writers had been, and certainly wished to stress it less.

The Q source (and hence Matthew and Luke, but not Mark) tells that during his imprisonment the Baptist sent his disciples to ask Jesus whether he was the Messiah (Matthew 11:2-6; Luke 7:18-23. In the fourth gospel, there is no such enquiry, for there the Baptist's acceptance of Jesus's exalted status remains unwavering). Matthew, for instance, first makes John hear the "voice out of the heavens" saying, at Jesus's baptism, "This is my beloved Son, in whom I am well pleased", but then makes him inquire from prison whether Jesus is "he that cometh", or whether they are to "look for another". The discrepancy can be explained if we assume: (i) that the historical Baptist did not regard Jesus as the coming one, and that Mark and Q, reworking the Baptist traditions that reached them, introduced this idea; (ii) that at some stage (represented in the material which went to form Q) Christian tradition could not believe that the historical Baptist did not have at least an inkling of who Jesus was, and so made him inquire from prison whether Jesus might be the Messiah. Later tradition did not rest satisfied with this much discernment on John's part, and Luke's infancy narrative makes him, still in his mother's womb, leap for joy when confronted with the also as yet unborn Jesus (Luke 1:41, 44).

Jesus replies to the Baptist's query from prison by alluding to his own miraculous powers—we are meant to infer that these authenticate him as the Messiah—and he then declares that John, although greater than any ordinary mortal, is inferior to the least in the kingdom of heaven (Matthew 11:11; Luke 7:28). Those in the kingdom are surely, for these two evangelists, the members of the Christian community; and the view here ascribed to Jesus is intelligible as a Christian attempt to subordinate to him a man venerated by a rival group. (That the Baptist had his own 'disciples' is implied by repeated references to them in the gospels. We learn, for instance, that after his execution, "his disciples" came and buried him: Mark

6:29; Matthew 14:12). A narrative in Acts betrays the same tendency very clearly. It tells of a convert to Christianity in Ephesus who knew "only the baptism of John" (18:25) and had in consequence never heard of the Holy Spirit. Paul then explains to the Ephesians generally that John had taught belief in one who was to come after him: and they thereupon allowed themselves to be "baptized into the name of the Lord Jesus . . . And the Holy Ghost came on them" (19:4-6). The point of the story is to make Christians immune to the attractions of the Baptist sect.

In Elliott's view, rivalry occurred not between John and Jesus, but after their deaths between their supporters (p. 20); for the Baptist sect reached its zenith at the end of the first century.[10] This would explain why there is no allusion to it in the stages of Christian tradition that are earlier than the gospels.

One further matter. If in the previous chapter we saw that Mary's Magnificat may not be hers at all, but may have referred originally to the Baptist, we may note in this one that the so-called Lord's prayer may derive from the Baptist. Elliott thinks that the introduction to the prayer at Luke 11:1 betrays as much. He writes:

> There the disciples ask Jesus to teach them to pray *as John taught his disciples*. Now, as Jews, Jesus' disciples would know *how* to pray – and, in fact, in several places in the gospels Jesus assumes that they will pray. What is meant in Luke 11:1 is that the disciples of Jesus ask for the special prayer that John is known to have used. From this Baptist background, therefore, came the so-called Lord's prayer (p. 28).

Did the historical Baptist ever meet Jesus? Josephus does not suggest that he did. The account of the collaboration of the two men in the fourth gospel is prompted by theological motives and in many respects at variance with what is said on the subject in the other three. As Scobie notes (p. 149) these three "give us no sayings of John which are directly applied to Jesus". And Brown thinks that "the idea that he was preparing the way for the Messiah whom he identified as Jesus (John 3:28 most explicitly) is a Christian adaptation of the Baptist's own thought that he was preparing the way for God". Brown adds that, "as part of this Christian reinterpretation, the Baptist was attributed the role of Elijah through an exegesis of Malachi . . . combined with Isaiah 40:3, with Jesus seen as the Lord whose coming was thus heralded" (pp. 283-84).

Jesus's baptism by John has nevertheless been classed among "the best attested data of his life".[11] The argument is that, since evangelists later than Mark found the sinless Jesus's submission to John's "baptism for the remission of sins" embarrassing, and tried to explain it or cover it up, Mark's statement on the matter cannot be a Christian invention. However, what embarrassed later Christians need not have embarrassed him. Justin Martyr, writing about AD 150, betrays that it was the Jewish notion that the Messiah would be unknown as such to himself and others until Elijah as his forerunner should anoint him;[12] and Morna Hooker concedes (p. 80) that Mark, who implies that the Baptist is Elijah, may have been influenced by a tradition of this kind. Apart from this possibility, if Jesus was to be brought into contact with John, baptism would have to be involved, as it is clear from Josephus that the principal thing known about John was that he baptized. Mark could unthinkingly have made Jesus come to him for baptism because opportunity was thereby provided to introduce the heavenly voice proclaiming Jesus's supernatural status as God's son. It is this supernatural aspect of the proceedings which Mark stresses, not the actual baptism (which is dismissed in half a dozen words), and he obviously did not pause to ask himself whether the baptism could be taken to put Jesus's sinlessness in question. In the earliest Christian tradition of which there is a record, the Resurrection was the moment when his true status as Son of God in power through the Holy Spirit was revealed (Romans 1:4). But Christians came in time to think that he must always have been what he was at that moment disclosed to be; and so, as Brown observes (p. 181), the revelation of who he is was brought back first to his baptism and, later still, in the infancy narratives, to his conception. Furthermore, early Christian communities, believing as they did that baptism imparted the Spirit, could not unnaturally suppose that Jesus himself had received it at baptism, "as a dove descending upon him" (Mark 1:10). Hence Haenchen can say that Mark's account is based "not on an old historical tradition, but on the projection of early Christian experience onto the life of Jesus" (p. 62). When baptism had become a universal Christian practice, the belief could naturally arise that Jesus had commended and consecrated it by his own example. Enslin has said that such "reading farther and farther back" of an important rite "is invariably the case in a religion which takes itself seriously as one of revelation. What is now under God's blessing must always so have been". He finds a parallel to such thinking in the standpoint of the 'priestly' material of the Pentateuch, dating from the Exile or after, but ascribing current religious law and ritual to the initiative of Moses, hundreds of years earlier.[13]

ii. THE TEMPTATION

At Jesus's baptism "he saw the heavens rent asunder and the Spirit as a dove descending upon him" (Mark 1:10). For the author of this story, the heavens "form a solid firmament, and above it is the abode of God; they must be 'opened' if the Spirit of God is to 'descend' " (Beare, p. 100). If Jesus was to see this spirit, it had to take some visible form; and as the author would not suppose it to have dropped like a stone, he would naturally think of the flight of a bird — not, of course, some savage bird of prey, but a creature of complete innocence. Haenchen refers in this connection (pp. 53–54) to Matthew 10:16, where the disciples are exhorted to be "harmless as doves".

Mark continues:

And straightway the Spirit driveth him forth into the wilderness. And he was in the wilderness forty days, tempted of Satan; and he was with the wild beasts; and the angels ministered unto him. (1:12–13)

There is no reference here to fasting or hunger, which, as we shall see, are integral to Q's version of Jesus's Temptation, preserved by Matthew and Luke. On the contrary, the 'ministry' of the angels (which the tense of the Greek verb shows to have been continuous) could only have consisted in supplying food, as angels fed Elijah (1 Kings 19:3–8) when he was in the wilderness for 40 days. Altogether, 40 is a suspiciously sacred number. Moses fasted 40 days and nights on Sinai (Exodus 34:28; Deuteronomy 9:9), and Israel spent 40 years being tested by God in the wilderness (Deuteronomy 8:2). We recall too that, according to Acts 1:3, Jesus's Resurrection appearances lasted for 40 days.

Mark's statement that during the 40 days Jesus "was with the wild beasts" is agreed even by conservative commentators to be "an imaginative element" in the narrative.[14] Some take it as suggesting that Jesus, as Messiah, restores the conditions of Paradise before man's fall, when he lived in harmony with the beasts. Adam was tempted and succumbed, but Jesus withstood temptation and is in that regard the antitype of Adam. Others, perhaps more plausibly, think that the beasts have affinity with Satan in that they are the associates of demons, as is already suggested in the Old Testament: Isaiah links "wild beasts of the desert" with "satyrs" (13:21; cf. the Septuagint of Isaiah 34:11–15, where "devils shall meet with satyrs" and both are associated with animals).[15] Although Mark (unlike Matthew and Luke) does not state wherein Jesus's Temptation consisted, the wilderness is the traditional haunt of evil spirits (cf. above, p. 89), and the background to Mark's story is "the current belief that the Messiah was the divine agent for the overthrow of Satan and all his powers, and that therefore a tremendous battle, or trial of strength, between him and Satan would form an integral element in the last days" (Nineham, p. 63; cf. above, p. 16).

Belief in angels and demons is generally considered to have entered Jewish religious thinking from Zoroastrianism from the time of the Babylonian exile. By New Testament times, the Jews were so conscious of evil in the world that they repudiated the Old Testament view that Satan and other supernatural powers were subservient to God, and supposed instead that these demonic forces had seized control of the world. In the apocalyptic literature of this time, "Satan's dethronement was anticipated as a cosmic event",[16] to be effected, in Christian understanding, by Jesus, who showed that he had the capacity to do so by facing up to him from the first, and then by giving his disciples "authority to cast out devils" (Mark 3:15) and "authority over the unclean spirits" (6:7). At Mark 1:24 one of these actually asks him: "Art thou come to destroy us?"

Best has pointed in this connection to the significance of the dialogue between Jesus and the scribes at Mark 3:22–30. They accuse him of himself having an unclean spirit, in a context which makes clear that it is in fact the "Holy Spirit" which enables him to cast out devils (verses 29–30). For his part, he implies that he has "bound", i.e. rendered powerless, "the strong man", clearly meaning Satan (verse 27), and it was presumably on the occasion of his confrontation with Satan at his Temptation that he did so. The temptation narrative therefore shows that "Satan is overcome: the demonic exorcisms of the remainder of the ministry . . . are mopping-up operations of isolated units of Satan's hosts and are certain to be successful because the Captain of the hosts of evil is already . . . immobilised."[17] If Best is right, Mark attached the defeat of Satan to the Temptation, and not, as Paul had done (cf. above, p. 16), to the Passion.

Matthew and Luke give the temptation story not as a narrative, but as a dialogue between Jesus and the Devil in which the two speakers contrive to settle disputed points by regaling each other with Old Testament quotations. No witnesses are present, and those who regard the exchange as authentic have to suppose that, on some 'holy occasion', Jesus confided its content to his disciples. Against authenticity is, first, the fact that all the quotations agree with the Septuagint, not with the Hebrew Old Testament, suggesting that the dialogue was drawn up in a Greek-speaking Christian environment, not in a Palestinian one; and, second, that none of the quotations are really to the point. They appear relevant only because they have been made to bear a meaning alien to their Old Testament context. What the evangelists are here giving us is "a learned dispute", in the manner of the rabbis of the time, who characteristically argued in this way.[18] We have seen Matthew doing this in his comments on Jesus's birth and infancy, but here it is Jesus himself who is made to follow this same method.

In these two accounts, the words of Jesus (absent from Mark) are practically identical, and so derive from Q, which, we recall, was essentially a collection of Jesus's sayings, with minimal indication of the circumstances in which they were spoken. The two narrative frames, however, are different, and each of them therefore represents the work of the respective evangelist, with also some assimilation of the brief Marcan material. The first four verses are as follows:

Matthew 4:1–4

(1) Then was Jesus led up of the Spirit into the wilderness to be tempted of the devil.

(2) And when he had fasted forty days and forty nights, he afterward hungered.

(3) And the tempter came and said unto him, If thou art the Son of God, command that these stones become bread.

(4) But he answered and said, It is written, Man shall not live by bread alone, but by every word that proceedeth out of the mouth of God.

Luke 4:1–4

(1) And Jesus, full of the Holy Spirit, returned from the Jordan, and was led by the Spirit in the wilderness (2) during forty days being tempted of the devil.

And he did eat nothing in those days: and when they were completed he hungered.

(3) And the devil said unto him, If thou art the Son of God command this stone that it become bread.

(4) And Jesus answered unto him, It is written, Man shall not live by bread alone.

We notice that Mark's reference to wild beasts has been dropped, but not his mention of the wilderness and the 40 days. Matthew adds "and forty nights", thus pressing the parallel with Moses's fast of "forty days and forty nights" on the wilderness mountain. New altogether compared with Mark is Jesus's fasting, leading to his hunger which gives the Devil occasion to tempt him. According to Matthew, there was no tempting during the 40 day fast, but only subsequently, as an attempt to exploit Jesus's hunger. This was presumbly the situation as presented in Q. Luke rather clumsily retains (verse 2) Mark's idea that the tempting was spread over 40 days, yet also follows Q in restricting it to the Devil's later approach initiated by Jesus's hunger after this period.[19] Luke also has (verse 3) "this stone" (singular) and the singular of "bread" in the Greek (i.e. 'command this stone that it become a loaf'), instead of the corresponding plurals, as in Matthew. The inference is that Matthew retained these from Q, but Luke changed them "in the interest of plausibility . . . Since Jesus is alone, the changing of one stone to a loaf would satisfy his need and reduce the grotesque image of a desert full of loaves" (Fitzmyer, p. 515). This small detail shows how rationally and deliberately a sacred writer can go to work in 'editing' his material.

Jesus responds (verse 4 of both accounts) with words from Deuteronomy 8:2–3, where the people of Israel are being reminded that, although God afflicted them by letting them hunger in the wilderness, he then provided food of a miraculous kind:

> He humbled thee, and suffered thee to hunger, and fed thee with manna . . . that he might make thee know that man doth not live by bread only, but by everything that proceedeth out of the mouth of the Lord.

The reminder is thus intended to show that life depends not only on material sustenance, but on reliance on God; and the Deuteronomist's point is: even where a natural food supply is wanting, God can sustain those who trust him with miraculous food. The point the evangelists are making, however, is: it is not permissible to sustain life miraculously because God can keep man alive by other means. As Haenchen has noted, the evangelists (and their predecessor, the compiler of Q) can make Jesus use the Old Testament passage only because they are following not its sense but its wording, in the manner of rabbinic exegesis (p. 67). If Jesus really held that working miracles implied an improper lack of trust in God, it is strange that the evangelists go on to make him work so many.[20]

The two further temptations are given in reverse order in the two gospels, and I quote next what Matthew gives as the second, with its Lucan parallel where it figures as the third:

Matthew 4:5-7	*Luke 4:9-12*
(5) Then the devil taketh him into the holy city; and he set him on the pinnacle of the temple (6) and saith unto him, If thou art the Son of God, cast thyself down: for it is written, He shall give his angels charge concerning thee: And on their hands they shall bear thee up, Lest haply thou dash thy foot against a stone. (7) Jesus said unto him, Again it is written, Thou shalt not tempt the Lord thy God.	(9) And he led him to Jerusalem and set him on the pinnacle of the temple and said unto him, If thou art the Son of God, cast thyself down from hence: (10) for it is written, He shall give his angels charge concerning thee, to guard thee: (11) and, On their hands they shall bear thee up, Lest haply thou dash thy foot against a stone. (12) And Jesus answering said unto him, It is said, Thou shalt not tempt the Lord thy God.

Whereas in the first temptation Jesus, being hungry, might be supposed to be willing to supply himself with food, he is given no motive that would lead him towards succumbing to this further temptation. Some commentators have tried to make good this deficiency by supposing that he is being asked to give an exhibition miracle, a public display of God's care of him, thus authenticating himself as Messiah. But no public is said to be present to be impressed by such a demonstration. The Devil does not say: do this so that people will believe in you, nor does Jesus's answer imply that this is what was meant.

The Devil here quotes a psalm which, in a series of images, represents God's protection of the Israelite who has "made him his refuge". In one image this protection is pictured as aid to a traveller walking along rough and rocky paths: the angels will hold him up to keep him from tripping over a stone. The Devil wisely omits the phrase (italicized below) which refers to these paths so that he can apply the passage to the quite different situation of jumping from a height:

For he shall give his angels charge over thee,
To keep thee in all thy ways.
They shall bear thee up in their hands,
Lest thou dash thy foot against a stone
(Psalm 91:11-12).

If Jesus were to object that, as the Psalm does not promise protection to those who jump from a height, he cannot feel any inclination to do so, the whole story — which presupposes that he is meritoriously resisting what he feels as a real temptation — would be ruined. And so instead of objecting to the Devil's distortion of Scripture, he replies in the same vein with Deuteronomy 6:16: "Ye shall not tempt the Lord your God, as ye tempted him in Massah." This alludes to the situation described in Exodus 17:2ff, where the Israelites, thirsting in the desert, doubt God's willingness to preserve them. They are here said to "tempt" the Lord, instead of trusting in him, and he responds by miraculously supplying water from a rock. But if the people here 'tempt' God by *not believing* that he will save them, the exact opposite is implied by Jesus's use of the verse from Deuteronomy; for he says that he will not tempt God by *believing* that God will come to his rescue.

We pass on to what in Matthew is the third and final temptation, and in Luke the second:

Matthew 4:8-11

(8) Again, the devil taketh him unto an exceeding high mountain, and sheweth him all the kingdoms of the world, and the glory of them;

(9) and he said unto him, All these things will I give thee,

if thou wilt fall down and worship me.

(10) Then saith Jesus unto him, Get thee hence, Satan; for it is written, Thou shalt worship the Lord thy God, and him only shalt thou serve.

Luke 4:5-8

(5) And he led him up, and shewed him all the kingdoms of the world in a moment of time.

(6) And the devil said unto him, To thee will I give all this authority, and the glory of them: for it hath been delivered unto me; and to whomsoever I will I give it.

(7) If thou therefore wilt worship before me, it shall all be thine.

(8) And Jesus answered and said unto him, It is written, Thou shalt worship the Lord thy God, and him only shalt thou serve . . .

(11) Then the devil leaveth him; and behold, angels came and ministered unto him.

(13) And when the devil had completed every temptation, he departed from him for a season.

Matthew's final verse introduces the angels of Mark's brief narrative—Luke omits them altogether—but adapts them to the situation he has constructed. They do not, as in Mark, minister to Jesus during the whole 40 days, but are appropriate and acceptable heavenly ministers to him at the end of his three trials.

In this temptation, the Devil does not, as before, introduce his proposal with "if thou art the Son of God". To have done so would have exposed it as ridiculous—offering the rulership of the world to him who, as Son of God, was destined to rule and judge it anyway. A mountain from which "all the kingdoms of the world" (Matthew's verse 8) are visible can only be mythical. This is possibly why Luke deleted it, making the Devil simply 'lead Jesus up', that is, into the air for a bird's eye view; for in Luke (as against Matthew) the two speakers are at this point standing on the pinnacle of the temple. In Matthew the view from the mountain discloses not only all kingdoms, but also "the glory of them". This was obviously too much for Luke, who transfers this phrase from the narrator (Matthew's verse 8) to the Devil (Luke's verse 6), leaving the pronoun 'them' with no antecedent in the Devil's speech: the antecedent ("all the kingdoms of the world") has been left (verse 5) with the narrator. The Devil's next sentence in Luke's verse 6 is altogether unrepresented in Matthew (occurring neither as narrative nor as dialogue there), and expresses very clearly the belief, common in New Testament times, that the world is in the power not of God but of the Devil. Although he came into Jewish thinking much later than the time of Deuteronomy, Jesus is made to repudiate him at the end of this temptation with Deuteronomy 6:13-14, where Israel is forbidden to worship the gods of other peoples.

Early this century J. M. Robertson suggested how this story, where the Devil offers all the kingdoms of the world in return for worship, could have originated. He was stressing the effects of pagan art on Christian believers. Paintings or sculpture, originally representing some event, historical or imaginary, coming to the eyes of those who know nothing of the real subject represented, may be freshly interpreted by such people in accordance with their own prepossessions. Robertson refers to a story (recorded by Evemeros) of the young Jupiter, led by Pan to "the mountain which is called the pillar of heaven; whereupon he ascended it and contemplated the lands afar; and there in that mountain he raises an altar to Coelus (or Heaven). On that altar Jupiter first sacrificed; and in that place he looked up to heaven".[21] In a picture or sculpture representing this story, Pan would be given horns, hoofs and tail, and would stand beside the divine youth at the altar. Christians who saw such a picture would take Pan for the Devil and suppose that, standing by the young divinity at the altar on a mountain top, he was asking to be worshipped in return for the kingdoms of the Earth to which he was pointing. This would give rise to a narrative where the Devil takes Jesus to an "exceeding high mountain" and tempts him.

Since Robertson, the view that ideas were transmitted to early Christianity by pictures has been taken up (without reference to him) by Toynbee, who stressed the importance of visual representations in conveying ideas among illiterate people.[22] Robert Graves believed that some Greek myths themselves originated from misinterpretations of a sacred picture or dramatic rite. He called such a process "iconotrophy", and declared that "examples of it can be found in every body of sacred literature which sets the seal upon a radical reform of ancient beliefs".[23]

Arnold Meyer noted in 1914 that, in the whole temptation dialogue, the real meaning of the Old Testament quotations is "completely fudged" (ganz verwischt).[24] Jesus and Satan, says Beare, are no more interested in the original setting of a text than a rabbi, and "the use of Scripture . . . on both parts is like nothing so much as the way in which a pair of rabbis would proceed in a disputation . . . The debate is the creation of someone who was trained in the methods of the rabbinical schools" (p. 111). Its author, as Strauss noted, was concerned to make Jesus the antitype of the people of Israel.[25] In the Old Testament, Israel, called God's son (We recall Hosea's "out of Egypt have I called my son"), is subjected to trials in the wilderness and found wanting; in the temptation dialogue, Jesus, as God's true son, is tested and stays faithful to his calling.[26] The kind of curiosity which led to the formation of infancy stories (cf. above, p. 56) could well have led to such learned expansion of a bare tradition (resembling the account preserved in Mark) that Jesus had confronted Satan. "Once it had come to be said that Jesus was tempted, people wanted to know in what manner."[27] On this view, the dialogue is a legend about Jesus's confrontation with the forces of evil, based on fairy-tale motifs and arbitrary interpretation of Jewish scripture. "All three incidents", says Haenchen, "collapse when deprived of the quotations wrongly interpreted in the manner of rabbinic dispute" (p. 71).

Many commentators have discerned more specific motives as underlying the temptation dialogue, and have regarded it as an attempt to explain to orthodox Jews, critical of Christianity, why Jesus had not performed some of the signs and miracles which, in Judaism, were expected of the Messiah; why he had not provided manna in the wilderness, nor given a showy display of his divine authorization, nor sought to achieve world sovereignty by political means.[28] Other commentators think that the dialogue is not a mere legend, concocted to refute Jewish charges, but is based on what went on in Jesus's own mind. Dodd, for instance, argues that gaining power by "doing homage to the devil" means "in realistic terms, exploiting the latent forces of violence to wrest from Rome the liberation of his people";[29] and that Jesus did go into the wilderness after receiving the spirit at his baptism in order to ponder whether his vocation as Messiah implied that he should act in this manner. Alternatively it is supposed that he wrestled with such questions not once but throughout his ministry, so that the biblical story is "a commentary by the later Church, couched in mythological imagery", on temptations with which he "must often have had to contend" when he wondered how best to assert his authority.[30] But we are in fact told nothing of such psychological processes in the texts, and have no more right to suppose that Jesus went into the wilderness to wrestle with the problem of Messiahship and to work out his future course of action than we are entitled to speculate that Paul withdrew to Arabia after his conversion to Christianity (Galatians 1:17) in order to think out the Christian faith and his future work as an apostle.[31]

In any case it is more than doubtful whether Jesus's temptations were Messianic. In the first of them there is no question of his 'supplying manna in the wilderness' to a crowd, but of satisfying his own hunger; and we saw already that no audience is provided in the gospels to be impressed by an exhibition miracle. A view that has found some favour is Bultmann's suggestion that these elements in the story are a reply to the charge that Jesus was a magician. The kind of miracles the Devil here invites him to work are what might be expected of a magician; and the story tries to show that only miracles which serve the will of God, not magical ones which serve human ends, are acceptable. However, certainly on this matter is not to be had. The temptation story, says one of its most recent students, is "polyvalent and permits many applications: as a paradigm of obedience, as a polemic against false christologies, as a recapitulation of Israel's wilderness experience, to mention only a few".[32]

Jesus's Temptation is not mentioned in the fourth gospel, even though the Devil is by no means ignored in it, and even though Jesus there thrice refers to "the prince of this world" (John 12:31, 14:30, 16:11), obviously meaning the Devil and assigning to him the function he performs in one of the passages from the Q dialogue. The fourth evangelist characteristically omits details which might be taken to depress Jesus's dignity—these include the scene describing his baptism, his prayer in Gethsemane and his forsaken cry from the cross (Mark 15:34 = Matthew 27:46)—and makes him stoutly declare that the prince of this world "has nothing in me" (14:30), i.e., has no power over me.

As the 'tempting' specified in the epistle to the Hebrews refers to Jesus's suffering and death,[33] there are no references elsewhere in the New Testament to the temptation situations as given in the first three gospels. It seems clear that Mark's brief narrative is independent of the Q dialogue, and since the two agree as to the bare fact that Jesus was tempted by the Devil, apologists have inevitably claimed that "it is probable that the incidents have some basis in fact".[34] By the same kind of reasoning, we should have to believe in Jesus's virgin birth and Resurrection, not to mention the historicity of Wilhelm Tell.

Morna Hooker observes that, if the ideas in Mark's temptation narrative seem "fanciful", this is "because we no longer think, as Mark and his contemporaries did, of a world dominated by demons" (p. 15). Quite so. For Beare, not only the demons but also the Devil is "a mythological conception" which we cannot accept "without falling victim to superstition" (pp. 107–08). Once again we see modern theologians quietly setting aside what has been taught as literal truth for hundreds of years, but is no longer acceptable to educated audiences of today. Hell, linked with the Devil, is, in the disarming phrase of one of these theologians, today "not culturally available".[35] Such antiquated ideas are not normally dismissed as nonsense, but are made acceptable by reinterpretation, as when Caird grants that "the devil is a mythological figure", but holds that "myth . . . is a pictorial way of expressing truths".[36] Fitzmyer claims that the "theological import" of the temptation scenes is "in the long run of greater importance than any salvaging of their historicity" (p. 510). So much in the gospel narratives is now treated in this way. Morna

Hooker writes, even of the Passion, that "in terms of historical verisimilitude, many of Mark's scenes creak". Yet of course they have great "significance for Christian believers" (p. 92). The 'theological import' and the 'significance' of the narratives used to be founded on their historical truth. It is not easy to see what remains — apart from pious fantasies — once this has been ceded.

The Passion

i. FROM THE PREDICTION TO THE ARREST

a. The Prediction

Many suppose that, however unsatisfactorily earlier incidents in Jesus's life may have been reported, his experiences in Jerusalem leading to his arrest and crucifixion must have made an indelible impression on his followers, and that here if anywhere we may expect a narrative which goes back to eyewitnesses of the events. In fact, however, for early Christian communities what God himself was understood as having said in the Jewish Scriptures by way of prophecy about Jesus's sufferings was of far greater account than what any human witnesses might say. For instance, in the first of the two epistles ascribed (misleadingly, as we saw above, p. 12) to Peter, the Passion is described not with reference to any traditions about Jesus's life on Earth, but from the sufferings of the servant of Yahweh detailed in Isaiah 53. Hoskyns and Davey have compared the relevant passages and have justly concluded that "the language is so similar that the resemblance cannot be fortuitous".[1] In the gospel Passion narratives, as commentators have come to recognize, reflection on the Old Testament likewise plays a decisive role. In chapters 11–16 of Mark, says Kee, "there is pervasive stress on the events that occur as the fulfillment of Scripture",[2] and features of these events that derive from the Christologically interpreted Scriptures are not always made readily identifiable by explicit reference to the relevant Old Testament passages. Furthermore, it is not only that reflection on what were taken for Messianic prophecies led to the conviction that Jesus, as Messiah, must have behaved in certain ways. There were also traditions, independent of the Scriptures, that he had done or suffered this or that, and the belief that all that he did had been scripturally foretold prompted search for supporting passages, some of which needed adaptation if they were to serve a Christological purpose. Hence Kee adds that "the critical reader cannot tell whether the events have been conformed to Scripture or (as seems likely in several cases) the Scripture has been modified to fit the event". I prefer to speak of the tradition that there was an event, rather than of the event as an unquestionably historical fact.

Let us begin with what in Mark is Jesus's third prediction of his Passion, said to the twelve as they all journeyed towards Jerusalem, and with Luke's adaptation of this pericope, where reference to the importance of prophecy is explicit.

Mark 10	*Luke 18*
(33) Behold, we go up to Jerusalem; and	(31) Behold, we go up to Jerusalem, and all the things that are written by the prophets shall be accomplished unto the Son of man. (32) For he
the Son of man shall be delivered unto the chief priests and the scribes; and they shall condemn him to death, and shall deliver him unto the Gentiles: (34) and they shall mock him, and shall spit upon him, and shall scourge him, and shall kill him; and after three days he shall rise again.	shall be delivered up unto the Gentiles, and shall be mocked and shamefully entreated and spit upon: (33) and they shall scourge and kill him: and the third day he shall rise again. (34) And they understood none of these things . . .

Luke omits (his verse 32) Mark's statement that the Jewish authorities will condemn Jesus to death. Mark (and Matthew) will go on to make the Sanhedrin condemn him, although they will make this council take no steps to carry out the sentence. Luke, however, will nowhere mention any formal sentence passed by the council. He does not mean thereby to diminish Jewish responsibility for Jesus's death. On the contrary, the fact that Jewish authorities, "though they found no cause of death in him, yet asked they of Pilate that he should be slain" (Acts 13:28, also written by Luke), makes their behaviour morally worse than if they had achieved his condemnation in a court of law. In Luke's passion narrative their malice is emphasized when Pilate, facing them and finding Jesus innocent, does not merely "deliver him to be crucified" (Mark 15:15 and Matthew 27:26), but "delivers him up to their will" (Luke 23:25).

As we saw (above, p. 42), if Jesus had actually given such a detailed forecast as in the passages I have quoted, his disciples would not have reacted to his arrest and execution with bewildered incomprehension. Here (as against 9:32) Mark does not even try to make their later behaviour plausible by alleging that they failed to understand the predictions. On the contrary, his next story—that, to the anger of the other ten disciples, James and John asked for the most privileged places at his side in his "glory", i.e. after his Resurrection, and that they were prepared to "drink the cup" that he will first have to drink—shows that they had understood him very well. (That the 'cup' means martyrdom is later explicit in Mark (at 14:36), and the image derives from the Old Testament: for instance, at Ezekiel 23:33-41 Jerusalem is promised the "cup of desolation" that Samaria had already had to drink.) Luke, who does allege that they had not understood, significantly omits the further story about James and John.

b. The Entry into Jerusalem

When the party comes near to Jerusalem, Jesus sends two of them on to a village where—so he predicts with miraculous foresight—they will be able to impress for his use "a colt whereupon no man ever yet sat" (Mark 11:2). That he thus selected an unbroken mount for his ride into the city makes no sense as historical fact, but is intelligible as an echo of the Septuagint of Zechariah 9:9: "Behold the king is coming . . . riding an ass and a young [lit. new] foal". This prediction of a divinely empowered ruler occurs in a section of Zechariah which speaks doom to Israel's neighbours and promises prosperity to her, restored to her land. It came to be understood as a Messianic prophecy before Christian times. It also specifies the acclamation of the crowd: "Rejoice, . . . daughter of Jerusalem". Mark's narrative is thus "not an eyewitness report of Jesus' entry into Jerusalem, but a story told by the later Christian community which allowed the Old Testament to provide the material" (Haenchen, p. 378).

Matthew makes reference to the Old Testament explicit by quoting (21:5) a mixture of Isaiah 62:11 and Zechariah 9:9. As he mistakenly supposed that two animals are here specified (Zechariah tells that the king will come "riding upon an ass, even upon a colt the foal of an ass"), he goes on to make Jesus sit astride both—to the embarrassment of many commentators, some of whom are reduced to conjecturing (against the plain statement of the text) that he used each animal alternately for his ride. The incident in fact shows how much more important to early Christians the Old Testament was than were any considerations of plausibility. What God was understood to have prophesied had to occur.

As Jesus rides towards the city, "many spread their garments on the way" (Mark 11:8), as had been done for Jehu when he was proclaimed king (2 Kings 9:13). Mark adds that "they that went before and they that followed cried, Hosanna; Blessed is he that cometh in the name of the Lord". This final sentence is from Psalm 118:26, where 'he that cometh' is a collective designation of pilgrims coming to a religious festival in Jerusalem. In the Psalm these words are preceded by "Save now, we beseech thee, O Lord", and the Hebrew for 'save now' is the original of the word 'hosanna', which, most scholars suppose, was misunderstood when it passed into the early Church and taken as a shout of homage or greeting—'Hail' or 'Glory to'.[3]

There could hardly be more Old Testament than all this in Mark's narrative of Jesus's triumphal entry into Jerusalem, and it is interesting to see how it is adapted in different directions by Matthew and by Luke. Mark says that the crowd cried: "Blessed is the kingdom that cometh, the kingdom of our father David". Jesus is thus not here called 'son of David'; the crowd does but claim David as *their* father. Matthew, however, has made Jesus son of David in the elaborate genealogy of his birth and infancy narrative, and obviously felt that these words in Mark were not good enough; for he changes them so as to make "the multitudes" cry "Hosanna to the son of David" (21:9). Luke, on the other hand, deletes all reference to David and his kingdom, and makes only the disciples (not a crowd) greet Jesus with thanks to God for all the miracles they had witnessed (19:37, unrepresented in Mark). They do indeed hail him as "the king that cometh in the name of the Lord" (verse 38), but continue with: "Peace in heaven and glory in the highest". So instead of the Marcan hope for the coming kingdom of David, Luke has a thoroughly non-political reminiscence of what he made the heavenly host say at Jesus's birth: "Glory to God in the highest, and on earth peace".

This is in line with Luke's general tendency to delete anything that could be construed as militant Jewish Messianism, and so to advocate a harmonious relationship with Rome. He tones down some of

Mark's references to persecution—replacing, as we saw (above, p. 95) Mark's injunction to 'take up one's cross' with 'take up one's cross daily', thus making a reference to martyrdom into one suggesting the frustrations to which Christians are exposed in ordinary living. Perhaps he hoped that some of the storm-clouds of persecution to which the Marcan community had been exposed had passed, at least temporarily, and that the Church might begin to develop what Walaskay calls "a dialogue with the local magistrates".[4]

Many Christians of about this time did not share this pro-Roman perspective. Walaskay notes: "There was a tendency for some to deprecate the imperial government. A speedy and catastrophic end of the empire was anticipated; the kingdom of Caesar would be replaced by the kingdom of Christ. At best the government could be tolerated, . . . at worst Rome was a ravenous beast" (p. 65). Such anti-Roman sentiment is very evident in the New Testament apocalypse or book of Revelation, and Luke may have been concerned to counter it, seeing it as "the primary internal threat to the Christian movement" (p. 67). Maddox is probably right to say that persecution was a possibility for Christians in Luke's world and that his purpose was to discourage them from actively seeking it. "The proper business of Christians is to live at peace with the sovereign power, so far as possible, and not to play the hero".[5]

According to the fourth gospel, the chief cause of the applause that greeted Jesus's entry into Jerusalem was his raising of Lazarus from the dead (John 12:9–18)—his greatest miracle, as Lazarus had already been dead for four days, so that "by this time he stinketh" (11:49). The other gospels know nothing of this miracle, just as John's knows nothing of their story of the raising of the deceased daughter of Jairus (Mark 5:22ff and parallels) nor of Luke's account of the raising of the widow's son at Nain (cf. above, p. 19). Here, as with the virgin birth and the Resurrection, there will first have been a tradition that raisings had occurred, and later imaginative accounts supplied details.

c. Activity in Jerusalem

Mark follows Jesus's triumphal entry into Jerusalem with his cursing of a fig tree for not supplying him with figs, even though "it was not the season for figs" (11:13). Was Jesus a child who would kick an object that offended him? For Haenchen (p. 382), the story is of interest as illustrating that even the gospel passion narratives are not lacking legendary features. A little later, Mark reports that the next day the tree was seen to be withered (11:20-24), and this gives occasion for Jesus to laud faith, saying that it can even move mountains. At 1 Corinthians 13:2 Paul mentions faith sufficient to remove mountains, but does not suggest that Jesus ever spoke on such lines. But faith was so important to early Christianity that it will have been natural to invent a story in which he inculcates it. The occasion for the legend may have been some prominent withered fig tree near Jerusalem which invited an account of how it came to be in this state. If the story was not originally set at Passover, the words "it was not the season for figs" will not have formed part of it. But as Mark makes Jesus come to Jerusalem on one occasion only, and at Passover, he will have seen fit to add them.

In between the cursing of the tree and the report of its having withered Mark places Jesus's so-called cleansing of the temple, on which I have commented elsewhere.[6] Luke did not much like this act of violence and at 19:45 deleted Mark's statements (11:15-16) that Jesus "overthrew the tables of the moneychangers, and the seats of them that sold the doves; and he would not suffer that any man should carry a vessel through the temple". Luke's Jesus is here said only to have "cast out them that sold" (not, as in Mark, both "them that sold and them that bought in the temple"). According to Mark 11:18 it was this event which made "the chief priests and the scribes" seek "how they might destroy him". Luke, having all but eliminated Jesus's violence, attributes their hostility to dislike of his teaching. In the fourth gospel the whole incident is placed at the beginning of his ministry (2:13-22) and has no outward consequences.

In Mark's next incident after Jesus's words about faith he is "walking in the temple" (11:27) – the day after his violent behaviour in it. If it is difficult to believe that the temple authorities permitted such violence, it is even harder to accept that they would have allowed the perpetrator to walk unimpeded in the temple area so soon afterwards. The incident introduced in this way may, then, like so many others in Mark (cf. above, p. 12), represent a tradition that was independent of the setting here given to it. It consists of a challenge from the "chief priests and the scribes and the elders" in the form of the question: "By what authority doest thou these things?" These things' cannot refer to his walking about in the temple. If the whole pericope was originally independent of its present setting, the reference might be to his miracles, involving as they did the dislodging of evil spirits from sick persons. (Earlier, at Mark 3:22, the scribes accused him of achieving such spectacular effects with the help of "Beelzebub, the prince of demons".) In the context which Mark gives, however, "these things" which Jesus is "doing" can really refer only to his violent behaviour in the temple the previous day. In the fourth gospel a somewhat differently worded challenging question follows this violence directly and cannot but refer to it, although the whole scene there (John 2:13–18) is, as so often in the fourth gospel, differently imagined, and Jesus gives a quite different answer to his questioners.

The situation in which Mark has the question put to Jesus really implies that he was continuing to make impossible any buying and selling in the temple. Otherwise we should have to assume that, having the previous day expelled both buyers and sellers and overthrown "the tables of the moneychangers and the seats of them that sold the doves", he allowed them back and let them proceed with their trafficking while he walked about. Called to account, he replies with a counter-question, as was customary in rabbinic debates: "The baptism of John, was it from heaven or from men?" The priests are afraid to affirm either alternative and say among themselves — one is not supposed to ask how Mark came to know of their private deliberations — that acknowledgement of John's baptism would ill accord with their hostility to him, while failure to acknowledge it would put them at odds with the people, who revered him as a prophet. They were not very intelligent if they were in fact thus stumped, and might easily have countered Jesus with some counter-question of their own about *his* attitude to the Baptist, in the manner of the question the Pharisees put to him at Mark 2:18.

The tension between Jesus and the Jewish leaders is again brought to a head when, in Mark's next incident, they realize that his parable in which the tenants of a vineyard kill the owner's son, and are then themselves dispossessed and killed, was aimed at them. In consequence they "sought to lay hold on him" (Mark 12:12 and parallels in Matthew and Luke). They are not, in these gospels, given any further motive for proceeding with this resolve. This parable, like the parables generally, is absent from the fourth gospel, which gives a quite different account of their motives. According to John 11:45–53, when the Pharisees heard of the raising of Lazarus, they decided that Jesus would soon command universal assent because of his many miracles, and the Romans would then come and subjugate the country (presumably from fear of a Messianic uprising). We have seen already how this fourth gospel makes the raising of Lazarus the chief reason for the applause that greeted Jesus as he entered Jerusalem. Now it is made into the key to his Passion. Yet it is unknown to the other gospels.

Mark follows the parable of the wicked tenants with some doctrinal altercations between Jesus and representatives of Judaism, and then with a warning against the hypocrisy of the scribes (12:38–40). Matthew expands this in his chapter 23 into a ferocious denunciation of "scribes and Pharisees" typical of the kind of sectarian hatred which Christians would be the first to deplore in any literature other than their own. Mark concludes his criticism of the scribes by complaining that they "devour widows' houses", and it seems to be this mention of widows that led him to append a brief narrative where Jesus watches a widow casting "two mites which make a farthing" into the temple treasury, and comments on her generosity in thus donating "all that she had, even all her living" (12:41–44). The positioning of this pericope is a good example of what theologians call a 'catchword connection': two traditions come to be linked not because of any chronological or thematic relation between them, but simply because they have some word in common.

The Marcan Jesus then (chapter 13) delivers his great apocalyptic discourse. I have commented in HEJ (chapter 4) on the way in which both Matthew and Luke, in their different ways, rewrote and reinterpreted it. It is of course entirely absent, as are other such apocalyptic elements, from the fourth gospel.

d. The Anointing

Next in Mark comes a story of Jesus being anointed by a woman. This is represented, in radically different forms, in all four gospels, and the differences well illustrate the way in which traditions about him proliferated. Both Mark and Matthew make the story part of their Jerusalem-based passion narratives, whereas Luke places it earlier in Jesus's ministry and in Galilee. ("The city" from which, according to Luke 7:37, the woman hails must be understood as Nain, where he had, a little earlier in the same chapter, raised a young man from the dead.) Once again, then, we see how a story about Jesus could be told with little respect to chronological or geographical setting.

Mark, followed by Matthew, has Jesus interpret the woman's action as the anticipatory anointing of his dead body: "She hath anointed my body aforehand for the burying" (Mark 14:8). We have seen what trouble Mark takes to make him supernaturally aware of what is going to happen to him at his Passion: apart from his predictions of it, we saw how he sends two disciples ahead knowing exactly in what circumstances they will be able to impress an animal for his ride into Jerusalem. This incident is doubled at 14:12–16, where he again sends two ahead knowing that they will meet a man carrying a pitcher of water who will direct them to "a large upper room" to be put at his disposal for the Passover. He also knows who will betray him and that Peter will deny him thrice.

Elliott has pointed out that Mark's positioning of the anointing in the last two days of Jesus's life enables him to interpret it as evidencing Jesus's supernatural foreknowlege that his body will not be anointed at burial.[7] In Mark there was no time for this after his death (15:46), and the intention of the women visitors to the tomb two days later to make good this omission (16:2) is frustrated by the Resurrection. Only in the fourth gospel is the body accorded the proper burial rites immediately after being brought down from the cross, and so here the anointing does not need to be so close in time to the death; John has in fact placed it immediately before the triumphal entry into Jerusalem.

Mark and Matthew site the anointing at a meal in the house of Simon the leper. Luke, however, has it happen at the house of a Pharisee (also called Simon) who has invited Jesus for a meal. In Mark and Matthew the anointer is simply "a woman", but Luke makes her "a woman of the city who was a sinner" (i.e. a harlot) who weeps over Jesus's feet, wipes them dry with her hair, kisses them and then anoints them. In Mark and Matthew the ointment is poured over his head, not his feet, and there is no mention of the woman's tears and hair. Mark makes some anonymous observers express indignation at the waste of precious ointment; Matthew ascribes the protest to "the disciples" (obviously thinking: who, other than they, would be in Jesus's company?); and the fourth gospel introduces sophistications by making the protest a hypocritical comment from Judas, who wants the perfume sold, ostensibly for the benefit of the poor, but in fact (as treasurer of the group) in order to pocket the proceeds (John 12:4–6).

Luke, however, does not suggest that the disciples were present and, in his version, it is the Pharisee who complains—not of waste (which is not mentioned), nor of the woman's behaviour, but of Jesus's failure (when he is supposed to have the discernment of a prophet) to realise what sort of woman is tending him. (We saw that only Luke makes her a harlot.) Although Luke's Pharisee does not speak this criticism aloud, Jesus of course knows his thoughts and replies with a parable of two debtors. This, like so much of the rest, is unrepresented in the other gospels. The one debtor is said to have owed 500 denarii and the other 50, and both were excused their debt. Which one, Jesus asks, will love their creditor more? The Pharisee replies: "He, I suppose, to whom he forgave the most" (Luke 7:43). Jesus approves this and so endorses the view that the loving deed of the sinful woman is a *consequence* of God's having forgiven her "many" sins. Here Luke may well be incorporating a tradition unknown to the other evangelists; but what comes next is surely an insertion of his own which teaches a different lesson, namely that her love is the *condition* of God's forgiveness. Commentators (e.g. Creed, pp. 109–110) admit to a "serious inconsistency of thought in the narrative" here. Before Luke manipulated the passage, it probably ran: "And turning to the woman, he said 'go in peace' ". I have emphasized this probable original in the following quotation, which gives Luke's expansion of it. Readers will observe that in verse 44 Jesus turns to the woman, but addresses her only in verse 50. Up to then, he addresses Simon, and his initial words to him ("Seest thou this woman?") look like Luke's attempt to smooth over this discrepancy:

> (44) *And turning to the woman, he said* unto Simon, Seest thou this woman? I entered into thine house, thou gavest me no water for my feet; but she hath wetted my feet with her tears, and wiped them with her hair. (45) Thou gavest me no kiss: but she, since the time I came in, hath not ceased to kiss my feet. (46) My head with oil thou didst not anoint: but she hath anointed my feet with ointment. (47) Wherefore I say unto thee, Her sins, which are many, are forgiven; for she loved much: but to whom little is forgiven, the same loveth little. (48) And he said unto her, Thy sins are forgiven. (49) And they that sat at meat with him began to say within themselves, Who is this that even forgiveth sins? (50) And he said unto the woman, Thy faith hath saved thee: *go in peace.*

The idea that the forgiveness is dependent on her loving deed is particularly clear in verse 47. Already Johannes Weiss (who died in

1914) held that verse 49 must be Luke's own composition because it resembles what he had written (in recasting Mark) at 5:21 (" 'Who is this? . . . Who can forgive sins but God alone?' "); and that in verse 50 in the passage quoted above Luke seems to be echoing what he had read at Mark 5:34 ("Daughter, thy faith hath made thee whole; go in peace and be whole of thy plague"). Luke has included this even though it does not harmonize well with his suggestion in verse 47 that it was the woman's love, not her faith, that mattered.

More recent commentators concede that the earlier verses (44–45) of the inserted passage are so full of implausibilities that they cannot be based on an actual incident in Jesus's life. Here, says Haenchen, Luke does not know what he is talking about ("schreibt ohne wirkliche Anschauung", p. 471). The Pharisees were most meticulous about cleanliness, and that one of their number should offer a guest no water and neglect other ordinary duties of hospitality is, as Creed puts it, "most unconvincing" (p. 109). Jesus's rebuke to a man who was, after all, entertaining him to dinner is considered by the same commentator to be "equally unsatisfactory". Haenchen argues that Luke made the whole insertion because he, and the Christian community of his day, "regarded deeds of love as the condition for the remission of sins, and Jesus as the one who remits them". "Of all this", he adds, "nothing was said in the older tradition to which Luke was here adding", and the pericope shows how easily theological ideas of a later age could be put into Jesus's mouth.

Another element in the story which is probably Luke's own invention is its setting in a Pharisee's house; for twice elsewhere (in contradistinction to Mark and Matthew) Luke makes Jesus the guest of a Pharisee when denouncing Pharisees in terms familiar from other gospels (Luke 11:37ff and 14:1ff. The denunciations in the latter passage are, in Mark and Matthew, directed not specifically at Pharisees, but at Jews of the synagogue.) Ziesler has suggested that Luke's purpose in thrice making Jesus eat with a Pharisee was "deliberately to modify his inherited anti-Pharisaic tradition"— although, as Ziesler adds, what happens or is said on such occasions is critical of the Pharisees, "so that there is some measure of incompatibility between settings and what occurs within them". He supports this view by adducing Luke 13:31 where "some Pharisees" give Jesus a friendly warning to leave town because Herod is out to have him killed. "There is nothing like this outside Luke, who certainly did not get it from Mark", where the Pharisees are aligned with the Herodians. He continues: "The Pharisees in Luke may doubt Jesus's prophetic status, but they are not involved in the guilt of the cross, quite the contrary". He notes too that even in Mark they disappear from the scene when the passion story begins. (Only John — at 18:3 — has it that Jesus is arrested by a band which includes some "officers from the chief priests *and the Pharisees*"). Ziesler can thus fairly comment that Luke's general tendency is to "soften the opposition" between Jesus and the Pharisees in the material he took from Mark.[8] Sanders, in a recent very detailed study, shows that one of the several ways in which Luke uses the Pharisees is "to let them represent those people who do make at least a superficial response to Jesus, who desire his presence and to be in his presence, but who object to his allowing into his company persons who are not properly righteous in the Pharisees' understanding". He adds that "this aspect of Luke's portrayal of the Pharisees . . . is unique in early Christian tradition and is remarkable in view of the portrayal of them in other early Christian literature". He thinks that this is Luke's "way of criticizing the Jewish Christians of his own day, who are of the opinion that being a Christian does not release one from the obligation to obey the Torah (cf. Acts 15:5; Galatians 2:11–14)".[9]

The way the incident of the anointing is treated in John's gospel well illustrates how its author, far from drawing (as some conservative scholars allege) on material which is more ancient and more reliable than that of the other evangelists, made use of more developed, more exaggerated and sometimes degraded forms of the traditions represented in them. He does not leave the woman anonymous, but names her as Mary, the sister of Martha and Lazarus. The latter is unmentioned in the other gospels,[10] and the two sisters Martha and Mary appear in another context in Luke (10:38–42), but are not identified with the woman of the anointing. It is in accordance with John's practice to name personages who are merely anonymous in the other gospels, and relatively late tradition often makes earlier tradition more specific in this way. Exaggeration is obvious when this Mary is made to pour a whole pound of ointment on to Jesus's feet. There is no mention of her tears, and it is the ointment that she wipes away with her hair (John 12:3–8). An equally senseless act, betraying John's use of a degraded tradition, is Jesus's statement (after Judas has protested that she has wasted all the oil); "Suffer her to keep it against the day of my burying".

Christian tradition later than the gospels has developed their material yet further, and has identified the anonymous harlot of Luke's story with Mary Magdalene, mainly because the latter is among the women named in the next phase of Jesus's ministry mentioned by Luke (8:2), even though Mary is not described as a harlot.

These stories of Jesus's anointing illustrate what is true also of theologically much more important ones about him, such as the virgin birth and the Resurrection, namely that minimal agreement between them suggests some tradition underlying all the variants — in all four Jesus is anointed by a woman and quashes objections made on the occasion — but that this tradition has been developed in different directions so that different personages voicing different comments propound different theologies. In the oldest gospel it is Jesus's head that is anointed, and this may go back to a tradition that he was consecrated as Messiah-king (Messiah = 'the anointed one'). Elliott argues for the historical truth of such an underlying tradition. But if stories about Jesus could rapidly assume radically different forms, it is rash to suppose that the earliest version extant, or inferable from what is extant, is any more reliable than the later. It may simply represent a link in a chain of developing tradition, the earlier links of which have been lost, and the very earliest of which may have been based on conjecture or theological need rather than on historical reportage. Elliott himself shows very clearly that "as the gospel tradition developed, the story of the anointing was adapted and altered to suit the theological needs of the individual evangelists".[11] Their predecessors may well have treated their material in the same way.

e. Gethsemane and the Arrest

After Judas's plans to betray him and the last supper (both of which I have discussed elsewhere: DJE, pp. 132–140; HEJ, pp. 26–29) Mark next records Jesus's agony in Gethsemane. He tells all the disciples except Peter, James, and John to "sit here while I pray" and then goes further ahead with these three, telling them, in what must be meant as a particularly intimate disclosure from which the others are excluded, that "my soul is exceeding sorrowful even unto death" (Mark 14:34). He then bids the three stay behind while he goes a little further forward and prays that, if possible, "the hour might pass away" and "the cup" be removed from him. (We have met 'the cup', as a designation of the suffering leading to his death, at Mark 10:39. The use of 'the hour' in this same sense is more characteristic of the fourth gospel than of Mark). After these few words he returns to the three and finds them asleep. That they should all have fallen asleep at all (let alone in such a short time) in the given circumstances makes no sense as realism. (Nor, if they did, could they — or anyone else — have learned of the words of his prayer; for at the end of this incident "they all left him and fled" at his arrest (14:50) and never rejoined him). It is strange that he admonishes only Peter (although he had found all three asleep) and then tells them all to "watch and pray, that ye enter not into temptation; the spirit indeed is willing, but the flesh is weak". What kind of temptation can here be meant is unclear. He then leaves them in order to "pray the same words" as before, and on returning finds them all asleep again: and "they wist not what to answer him" (although he has, on this occasion, said nothing to them. Matthew smooths the narrative by omitting these words). He then leaves them and returns a third time saying, first "sleep on", but then "arise".

The point Mark seems to be trying to make with this muddled narrative is: what a tremendous thing Jesus has done for us; for the burden which God is placing upon him in the form of his imminent suffering is so heavy as to make even him waver — in spite of his own previous detailed predictions that he must suffer and die, and in spite of his superior moral fibre, brought out by contrast with his intimates, who were incapable even of "watching one hour".

This obviously legendary material is manipulated very differently in later Christian tradition. Luke simplifies it by not dividing the disciples into two groups (Jesus goes forward "about a stone's cast" from them all) and by telescoping it into one prayer and one admonition (addressed not just to Peter but to them all). The result is even greater implausibility, as the whole body of disciples is now represented as having fallen asleep. More importantly, Luke magnifies Jesus's agony, saying (in passages unique to his gospel) that "his sweat became as it were great drops of blood falling down upon the ground". So great was his need that "there appeared unto him an angel from heaven, strengthening him" (Luke 22:43–44).

The fourth gospel takes exactly the opposite course, and all but eliminates the whole incident as incompatible with Jesus's majesty. The setting in Gethsemane is dropped, as are the exchanges with the disciples. All that remains is a mere flicker of weakness when, in a different context, Jesus confesses "my soul is troubled" and asks himself whether to say "Father, save me from this hour". He decides to do no such thing, since "for this cause" — to redeem mankind—"came I unto this hour"; and he says instead: "Father, glorify thy name" (John 12:27–28)—through his obedience to him unto death. Haenchen notes (p. 497) how this evangelist has likewise transferred the saying about 'the cup' to a different context and transmuted it in the same spirit, making Jesus justify his refusal to resist arrest by saying: "The cup which the father has given me, shall I not drink it?" (18:11). In this gospel, the Passion is a 'glorification' of Jesus and of God, not a humiliation, nor an acceptance of almost intolerable suffering.

To conclude the Gethsemane incident, the Marcan Jesus, with his usual foreknowledge, declares: "Behold, he that betrayeth me is at hand". Eta Linnemann has used the next eight verses, narrating his arrest, to illustrate her very important thesis that Mark compiled his whole passion narrative, as he did the rest of his gospel (cf. above, p. 12), from individual isolated units of tradition, and that he was not able to draw on an existing unified account even of the Passion. These verses are as follows:

(43) And straightway, while he yet spake, cometh Judas, one of the twelve, and with him a multitude with swords and staves from the chief priests and the scribes and the elders.

(44) Now he that betrayed him had given them a token, saying, whomsoever I shall kiss, that is he: take him and lead him away safely.

(45) And when he was come, straightway he came to him, and saith, Rabbi; and kissed him.

(46) And they laid hands on him and took him.

(47) But a certain one of them that stood by drew his sword, and smote the servant of the high priest, and struck off his ear.

(48) And Jesus answered and said unto them, Are ye come out, as against a robber, with swords and staves to seize me?

(49) I was daily with you in the temple teaching, and ye took me not: but this is done that the scriptures might be fulfilled.

(50) And they all left him, and fled.

One would have expected the act of violent resistance (verse 47) to come from one of the disciples, not merely from a bystander. (Luke, by omitting the words 'that stood by', implies as much). Strangely, it is not suggested that the armed multitude took any counteraction.

Even stranger is that Jesus himself makes no comment on the violent action done on his behalf, but merely tells his attackers that they need no weapons to effect his arrest (verse 48). But by this time — contrary to the implication of this verse — he has already been arrested, and this verse 48 would make better sense if it followed immediately after verse 43. Such unevennesses are intelligible, says Linnemann, if these eight verses represent Mark's combination of three originally independent traditions concerning Jesus's arrest: (i) that he was arrested like a criminal, thus fulfilling the Scriptures (verses 43, 48–49); (ii) that he was betrayed by a close disciple (verses 44–46. Mark has brought verse 43 into line with this by introducing there a reference to Judas. The earlier tradition underlying verse 43 will simply have specified an armed multitude, sent by the priests); (iii) that some attempt was made to prevent his arrest (verses 47, 50).[12]

Luke specifies that it was the right ear of the high priest's servant that was cut off, and that Jesus then miraculously healed it. John names both the swordsman (as Peter) and the victim (as Malchus). "The latest legend specifies the most details" (Haenchen, p. 502n.).

Matthew's additions to Mark are different from Luke's and betray anxiety to convince his readers that it was not helplessness that led to Jesus's arrest — "more than twelve legions of angels" were at his disposal (words of Jesus, unique to Matthew, at 26:53) — but necessity that "the scriptures be fulfilled". Matthew also remedies the Marcan Jesus's failure to comment on the swordsman's action against the servant of the high priest, and makes Jesus respond to this by saying: "Put up again thy sword into its place; for all they that take the sword shall perish with the sword". The evangelist thereby tells his community that no Christian is entitled violently to resist arrest.

The hostile party is led by Judas in all four gospels. In the fourth he "took" (Greek of John 18:3) not a Jewish "multitude", as in the other three, but a Roman cohort (i.e. 600 or, at any rate 200 men) — as if Pilate, who in any case as yet knows nothing of charges against Jesus, would have entrusted it to a Jewish civilian. Judas has no need to identify Jesus with a kiss, as in the other gospels, for Jesus himself declares that he is the man they are seeking with the words "I am he". These could be simply words of identification, but in the Bible they can also be the language and title of God himself (cf. Exodus 3:14: "And God said unto Moses, I am that I am"); and it can only be for this reason that the whole cohort then falls to the ground (John 18:6). The evangelist's message, then, is: if the enemy is mightily strong,

Jesus is yet stronger. To allow an arrest to occur at all in the face of such majesty, Jesus has to be made to repeat his declaration, but with plainer words of identification, saying: "I told you that I am he" (verse 8). As we saw, in John Jesus's death is his glorification, not his humiliation, and "no narrative typifies this more than the Johannine account of his arrest".[13]

With the cohort on its feet again, the story can proceed. The disciples do not flee, as in Mark, but are allowed to leave unmolested. Peter then cuts off Malchus's ear, but, strangely, he is not penalized for this, but is able to follow when Jesus is led bound to the court of the high priest (18:15).

ii. THE TRIAL

a. Peter's Denial

All four gospels combine an examination of Jesus by Jewish authorities with Peter's denial of Jesus; and in all four Jesus, with his miraculous knowledge, prophesies that Peter will deny him. In Mark, this foretelling is placed in chapter 14, immediately before the scene in Gethsemane:

> (27) And Jesus saith unto them, All ye shall be offended: for it is written, I will smite the shepherd, and the sheep shall be scattered abroad. (28) Howbeit, after I am raised up, I will go before you into Galilee. (29) But Peter said unto him, Although all shall be offended, yet will not I. (30) And Jesus saith unto him, Verily I say unto thee, that thou today, even this night, before the cock crow twice, shalt deny me thrice.

Verse 28 is widely regarded as inserted by Mark into a pericope which originally lacked it, for it is hardly likely that Jesus would have spoken of his being "raised up" in this casual way, as if his audience would find nothing unusual or unexpected about it. Nor, if he did so speak, is it likely that Peter would have ignored the whole matter, as he does in his reply in the following verse. It looks, then, as if Mark inserted verse 28 so as to match what he makes the women at the empty tomb be told at 16:7 ("He goeth before you into Galilee"). Commentators suspect that the second half of verse 27 (from "it is written") is likewise a Marcan insertion; for if both this 27b and 28 are deleted, the 'shall be offended' of 27 is picked up naturally in verse 29, and we are left with "a clear and unified account of Peter's denial".[14] Lindars has observed that 27b (which refers to Zechariah 13:7) can be accounted for from the needs of Mark's narrative plot: Jesus will be made to say at his arrest: "This is done that the scriptures might be fulfilled" (14:49), and the following verse reads "they all left him and fled". The evangelist therefore needs a passage from Scripture which will foretell the defection of the disciples when their leader is smitten; hence his earlier allusion to Zechariah 13:7. Of course, this identification of Jesus with Zechariah's shepherd and of the fleeing disciples with the scattered sheep is possible "only when the verse has been torn from its context".[15] In the early Church the verse seems to have circulated independently of the context Mark has given it, for it has influenced John 16:32.

We are left, then, with verses 27a and 29–30. Only Mark has "before the cock crow twice": the other three evangelists refer to a single cock-crow. Now there is some evidence that the keeping of cocks was forbidden in Jerusalem at the time in question (Nineham, p. 388). Possibly Mark is here assimilating some tradition about Jesus in which 'cock-crow' was used simply to mean early morning (as at Mark 13:35: "Watch therefore, for ye know not when the lord of the house cometh, whether at even, or at midnight, or at cockcrowing, or in the morning"). The evangelist may have taken the expression literally and on that basis have provided, in the sequel, an incident where Peter denies his master to the sound of crowing cocks. Haenchen says (p. 489) that the pre-Marcan tradition will have made Jesus say merely: 'You will soon leave me in the lurch', and that from this the subsequent scene of Peter's denial and the crowing was developed.

Luke has brought the prophecy of Peter's denial forward in time to form part of the farewell discourse at the last supper. As we saw (p. 27), he omits Mark's statement that the risen Jesus will go before the disciples into Galilee; and he also omits the statement that they will be "scattered" when their master is "smitten". Correspondingly, he does not make them flee at Jesus's arrest, as Mark does (Mark 14:50 has no equivalent in Luke). Acts 1:21–22 shows that Luke wants them as guarantors of the true faith, and it is surely for this reason that he omits this incident which would tend to discredit them.

Luke has also introduced the foretelling of Peter's denial with quite different words of Jesus, unrepresented elsewhere (22:31-34):

> (31) Simon, Simon, behold, Satan asked to have you [plural in the Greek], that he might sift you [plural] as wheat: (32) but I made supplication for thee [singular], that thy faith fail not: and do thou, when once thou hast turned again, stablish thy brethren. (33) And he said unto him, Lord, with thee I am ready to go both to prison and to death. (34) And he said, I tell thee, Peter, the cock shall not crow this day, until thou shalt thrice deny that thou knowest me.

If the two final verses here are roughly parallel to what is in Mark, the first two are peculiar to Luke. That they derive from a non-Marcan source is suggested by the use of 'Simon' in 31, as against 'Peter' in 34, which is the form which the name is given in Mark. (If 31-32 had been Luke's own composition, he would surely have harmonized and made Jesus say 'Peter'). There is, then, a case for considering 31 and 32 by themselves, without allowing their meaning to be affected by the prophecy of the denial in 33-34. The only link they appear to have with this denial is the words "when once thou has turned again" (32). These render a single word (*epistrepsas*) in the Greek, and without it 31-32 mean: all the disciples are to be tempted to renounce their Lord; Peter alone will hold firm — we are surely to understand that Jesus's "supplication", made on his behalf alone, was successful — and he will then "stablish", that is, strengthen the others and so win them back. This meaning would be the exact opposite of the defection of Peter foretold in 34, and Bultmann regards *epistrepsas* as Luke's insertion into the tradition represented at 31-32 — an insertion made to harmonize it with 33-34.[16] Some other commentators understand *epistrepsas* (a participle in the active voice) transitively and as going with the imperative verb 'stablish', giving the meaning: 'converting them (thy brethren, from their lapse), strengthen them'.[17] The overall meaning of 31-32 will then still be that the others lapsed but Peter did not; and we shall still have, at the pre-gospel stage, two contradictory traditions about Peter's behaviour.

It seems plausible, following Eta Linnemann (pp. 5-7) to regard these two verses as originally an utterance of one of the early Christian 'prophets' who were supposedly inspired by the spirit of the risen Jesus and who spoke in his name. Just as Old Testament prophets introduced their directives with 'thus saith the Lord', so early Christian ones "set in the Church", says Paul, by God (1 Corinthians 12:28), promulgated, as words of Jesus, what they thought the risen one was saying to them (details in DJE, pp. 28, 30, 69n. 34; HEJ, p. 30. And cf. above, p. 44). In Linnemann's view, Luke 22:31–32 represents what was originally such an utterance, occasioned by the prospect that the Christian community to which it was addressed would suffer persecution for its faith and so be in danger of renouncing it. That Jesus here prays only for Peter is intelligible only if he was the leader of such a community; and we know from Paul's letters that Peter (Cephas) was in fact an influential figure before AD 70.

Coming now to the actual denial, we find that, in Mark, Peter follows Jesus, after his nocturnal arrest, to the courtyard of the high priest and sits with servants by the fire there. The scene then switches, presumably to inside the house, where Jesus is maltreated by his Jewish accusers. We then return to Peter in the courtyard. When one of the maids of the high priest challenges him, accusing him of being of Jesus's company, he declares that he does not know what she is talking about. Some manuscripts add here "and the cock crowed". This first cock-crow is necessary to Mark's story, but may have been omitted in many good manuscripts because copyists asked themselves why Peter, who must have recalled Jesus's prophecy, did not at once repent when he heard the cock. After a further challenge, he twice again denies all knowledge of Jesus, the second time with curses; and the cock again crows. He then remembers Jesus's prophecy and weeps (14:72).

Luke cannot incapsulate Jesus's trial with Peter's denial on the night of his arrest, as Mark does, for he places the trial on the following morning, and so represents the denial as completed before the trial begins. An added and obviously legendary feature is that when Peter, outside in the yard, speaks his denial, Jesus, although inside the house, turns and looks him in the face (Luke 22:61), to his shame. That the denial is a separate tradition, not an integral part of the passion narrative, is particularly clear in this gospel, where it fits awkwardly between the arrest and the maltreating of Jesus. 22:54 records the arrest: "and they seized him, and led him away, and brought him into the high priest's house". The natural continuation comes only at verse 63: "And the men that held him mocked him and beat him". This 'him' is clearly meant to refer to Jesus, but does so only if the denial incident is deleted; for that has just terminated (verse

62) with: And he [Peter] went out and wept bitterly". Thus, as the text now stands, 'him' of 63 refers *grammatically* to 'he' of 62, but its *sense* links it with 'him' of 54.[18]

The author of the fourth gospel has complicated the story by making "another disciple" as well as Peter follow Jesus to the high priest's house and thus deprive him of being the only one with the courage to do so. My box outline round this new material shows that, if it is excised, we are left approximately with the story as given in the other three gospels:

(18:15) And Simon Peter followed Jesus and so did another disciple. Now that disciple was known unto the high priest, and entered in with Jesus into the court of the high priest; (16) but Peter was standing at the door without. So the other disciple, which was known unto the high priest, went out and spake unto her that kept the door, and brought in Peter. (17) The maid therefore that kept the door saith unto Peter, Art thou also one of this man's disciples? He saith, I am not.

In the material in the box outline, the recommendation of the 'other disciple' to the maid puts Peter in the clear (verse 16). But when we leave this new, inserted matter, she challenges him to clear himself, as in the older tradition.

In the other gospels there is admittedly no guard on the door: Peter enters the courtyard unhindered and a maid of the high priest comes and questions him there. In the new material of the fourth gospel, the other disciple is allowed to pass through the door because he was "known to the high priest". He then returns to it, and it is his good offices alone which get Peter through it. Having thus been shown as the more influential of the two, he disappears from the narrative. This is not the only passage in this gospel which is designed to subordinate Peter to another disciple. The preferred disciple is sometimes called the one "whom Jesus loved" (13:23), but not here, probably because the evangelist felt that a connection with the high priest would be a questionable recommendation for a close disciple of Jesus, however convenient for the exigencies of the narrative at this point.

Concerning the historicity of Peter's denial, apologists claim that no Christian community would have invented a story which humbled him so deeply unless something of the sort had actually taken place. But critical scholars have suggested possible motives for the story as legend: by stressing Jesus's isolation in his Passion, it seems to show the magnitude of the burden he shouldered for our salvation. Again, Mark's studied juxtaposition of Peter's weakness with Jesus's fortitude may have served the needs of a Christian community fearing or suffering persecution by pointing the moral: stand firm under duress, as did Jesus; do not deny your faith, as did Peter. Against the historicity of the incident is that Paul, anxious in Galatians to discredit the Peter with whom he contended, seems to have no knowledge of it, for he does not mention it. (He does not even suggest that there had been a historical Jesus in his own lifetime with whom Peter had had contact.) Certainly ignorant of it is the author of the epistle to the Hebrews; for he takes the stern view that there can be no second repentance, that apostates can never be forgiven (6:4–6). A Christian community which was anxious to deal more charitably with apostates, and to usher them back into the fold, may have helped to preserve the story once it had become current: if even Peter had given way under interrogation, they might be excused for having done the same.

b. The Jewish Trial

In Mark, Jesus is led to the high priest's house, where his trial proceeds as follows (Mark 14:55–64):

(55) Now the chief priests and the whole council sought witness against Jesus to put him to death; and found it not.

(56) For many bare false witness against him, and their witness agreed not together.

(57) And there stood up certain, and bare false witness against him, saying,

(58) We heard him say, I will destroy this temple that is made with hands, and in three days I will build another, made without hands.

(59) And not even so did their witness agree together.

(60) And the high priest stood up in the midst, and asked Jesus, saying, Answerest thou nothing? What is it which these witness against thee?

(61) But he held his peace and answered nothing. Again the high priest asked him and saith unto him, Art thou the Christ, the Son of the Blessed?

(62) And Jesus said, I am: and ye shall see the Son of man sitting at the right hand of power, and coming with the clouds of heaven.

(63) And the high priest rent his clothes, and saith, What further need have we of witnesses?

(64) Ye have heard the blasphemy: what think ye? And they all condemned him to be worthy of death.

(65) And some began to spit upon him, and to cover his face, and to buffet him, and to say unto him, Prophesy: and the officers received him with blows of their hands.

Linnemann has pointed to the following unevennesses which betray that this passage too is a combination of originally independent traditions: after verse 56 has summarised what happened, we do not really expect the details of 57–58, and 58 gives no evidence of the lack of agreement in the testimony that is then specified in 59; as both 56 and 59 maintain that only conflicting testimony, which was therefore worthless, was produced, Jesus has no case to answer, and so the high priest's question (60) why he does not answer the charges is unmotivated (pp. 109–110).

Reflection on the Old Testament underlies much in these verses. Almost every word in verse 65, says Nineham (p. 408) is taken from the Greek version of one or other of five Old Testament passages, and the main point is clearly to exhibit the fulfilment of 'prophecy'. Verse 62 is a saying constructed from Christian reflection on Daniel 7:13 ("I saw in the night visions, and behold there came with the clouds of heaven one like unto a son of man") and Psalm 110:1 ("The Lord saith unto my lord, Sit thou at my right hand"). Jesus' silence (verse 61) reflects Isaiah 53:7: "He was oppressed, yet he humbled himself and opened not his mouth; as a lamb that is led to the slaughter, and as a sheep that before her shearers is dumb; yea he opened not his mouth" (cf also Psalm 38:13–16). Yet in 62 Jesus breaks his silence, and this again suggests a combination here of originally independent traditions, only one of which represented him, on the basis of Isaiah 53, as completely silent. Linnemann reconstructs it as having consisted of verses 57–58, 60, and the first sentence of 61. If, as the Old Testament required, Jesus is here to be silent before his accusers, their accusations are best represented as false – particularly as the accusation of false witnesses is itself a biblical motif (Psalm 27:12 and 109:2–3). The charge they produce (verse 58) is really quite absurd.

Later evangelists were not altogether happy about any state-ment — even from false witnesses — that Jesus had promised to de-stroy the temple (verse 58); for Matthew tones down what they say to: "This man said, I am able to" — not, as in Mark 'I will' — "destroy the temple of God and to build it in three days" (26:61); and Luke saves all mention of the saying for Acts 6;14, and makes it very oblique: false witnesses say that Stephen said that Jesus said something of the sort ("this Jesus of Nazareth shall destroy this place"). John deletes all suggestion that the saying was falsely ascribed to Jesus, but also deprives it of all violence by interpreting it as referring to the Resur-rection: "Destroy this temple and in three days I will raise it up . . . But he spake of the temple of his body" (2:19-21).

If, then, we identify Mark 14:57-58, 60 and 61 (first sentence) as based on the tradition that Jesus was silent before his accusers, this leaves verses 55-56 and 61 (second sentence — the high priest's ques-tion) as the substance of a different tradition, namely that Jesus was condemned for claiming to be the Messiah. The form this takes in Mark is not historically plausible. He requires us to accept that the malice of the priests was accompanied by a hardly credible failure to brief their witnesses properly (verse 56). And the high priest would not have called the Messiah "the son of the Blessed" (verse 61), as this formulation is Christian, not Jewish (Haenchen, p. 511). Nineham thinks that the variant in Matthew ("the son of God") is likewise Christian, and that "the most likely explanation of all this is that, at any rate as now formulated, the high priest's question is due to the early Church" (p. 407). Moreover, according to Mark 11:15-19 Jesus had already violently 'cleansed' the temple and in consequence made the chief priests and scribes determined to kill him. His misbehaviour in the temple would surely have made a more effective indictment than the conflicting charges of false witnesses; yet it is not mentioned at his trial, probably because, by the time Mark wrote, Christians, convinced that the Jews had condemned Jesus for claiming to be the Messiah, could not imagine a condemnation on other grounds.

It has repeatedly been shown that the trial scene of Mark 14 does not stand up to criticism. In addition to features already mentioned as questionable, it "contravenes all the rules of Jewish legal pro-cedure, apart from the intrinsic improbability of such a session dur-ing the middle of the night."[19] Admittedly, rules can be broken; but it is hardly credible that the Jewish authorities should have found Jesus sufficiently important to warrant their alleged procedure, nor, if they did think the case important, that they needed to deal with it in such an irregular manner. The trial scene must in any case owe something to Christian guesswork, as no Christian witnesses are said to be present. As the early communities were primarily concerned with the Resurrection, this guesswork about the trial will not have begun until well after the event — if indeed there was an event.

After Mark's quite detailed account of the Sanhedrin trial during the night, culminating in the condemnation of the prisoner, he goes on to record another meeting of the Sanhedrin the following morning which makes no reference to the previous night's proceedings, nor to any charges or sentence, but simply has Jesus put in bonds and handed over to Pilate (15:1). Many commentators suppose that this verse represents all that the earliest tradition could say about his Jewish trial, and that the detailed account of the previous chapter is a later imaginative expansion of it which Mark took for the record of an independent series of events.

Luke differs from Mark by making Jesus be mocked and beaten before his trial begins, and may have felt that such rough behaviour could more plausibly be attributed to jailors than to the council. Another improving touch is that in Luke the trial takes place in the council chamber, in the official hall, not in the residence of the high priest. In Mark (and in Matthew) Jesus is taken to this private house and tried there immediately on arrival. The elders and the scribes were already there when he was brought in, and the trial proceeds during the night. In Luke, however, he is merely kept under guard in the house during the night, and at daybreak the Sanhedrin assemble and lead him away "into their council" (22:66). The high priest is not said to be present at the ensuing trial, so he is not there to rend his garments and declare the prisoner guilty of blasphemy. Nor do any witnesses appear. Instead the council immediately ask Jesus whether he is "the Christ", and "the son of God". When he replies "Ye say that I am", they declare they have no "further need" of witnesses (even though there have been none in this account), and, without first passing any sentence, bring him before Pilate.

If the Jewish trial is attenuated in Luke, it is practically eliminated in John. There, the high priest does not even ask whether Jesus is the Messiah, but merely questions him about "his disciples and his teaching" (John 18:19). As we saw, Mark makes Jesus say (14:62) that his second coming, when he will effect the final judgement, is shortly to be expected. If such apocalyptic ideas were an integral part of traditions about the Jewish trial, it is understandable that the fourth evangelist eliminates it, hostile as he is to apocalypticism. Already in Luke the suggestion of imminence is removed. The reader is no longer told that he will "see" Jesus at his second coming, but simply that "from henceforth shall the Son of man be seated at the right hand of the power of God".

In the fourth gospel Jesus, in reply to the high priest's question about his disciples and his teaching, gives no information about his disciples and, as to his teaching, declares that they rather than he had better be questioned on the matter. One of "the officers standing by" regards this as impudence and strikes him (verse 22). All this is represented as having occurred before the high priest, named as Caiaphas as early as verse 13. But Jesus, at this stage, is said not to be with him, but with his father-in-law, Annas, who sends him on to "Caiaphas the high priest" only at verse 24. Bultmann supposed, probably correctly, that in one of John's sources Annas was, wrongly, represented as high priest and that the evangelist has tried to combine two incompatible versions of the incident.

When Jesus is sent on to Caiaphas at verse 24, no charges have as yet been made and no sentence passed. Instead of then telling us how Caiaphas dealt with him, the evangelist relates the final part of the story of Peter's denials and follows it immediately with Jesus being led to Pilate's palace (verse 28). This makes it likely that the reader will not realize that he has been told nothing at all about the confrontation between Jesus and Caiaphas. John clearly wishes to eliminate the Sanhedrin trial and place all emphasis on the trial before Pilate.

c. Jesus Before Pilate

Mark 15 opens with a brief mention of Jesus's Jewish trial (cf. above, p. 135) and continues with his appearance before Pilate:

(1) And straightway in the morning the chief priests, with the elders and scribes, and the whole council, held a consultation, and bound Jesus, and carried him away, and delivered him up to Pilate.

(2) And Pilate asked him, Art thou the King of the Jews? And he answering saith unto him, Thou sayest.

(3) And the chief priests accused him of many things.

(4) And Pilate again asked him, saying, Answerest thou nothing? Behold how many things they accuse thee of.

(5) But Jesus no more answered anything; insomuch that Pilate marvelled.

The first of these verses reminds us that Mark's gospel is not meant as a historian's account; for although Pilate is here mentioned for the first time in this gospel, "no attempt is made to explain who he was or how he came to be in Jerusalem" (Nineham, p. 415). As Mark was writing for Christians already familiar with the story, he did not find it necessary to explain who the major actors were, as a historian would. Matthew seems to have felt this as a defect, for in the parallel passage in his gospel he states that Pilate was "the governor" (27:2); and Luke indicates as early as the beginning of his third chapter who was what at the time: Tiberius was emperor, Pilate governor of Judaea, etc.

The second of the Marcan verses quoted above interrupts the natural sequence and seems to derive from a tradition (originally separate from that represented in the other verses) that Jesus was condemned for claiming to be the Messiah.[20] Without it we have a perfect example of Jesus's silence in the face of (unspecified) charges, and this — like the similar element in his Jewish trial will have been constructed on the basis of Isaiah 53:7 (quoted above, p. 133). "The tradition clearly contained no information about the precise content of the 'many charges' " of verse 3 (Nineham, p. 416).

The inserted verse 2 makes Pilate begin his interrogation before he has been informed what the indictment is. Only Luke remedies this, by supplying an entirely novel indictment, making the whole Sanhedrin tell him that Jesus was guilty of anti-Roman sedition, in that he stirred up the people and encouraged them to refuse tribute to Caesar, giving himself out to be "Christ a king" (Luke 23:2).

Commentators who wish to stamp Jesus as a political activist take this as historically accurate and suppose that Luke is here less circumspect than Mark and has betrayed the real reason for Jesus's condemnation (cf. DJE, chapter 7, entitled 'Was Jesus a Political Rebel?'). As political activism is today à la mode, it is widely felt that a revolutionary Jesus is more 'relevant' than the Jesus of the nineteenth-century liberal theologians who "went about doing good" (Acts, 10:38). Both these Jesuses simply reflect what in each case the commentators value most highly rather than the burden of the texts. If Jesus had been politically troublesome, his supporters would have been arrested with him. But there is no suggestion of this in any of the gospels.

Luke 23:2 is better understood in the light of what obtained in the late first century, rather than the twentieth, as Luke's answer to Jewish hostility towards Christians. Jews will have tried to discredit them by representing Christian communities to the Romans as revolutionary sects honouring Christ, not Caesar, as their king. Luke counters by making a Roman governor deny a Jewish charge that Jesus was politically guilty; for in the next verse (Luke 23:3) Pilate asks the question as formulated in Mark's verse 2 ("Art thou the King of Jews?") and receives the answer also given there ("Thou sayest"). To this Luke – and only he, not Mark or Matthew – makes Pilate reply: "I find no fault in this man" (23:4). In the Jewish trial, as given in Luke and in Matthew, the formula "thou sayest" is understood as an affirmtion; but even if it is mere equivocation, a Roman governor would not take it as evidence of the innocence of a prisoner charged with sedition, as Luke would have us believe.

In sum, Pilate's declaration is not only absent from the parallel passage in Mark (and in Matthew), but its context (a governor's response to suspected sedition – a charge also absent from these other gospels) makes it quite incredible. What, then, was Luke's purpose in attributing such an implausible reaction to Pilate? Surely to suggest that he understood straightway that Jesus was the Christian Messiah and as such politically harmless. This is in accordance with Luke's overall tendency to persuade his Christian readers that Rome need not be regarded as necessarily hostile to them (cf. above, pp. 114f).

At this point Luke inserts a story that Herod the ruler of Galilee (i.e. Herod Antipas, who ruled there until AD 39) happened to be in Jerusalem and that Pilate therefore passed Jesus, as a Galilean, to him for questioning. This story rests on no early tradition, otherwise it would have appeared in Mark. But although absent from all the canonical gospels other than Luke's, it is surely no invention of his, for a variant of it appears in the apocryphal gospel of Peter. How such a tradition originated is betrayed by Luke at Acts 4:25–28, where Psalm 2:2 ("the rulers take counsel together against the Lord and against his anointed") is quoted as a Messianic prophecy, fulfilled when Herod and Pilate confronted Jesus. Once it had come to be believed that Jesus was a Galilean and had been crucified under Pilate, it would be natural to suppose that he had been arraigned by the civil ruler of Galilee as well, in fulfilment of this Scripture. If, then, the tradition is pre-Lucan, Luke found it very serviceable as additional evidence that the real guilt for Jesus's death lies with the

Jews, not Romans; for Pilate is made to "call together the chief priests and the rulers and the people" — that he should summon 'the people' is extremely odd, and does not read like historical truth — and tell them that both he and Herod have "found no fault in this man" (Luke 23:14-15), so that the execution follows solely at the behest of the Jews.

After the narrative about Herod Antipas, Luke returns to the Marcan sequence, where the next incident concerns the release of Barabbas, at the insistence of the Jews, instead of Jesus. Mark tells that, at the festival, the governor was wont to release one prisoner at the people's request — scholars have found no trace of any such custom — and on this occasion offered to free "the King of the Jews" (15:9). If, then, we believe Mark, Pilate who, as we know from historians of this period, was constantly faced with the threat of sedition, has asked Jesus whether he is king of the Jews, has received an equivocal answer ("Thou sayest"), but nevertheless does his best to acquit this person whom he himself is made here, against all plausibility, to call "the King of the Jews". (A few verses later Mark is more circumspect and makes Pilate speak of "him whom ye call the King of the Jews", 15:12). But the crowd, incited by the chief priests, insists that he crucify Jesus and set free "one called Barabbas, lying bound with them that had made insurrection, men who in the insurrection had committed murder" (15:7). And the compliant Pilate, "wishing to content the multitude", released this man tainted with rebellion. This is intelligible not as history, but as the evangelist's indictment of the Jews (cf. DJE, p. 166), as is particularly clear in Luke's version of the incident (*Ibid.*, p. 168).

Pilate then "delivered Jesus, when he had scourged him, to be crucified" (Mark 15:15); whereupon Roman soldiers dressed him with purple, placed a crown of thorns on him, smote his head with a reed, "and did spit upon him, and bowing their knees worshipped him" (15:17-19). There are four other accounts of similar maltreatment and mockery of Jesus after his arrest and prior to his crucifixion. John (19:2-3) places such an incident before Pilate's final sentence, not after it, as here in Mark. Mark additionally has had Jesus spat upon and buffeted by some of the Sanhedrin at the end of his nocturnal Jewish trial (Mark 14:65). Luke (22:63-65) has it that this was perpetrated by the jailors before he was brought before the council (cf. above, p. 135). Luke also mentions a further mockery at the hands of Herod Antipas and his entourage (23:11) instead of Mark's account of a further mockery by Pilate's soldiers, which would have ill accorded with his desire to show that Rome is not basically hostile to Christianity. Luke's Pilate merely *offers* to satisfy the Jews by having Jesus scourged, but then released (23:16), and is even made to repeat this offer (verse 22), signifying how eager the evangelist is to represent the governor as doing his best to avoid a sentence of death. (The Lucan soldiers who mock Jesus during his actual crucifixion are arguably Jewish, not Roman.)

As Winter notes, "it is inherently unlikely that the same scene was enacted five times, with only slight differences, by the police, by members of the High Court, by Herod and his soldiers, and finally by the Roman legionaries before, as well as after the procurator had passed sentence." The oldest tradition will have recorded but one instance of such mockery, but, in the course of transmission, "the description of this incident was shifted to various places and thereby became attached to different situations".[21] As we saw, the same happened with traditions about the Jewish trial.

Matthew does but add to Mark's account of Pilate's dealings with Jesus what Evans calls "novellistic" features "which the tradition would surely have been better without",[22] namely a digression about the suicide of Judas (Matthew 27:3–10) and Pilate's wife's dream (27:19). More sinister is the added saying of "all the people", when Pilate is trying to resist their demand that Jesus be crucified: "His blood be on us and on our children" (27:25). This, says Evans (p. 187 n. 1), has "perhaps been responsible for more anti-Semitism in connection with the crucifixion than any other single statement"; and it has been particularly efficacious, as, since the second century, priority has been given to Matthew's gospel. That is why it is given as the first in our Bibles. Evans also notes that the charge of deicide in respect of the death of Christ against the whole Jewish people (retracted only at the Second Vatican Council) combines

> two fearful naivetes of popular thought and piety rolled into one. The first was that the divinity of Christ was a matter of plain observation, which is ridiculous by the standards of the New Testament itself, where it is consistently represented as veiled and as discerned by faith arising from the resurrection; and the second was that the responsibility of a whole people—if indeed there can ever be such a thing—was transmissible across the generations, which is lunatic by any standards. (p. 4)

It is a Christian theologian who is here telling us that uncritical interpretation of Matthew has been ridiculous and worse, and has had ap-
palling effects on Christian behaviour. Matthew 27:25, like so much
else in the Bible, needs to be understood in the light of the writer's
own situation (in this case at the end of the first century), not taken
as pointing to some timeless truth. What the evangelist here had in
mind was surely that the generation of Jews represented by the
'children' of the speakers in 27:25 bore the horrors of the Jewish War,
AD 66–73, and in this way paid for their fathers' murder of the
Messiah.

The account in the fourth gospel of Jesus before Pilate shows very
considerable divergencies from what is reported in the other three.
The Jews are represented as remaining outside Pilate's palace "that
they might not be defiled, but might eat the passover" (John 18:28).
Pagan houses were believed by some Jews to defile them for seven
days, although, according to Barrett, this was not the prevailing view
at the time represented, so that John's account is here an "anach-
ronism", and the motive he attributes to the Jews "questionable". Barrett thinks that we have here an example of "characteristically Johannine" irony: "Those who plot the murder of the Son of God mind to
the last detail their formal religious punctilio."[23]

In the chronology of the fourth gospel, the Jews will be eating the
Passover on the following day; but according to the other three they
have already eaten it, as there the Last Supper is represented as a
passover meal. This seemingly trivial difference in fact reflects different theological manipulation of tradition. John is anxious to represent Jesus himself as the true paschal sacrifice, and so he makes his
final supper with his disciples an informal meal (with no 'take, eat'
formula) "before the feast of the passover" (13:1–4); and he makes his
death occur on the day when the animals are slaughtered in prepara-
tion for the paschal meal (19:31). The idea is clearly that the old
sacrifice of a lamb has been superseded.

If in fact the Jews had refused to enter Pilate's palace, he would
have left them waiting, not gone out to them "like a stolid citizen
when someone knocks at the door".[24] Even less credible is the way he
is then represented as running to and fro like a receptionist between
the Jews outside and Jesus inside. First he goes out to them and asks
to know what charge they bring (18:29). He then returns inside (verse
33) and questions Jesus, after which he again goes out to them (verse

38), declares Jesus innocent and offers to release him; but they insist on having the "robber" Barabbas released instead. He then returns inside, has Jesus scourged and then takes him out to the Jews (19:4), again declaring him innocent and obviously hoping that they will agree that his scourging has been punishment enough. They, however, cry "crucify him". He then returns inside to question the prisoner further (19:9). At verse 12 he is again addressing the Jews outside, but by 13 he has returned inside and brings Jesus out again.

The purpose of this implausible scenario is, as Dodd noted, to provide two stages on which the drama is enacted, "a front stage and a back".[25] On the one, Pilate pleads the prisoner's cause in the face of the Jewish accusers; on the other he is alone with Jesus. (One is not supposed to ask who then recorded their conversation for posterity.) Jesus is silent when brought out to his accusers, as required by Isaiah 53:7, but gives quite full answers when he is alone with the basically sympathetic Pilate.

In the fourth gospel, what is said of the Jews is said also of "the world", meaning mankind. The world does not acknowledge Jesus (1:10), hates him (7:7 and 15:18) and cannot receive the spirit (14:17); and the Jews are "of this world" (8:22–23). They are so theologically blind that they have plotted to kill Lazarus after Jesus raised him from the dead (12:10). When Pilate faces them, we see him up against the unbelieving world which pays no heed to the voice of divine truth. When he faces Jesus, the evangelist can inform him, and us, that Christianity is no political movement, but something far more exalted: "My kingdom is not of this world" (18:36).[26]

At the beginning of this section of the narrative, then, Pilate comes out to the Jews (18:29). As in Mark, he is introduced without explanation (not having been mentioned before); the Christian audience the evangelist had in mind will have known that he was the Roman governor under whom Jesus was crucified. The Jews bring no charge, but are determined to secure a condemnation, saying: "If this man were not an evil-doer, we should not have delivered him up unto thee" (verse 30). The verb 'deliver up' is ominous. Paul had said that Jesus was "delivered up for our trespasses and was raised for our justification" (Romans 4:25), echoing the Septuagint of Isaiah 53, where the suffering servant of Yahweh is repeatedly said to have been "delivered up" for our sins.

Pilate tries to hand the case back to the Jews ("Take him yourselves, and judge him according to your law"), but they reply that they have no jurisdiction in capital cases. Commentators are divided on whether this is historically correct. Mark and Matthew mention no such restriction of the Sanhedrin's authority. John mentions it as occasioning fulfilment of what Jesus had said concerning "by what manner of death he should die" (19:32). The reference is to such sayings as "the Son of man must be lifted up" (3:14) and "I, if I be lifted up from the earth, will draw all men unto myself" (12:32: the next verse expressly links this with his manner of death). Roman crucifixion involved hoisting up the victim vertically, which as Evans says, "could be a symbol of . . . exaltation to God", whereas "to be knocked down flat by the Jewish method of stoning could not symbolise anything, at least anything to do with Jesus" (p. 58). Hence he must die at the hands of the Romans.

Pilate then goes inside and, although he has been informed of no charge, asks straightway: "Art thou the king of the Jews?" (John 18:33). The evangelist's Christian community were convinced that Jesus had been rejected as Messianic king by the Jews, and so will have felt sure that his kingship was the main topic in his exchanges with Pilate. Hence the governor is made to broach this decisive point at once. Jesus then asks whether Pilate has derived this idea — that he is king — from the Jews, and receives what is in effect an affirmative reply: "Thine own nation and the chief priests delivered thee unto me: What hast thou done?". The 'delivered up' again emphasizes that Jewish theological blindness, not Roman hostility, is responsible for the saviour's plight.

Jesus responds with a short course in Johannine theology:

> To this end have I been born, and to this end am I come into the world, that I should bear witness unto the truth. Every one that is of the truth heareth my voice (18:37).

The final sentence here emphasises that only those who are "of the truth" are open to his message. He himself is "the way, the truth and the life" (14:6), but not everybody can perceive this: "No man can come to me, except the Father which sent me draw him" (6:44). The Christian faith can therefore be accepted only by an elect, chosen by God for salvation. Haenchen thinks, probably correctly, that such predestinarian ideas were prompted by the experience of the evangelist, and of missionaries generally, that it is impossible to get the Christian message through to the obdurate; that unless an audience has a certain goodwill and predisposition to believe, the best of preachers is quite helpless.[27]

To show that Pilate, although sympathetic, is not of the elect, not "of the truth", the evangelist makes him respond with the uncomprehending question "What is truth?". He has obviously failed to realize that he is being addressed by "the way, the truth and the life"; but he still tries to do his best for the prisoner, and so goes out and tells the Jews: "Ye have a custom that I should release unto you one at the passover" (18:39), and offers to free Jesus on this basis. We note that here in John, as against Mark 15:8, it is Pilate himself who raises the subject of an amnesty. As Winter has observed (p. 60), "the stern Pilate grows more mellow from Gospel to Gospel". But the Jews insist on having Barabbas released. "Now Barabbas was a robber" (verse 40) – a sufficient condemnation of his advocates.

Pilate then "took Jesus and scourged him" (19:1) and the soldiers mocked him by dressing him with a crown of thorns and a purple robe. He is then taken out and shown to the Jews, with Pilate still declaring him innocent. We can now see why John has placed this scourging and mockery before Pilate's pronouncement on Jesus's fate, not after it, as in Mark (cf. above, p. 139). The transposition to an earlier stage reflects "the evangelist's aim to make Pilate appear to have exhausted all means of satisfying the vindictiveness of the Jews". He orders the scourging "in the vain hope of placating thereby their insatiable fury . . . and of saving Jesus from suffering a worse fate" (Winter, p. 101). The way tradition can grow and can be manipulated is exemplified also by comparison of Luke with John here. In Luke Pilate twice offers to scourge Jesus and then release him (Luke 23:16 and 22). In John he actually does have him scourged in the hope of thereby securing his release.

The Jews are then at last made to bring a specific charge: Jesus "ought to die, because he made himself the Son of God" (John 19:7). This frightens Pilate (verse 8), who fears he may be being pressed to kill some kind of deity. And so he goes inside again and asks "Whence art thou?" Jesus is silent. There is no form of words to declare his status that would be intelligible to this person who is not "of the truth". But when Pilate points out that he has the power to have him killed, he replies:

Thou wouldst have no power against me, except it were given thee from above: therefore he that delivered me unto thee hath greater sin (19:11).

We have twice in this narrative been told that it is the Jews who 'delivered' him to Pilate (18:30 and 35). It is they, then, who are the real culprits concerning his death. Pilate has been given power over him "from above" (i.e. what he is doing is permitted by the will of God) and so is simply playing out an (admittedly thankless) role which will lead to man's salvation by Christ's redeeming death. But the Jews are acting without divine sanction and are the really guilty party.[28]

Pilate still wishes to achieve Jesus's release (19:12), but the Jews tell him that this constitutes dereliction of duty, in that a man who claims to be any kind of king is really a rebel against Rome. Whereupon, in the wording of the RV:

> He brought Jesus out, and sat down on the judgement-seat . . . and he saith unto the Jews, Behold your King! (19:13–14).

The Greek *ekathisen*, here rendered 'sat down', can, however, be understood transitively to mean: he seated Jesus on the judgement-seat (cf. Evans, p. 61). The old manuscripts have no punctuation, and if the RV's interpretative comma after 'brought Jesus out' is deleted, we can construe: 'he brought Jesus out and seated (sc. him) on the seat'. This sense is not only permitted but is really required by the following words: "Behold your King!" Jesus is pointed to as the one in the seat of authority.

That Jesus could be represented in this way is clear from other records. In the apocryphal Gospel of Peter (3:7), the Jews "put upon him a purple robe and set him on the judgement seat and said 'Judge righteously, O King of Israel!' " And in the first *Apology* of Justin Martyr (chapter 35) it is said that the Jews "mocked him, as the prophet says, and set him on the judgement seat and said: 'Judge us!' " The 'prophecy' here alluded to is Isaiah 58:2: "They ask of me righteous ordinances"; and it was doubtless reflection on this passage that gave rise to this tradition. Haenchen thinks that John was aware of such a tradition and was concerned to correct it by alleging that, not the Jews (who had no such opportunity) but the Roman governor placed Jesus on the judgement-seat, and that his purpose was to make a final appeal to the Jews to accept him as their Messianic king.[29] But they cried: "Away with him, crucify him" (19:15). Pilate replies: "Shall I crucify your King?" He is still Jesus's advocate against theological blindness. But "the chief priests answered, We have no king but Caesar". The evangelist's point here is (as Evans notes, p. 61) that by proclaiming allegiance solely to the emperor like good pagan inhabitants of the empire, they have ceased to be God's chosen. They no longer believe that "the Most High ruleth in the kingdom of men" (Daniel 4:32). And in repudiating the very idea of a Messianic king they cannot be a Messianic people.

Pilate's resources are now exhausted, and "he delivered him unto them to be crucified" (19:16).

It is almost universally believed that Jesus, in the wording of the creed, 'suffered under Pontius Pilate'. This is regarded as an ir- refragable residual fact after criticism has done its worst with the re- maining traditions. In this section of this chapter we have seen that a good deal of what the gospels have to say on this matter is very un- convincing. It remains to note that Christian documents earlier than the gospels, or at any rate independent of them, do not in any way suggest that Jesus had fallen foul of a Roman governor. Paul, who never mentions Pilate, says that the governing authorities punish on- ly wrongdoers (Romans 13:1–7). Likewise, the author of 1 Peter urges his Christian readers to obey Roman governors, who, he says, have been sent by the emperor to punish those who do wrong and to praise those who do right (1 Peter 2:13–14). It is difficult to believe that a Christian writer who generalizes in this way about the beneficence of governors also believed that the founder of his religion had been ordered to his death by one of their number. It is significant in this connection that later epistles — written when the traditions in the gospels were becoming or had become firmly established among Christians — do not share this enthusiasm for Roman governors. Thus the pastoral epistle 1 Timothy, which, although ascribed to Paul, was by general consent written after AD 90, and which express- ly links Jesus with Pilate, urges its readers to pray that all in high positions behave themselves decently (1 Timothy 2:1–2). It is not said that they punish only wrongdoers. Here we have something like the fear of Roman authority expressed at Mark 13:9: "Before governors and kings shall ye stand for my sake." All this constitutes evidence that Pilate entered Christian thinking on Jesus only relatively late.

iii. THE CRUCIFIXION

a. Simon of Cyrene and the Inscription on the Cross
I shall follow the relevant narratives only as far as Jesus's death, as I

have discussed elsewhere (DJE, pp. 49–51; HEJ, pp. 187–192) the issue of blood and water from his side, the breaking of the legs of his fellow-sufferers (both incidents are recorded only in the fourth gospel), the role of Joseph of Arimathea in his burial, and the lists of women witnesses of the crucifixion and of the burial.

As we saw, in Mark and Matthew, immediately after Jesus has been "delivered" to be crucified, he is given a crown of thorns and mocked as King of the Jews. We saw too that Luke does not mention these incidents, while John places them before Pilate has been persuaded to pass the death sentence.

Mark and Matthew go on to tell how Simon of Cyrene was made to carry the cross (Mark 15:21; Matthew 27:32), and Luke agrees with this, returning here to the Marcan sequence (Luke 23:26). John, however, makes no mention of Simon and says that Jesus carried his cross himself (19:17). John may very well have known a tradition that Jesus had his cross carried for him and deliberately rejected it. Strauss noted that it would have seemed utterly perverse to him to introduce a substitute in the place of "the Lamb of God which taketh away the sin of the world" (John 1:29). We cannot meaningfully be asked to 'take up our cross and follow him' (Mark 8:34) if he did not take up his own cross.

In Mark, Simon is further described as "the father of Alexander and Rufus". Wood and others have instanced this detail, absent from the other gospels, as important evidence that Mark "is offering us early and genuine reminiscence of an actual historical event"; for, Wood adds, "such a reference to two living men could only have been made by a copyist who was writing for persons who knew them. It has no point otherwise." Matthew and Luke, "writing for other circles, not interested in Alexander and Rufus, naturally omit the reference."[30] This allegation that the two men were 'living' persons 'known' to the copyist, is gratuitous. Mark's reference to them may mean only that some tradition about them was known to the Christian community for which he was writing. They might, for instance, have been influential teachers of a previous generation, in which case his attempt to represent them as descended from someone acquainted with the historical Jesus would be a mere tendency-story to increase the credibility of his narrative. Nineham has noted that one of the aims controlling his account is "to show that the Christians had a trustworthy source of information" about the events, and that this aim is visible in the reference to Simon of Cyrene (p. 421).

Mark tells that, on the cross, "the superscription of his accusation was written over, The King of the Jews" (15:26). Winter says (p. 107) that 'accusation' here is a euphemism, the Greek (aitia) meaning 'cause of condemnation' or 'guilt'. The word is avoided by Luke, who has simply "there was a superscription over him" (23:38), a formulation more in accord with proper reverence. In any case, the title really expresses not Jesus's guilt, but the claims of early Christian communities concerning his true status. John evidently realized that it is inappropriate as a statement of his guilt, and so makes Pilate, as his advocate against the Jews, insist on writing it against the protests of the high priests, and in three languages (Hebrew, Latin and Greek) to announce his true dignity to the civilized world (John 19:19–22).

b. Use of the Psalms

A good deal in the gospel passion narrative was inspired by early Christian reflection on the Psalms. A whole group of them can be classified as individual laments, revealing the speaker as suffering in various ways; and early Christians, who believed in a suffering Messiah whose life had been largely foretold in the Jewish Scriptures, would naturally find such Psalms very much to their purpose. Psalm 22 has been particularly well quarried. The speaker asks God: "Why hast thou forsaken me?" and complains that "all they that see me laugh me to scorn." He compares his tormentors to fierce animals (bulls and lions), and then pictures them as a multitude of savage faces which enclose him like a ring of snarling dogs:

> For dogs have compassed me:
> The assembly of evil-doers have inclosed me;
> They pierced my hands and my feet.

The next verse compares them to brigands who strip the traveller of his clothing:

> They look and stare upon me:
> They part my garments among them,
> And upon my vesture do they cast lots.

The parting of the garments and the casting of lots upon them specify not two acts but one, in accordance with the *parallelismus membrorum* characteristic of Hebrew poetry; and this is how this verse of the Psalm is understood in the first three gospels. When Jesus is on the cross, the soldiers "part his garments among them, casting lots upon them, what each should take" (Mark 15:24 and parallels in Matthew and Luke). The fourth evangelist actually quotes the relevant passage from the Psalm, but misunderstood it, taking the 'parting' of the garments for a rending into pieces of some of them, and the 'casting of lots' for a lottery to decide who should appropriate a garment which had not been torn. First, he says, the soldiers, four in number, took Jesus's garments other than his coat, and "made four parts, to every soldier a part". This fulfils the first half of the Scripture. Then they took the coat, which "was without seam, woven from the top throughout. They said therefore one to another, Let us not rend it, but cast lots for it, whose it shall be: that the scripture might be fulfilled . . . " (John 19:23–25). The evangelist's misunderstanding of the Psalm has led to the invention of a supposedly historical incident. We saw that a similar misunderstanding of *parallelismus membrorum* underlies Matthew's version of Jesus's triumphal entry into Jerusalem (above, pp. 113f).

The mockery of Jesus by passers by and chief priests (Mark 15:29–32 and parallel in Matthew; in Luke "the people" merely "stood beholding", and only "the rulers scoffed at him") is another incident that seems to have arisen from Christian reflection on Psalm 22, where we read: "All they that see me laugh me to scorn: They shoot out the lip, they shake the head, saying, Commit thyself unto the Lord; let him deliver him, seeing he delighteth in him" (verses 7–8). Matthew 27:43 makes the crowd reproduce some of this verbatim.

c. The Words from the Cross

All four gospels represent Jesus as crucified between two others. In the first three gospels they are criminals. In the AV of Mark, this is said to fulfil the 'scripture' according to which "he was reckoned with transgressors" (Mark 15:28. The reference is to Isaiah 53:12). In the RV, this verse is relegated to a footnote because absent from the best manuscripts. Luke had regarded this particular 'prophecy' as fulfilled at Jesus's arrest (Luke 22:37).

According to Mark and Matthew, the two criminals join in the denunciation and mockery of Jesus. Luke, however, tells that, while one of the two mocked him, the other recognized him as Messiah, and asked him to "remember me when thou comest in thy kingdom" (23:42). Jesus replies: "Verily I say unto thee, Today shalt thou be with me in Paradise". Commentators attempt only a half-hearted defence of this as history. Creed, for instance, says: "How much is to be set down to Luke's own account it seems impossible to say" (p. 285). Jesus's words imply that he will rise straight from the cross into heaven, and this conflicts with the tradition that he was raised on the third day.

Jesus's words from the cross differ substantially in the different gospels. Mark and Matthew have only one saying: "My God, my God, why hast thou forsaken me?" (Mark 15:34). This is another quotation from Psalm 22, which begins with these words. It is not recorded by Luke or John. Many have supposed, with Wood (p. 123), that the idea of his being abandoned by God could not have been invented by early Christians, and that this episode is therefore authentic history. But Mark's intention in stressing that he died deserted by all—by his disciples from the time of his arrest—and mocked by all (even by his two fellow sufferers) is to show both how heavy was the burden he took upon himself for us, and that he bore it quite alone, with no help from any quarter. "Hence his isolation is no sign of weakness, but testifies to his dedication and to his strength" (Haenchen, p. 533).

Older tradition may have known no more about the circumstances of the crucifixion than what is recorded by Mark three verses after this quotation from Psalm 22, namely: "Jesus uttered a loud voice and gave up the ghost" (Mark 15:37). The saying of verse 34 would then be what Taylor calls a "secondary interpretation" (i.e. an imaginative expansion) of this death cry "in terms of Old Testament prophecy".[31] Mark will have known both traditions and have taken them as referring to separate events. We saw something similar in the case of the bare statement (at Mark 15:1) that Jesus was tried by the Sanhedrin, preceded by a more detailed account of the trial, understood as a different occasion.

Mark also records two taunts to Jesus on the cross (15:29–30 and 31–32, the first from passers by, the second from chief priests), and two references to the act of crucifixion, as follows:

(24) And they crucify him and part his garments among them, casting lots upon them, what each should take.

(25) And it was the third hour, and they crucified him.

(26) And the superscription of his accusation was written over, The King of the Jews.

The way in which "and they crucify him" (24) is repeated as "and they crucified him" in the following verse suggests that the intervening reference to the parting of the garments is an insertion that will have been lacking in an earlier account. It is evidence of this kind that led Taylor to say that Mark's crucifixion narrative, consisting of "short separate scenes strung together in rapid succession", gives "the impression of a comparatively brief foundation story, which has attracted to itself various items of tradition, some historical and others legendary, out of which a kind of crucifixion drama has been compiled to meet the religious needs of a Gentile church" (p. 587).

Mark's gaunt account of Jesus's dying in utter isolation was obviously too much for the other evangelists. Their mitigation of it is very evident in their versions of the words from the cross. Luke records three such sayings (all different from Mark's single one), namely: (1) "Father forgive them, for they know not what they do" (23:34). These words are, however, absent from some important manuscripts; hence, says Creed, "it is improbable that they were original in the Lucan text." (In plain English: they were added later.) (2) The speech to the malefactor, cited above; (3) "And when Jesus had cried with a loud voice, he said, Father, into thy hands I commend my spirit" (23:46) — a quotation from Psalm 31 (an evening prayer), introducing a note of tranquillity lacking in Mark. "Pathos and humanity" is here the dominant note, says Evans, as against "mystery and realism" in Mark. He adds: "It is . . . presumably essential to what Mark thought he was presenting that Jesus should die with a cry of dereliction on his lips, and presumably it was also essential to what Luke thought he was presenting that he did not" (pp. 47, 49).

The fourth gospel goes much further in lightening the gloom, with sayings that are again different. There is no mockery of the dying Jesus (neither by the two fellow sufferers, nor the passers by, nor the priests). On the contrary, the only persons said to be present, other than the soldiers, are sympathizers: "his mother, his mother's sister, Mary the wife of Clopas, Mary Magdalene" and "the disciple whom he loved" (John 19:25–26). In Mark, the disciples all fled when he was arrested (apart from Peter, who followed him as far as the courtyard of the high priest's house, only to deny him there), and they are not again mentioned until the women at the empty tomb are told to inform them of the Resurrection. There were a number of women sympathisers at the crucifixion — the names are not identical with those in

John — but they were all "beholding from afar" (Mark 15:40), not near enough to the cross for Jesus to be able to address them, as he does in John. (Luke, who omits Mark's statement that the disciples fled at Jesus's arrest, has them present at the crucifixion, but again standing only "afar off", with the women: Luke 23:49). In John, however, the dying Jesus gives his mother into the care of the beloved disciple (19:26–27). He then says "I thirst", but only "that the scripture might be fulfilled", and accepts vinegar (cf. Psalm 69:21 "In my thirst they gave me vinegar to drink"). Finally he declares "it is finished": all is accomplished, triumphant words anticipated in his use of the same Greek verb in his prayer to the Father at 17:4: "I glorified thee on earth, having accomplished the work which thou hast given me to do". In this gospel, he goes forward without faltering, even to the end:

> Jesus, knowing that his hour was come that he should depart out of this world unto the Father, having loved his own which were in the world, he loved them unto the end (13:1).

The cry of god-forsakeness, given in Mark's account, can obviously have no place in the majestic triumph into which John makes the crucifixion scene.

d. Matthaean and Lucan Specialities

Mark, Matthew and Luke all allege an unnatural three-hour darkening of the sun at the death of Jesus and declare that the veil of the temple was rent. Neither event is mentioned by any non-Christian writer of the time (On Thallus, cf. above, p. 23.) Matthew (and only he) supplements these miracles with an earthquake, the splitting of rocks, the opening of graves and the resurrection of the "saints" occupying them, who, however, did not emerge from their miraculously opened tombs until after Jesus's Resurrection, when they "entered into the holy city and appeared unto many" (27:51–53). This seems to be a clumsy attempt to harmonize this story of their resurrection at the time of his death with the widespread tradition (preserved in Acts 26:23 and Revelation 1:5) that he himself was the first to rise from the dead. Werner has noted that the miraculous signs specified by Matthew include clear motifs of an apocalyptic picture of the end of the world. The idea, then, was to suggest that the death of Jesus heralded the last days, when the world would come to a catastrophic end, in accordance with the expectations expressed in Jewish apocalypses.[32]

These miracles, new in Matthew, at least enable him to motivate the cry of the centurion at Jesus's death: "Truly, this man was the Son of God." In Mark the centurion says this for no adequate reason — early Christianity is surely here using him as its spokesman — but simply when he saw that Jesus "gave up the ghost" with a loud cry (Mark 15:37,39). Matthew, however, is able to say that the centurion's words were prompted by his witnessing the earthquake and the other miracles (27:54).

Turning now to Luke, we find that, in his gospel, Jesus, on his way to the place of execution, urges the "daughters of Jerusalem" to weep not for him, but for themselves and their children (23:27-31) — a good example of the way Luke represents the destruction of Jerusalem in AD 70 as a punishment for the Jews' treatment of Jesus. The same tendency is visible in an earlier passage, likewise unique to Luke, where Jesus weeps over the city as he approaches it, because by its blindness it is bringing upon itself the misfortune of siege and destruction (19:41-44; cf. HEJ, p. 117).

Luke's omission of the maltreatment of Jesus by Pilate's soldiers after the governor had passed sentence (cf. above, pp. 139f) comports well with clear indications in his gospel that Jews, not Romans, carried out the crucifixion. Pilate does not merely "deliver Jesus to be crucified", as in Mark and Matthew, but "delivers him up to their will" (Luke 23:25), 'they' being "the chief priests and the rulers and the people". As there is no scourging that follows this immediately, the Jews are still meant when Luke continues: "And when they led him away . . . they came unto the place which is called the skull; there they crucified him" (verses 26-33).[33] That some modern scholars do not recognize this as a fact is, says Sanders, "a matter of some amazement". It is, he adds, irrelevant to urge that crucifixion was a Roman form of punishment, for we are not here dealing with the historical question of what really happened, but with what Luke would like his readers to understand. Admittedly, in this crucifixion narrative Luke merely designates the culprits as 'they' and leaves us to look for the antecedent of this pronoun some verses back. He seems to have felt that he could not entirely alter the tradition clearly specified in Mark if he wanted to maintain credibility, and so, as Sanders says, he does "just enough rewriting to emphasize Gentile innocence and to imply Jewish guilt."[34] But in episodes unrepresented elsewhere, he could speak his mind freely: thus on the Emmaus road, in a narrative peculiar to Luke, disciples declare that it was the Jewish "chief priests and rulers" who crucified Jesus (24:20).

Only in Luke is it said that, when the crowd that had assembled for the spectacle of the crucifixion saw what happened ("darkness over the land" and "the sun's light failing") they went home "smiting their breasts" (23:48). Lampe has seen in this another of Luke's allusions to the fate of Jerusalem in AD 70. He says:

> Taken together with Luke's insistence on the responsibility of the Jews for Jesus's death after Pilate's threefold verdict of acquittal, these words imply that already, at the time of the crucifixion, the people of Jerusalem were expecting that divine retribution would be exacted from them. Later tradition makes this explicit. According to a 'Western' manuscript tradition [of Luke], the crowds cry, 'Woe to us for the things that have been done today on account of our sins; for the desolation of Jerusalem has drawn near'. This seems to be derived from the tradition in the Gospel of Peter (25) which enlarges on the guilt and terror of the Jewish leaders. After the begging of the body of Jesus, 'the Jews and the elders and the priests, knowing what great evil they had done themselves, began to lament and to say, "Woe for our sins; the judgement and the end of Jerusalem has drawn near".'[35]

Luke's altering the received tradition of the passion narrative in the direction of greater Jewish culpability represents what Sanders calls "more a theological tendency than any historical tradition" (p. 18) — a tendency arising from Luke's attempt to explain why Christianity, originally a Jewish movement, had by his day become predominantly gentile. In the opening scene of Jesus's ministry (Luke 4:25–29) and in the closing scene of Paul's (Acts 28:25–29), Luke cites or alludes to the Jewish Scriptures in order to show that God's salvation was never intended for the Jews, who are represented as theologically blind (Sanders, pp. 82, 167). In Acts "the same Jewish religious leaders appear . . . routinely . . . rather woodenly working the same mischief on the Church that they worked on Jesus" (p. 19). Whenever there is a disturbance in connection with the Christian movement, including, as Evans notes (p. 46), disturbances with a supposed political flavour, "it turns out to be the fault of the Jews, while the Romans say consistently that there is no case to answer".

iv. CONCLUSION

I began this chapter by noting the decisive role which the Old Testament plays in the New Testament references to the Passion. As Evans says (p. 13), what for us is a laborious matter of hunting in concordances, lexicons, and dictionaries was, for early Christians, "more immediate. It was in their heads and their hearts." He adds that this extensive use of the Old Testament means that "the celebrated argument from prophecy, which, along with its twin argument from miracle, has operated from the second century until the nineteenth as the chief pillar of Christian apologetic, collapses" (p. 14).

We saw that in Mark the Passion is a predominantly Jewish affair, and that Matthew in the main follows Mark. Luke, however, emphasizes the Roman side of the matter more (though not in order to exculpate the Jews) and John practically excludes the Jewish trial. These different versions cannot all be historically accurate. Furthermore, any one of them embraces material that is clearly supplementary. Evans concedes that the passion narratives, as they now stand, "would appear to have incorporated in them, and to have been filled out by, stories that could once have stood on their own feet and been told for their own sake, and some of which even now can be lifted out of the narrative without much difficulty and without unduly disturbing its sequence. Such stories could be the anointing at Bethany, the Last Supper, the prophecy of desertion, Gethsemane perhaps, and the denial of Peter" (p. 20). To the question: was there a pre-existing brief passion narrative without these?, he replies: "The possibility . . . has at least to be left open" that there was not (p. 21). Linnemann, as we saw (above, p. 125), insists that Mark's whole passion narrative, like the rest of his gospel, was compiled from isolated units of tradition (p. 171), and that there was no already existing account which gave the passion story as a unified whole (cf. DJE, p. 133). Furthermore, these isolated units are not, she says, historical reportage, but "kerygmatic accounts"—proclamations of what an early Christian community believed to have happened, intended for other believers. Against the commonly-held view that there was a ready-made historical account at any rate of the Passion on which Mark was able to draw, she notes:

> A consensus communis is not always brought about by convincing arguments for a particular view. Often it arises merely because no-one sees any need to question the thesis, as it fits everybody's preconceptions all too well. (p. 173)

Quite so.

It is sometimes argued, in favour of Mark's (the earliest) passion narrative that it is vitiated by a contradiction concerning Jewish and Roman involvement that no writer of fiction would have gratuitously invented. Anxious to blame the Jews for Jesus's death, Mark nevertheless does not make him die by sentence of a Jewish court (e.g. by stoning), but introduces the Romans and so thwarts his own purpose. The answer to this argument is that the evangelists (including Mark) were not making the whole story up, but reworking, so as to blame the Jews, an older tradition that blamed the Romans. We saw how Luke somewhat delicately effected an even further reworking in that direction of what he had read in Mark. Whether the older underlying tradition can be accepted as true depends on the extent to which it is substantiated by even earlier ones about Jesus's death. I have argued in DJE and HEJ that the gospel passion narratives represent the fourth stage in the development of Christian thinking about the death of Jesus; that according to the earliest documents (the Pauline and other early epistles) he was believed to have died obscurely some time in the not recent past; that next his death, understood as among the phenomena of 'the last days' (the final epoch of history), was on that basis taken as a recent event; and that the time was then made specific by supposing the event to have occurred under Pilate, so that Jesus's life came to be supplied with a precise framework in time and space, noticeably absent in the earliest documents. The gospels represent a yet further adaptation in that they exonerate Pilate and blame the Jews.

Apocalypses, Jewish and Christian

i. THE RISE OF APOCALYPTIC THINKING AMONG THE JEWS

After the reign of Solomon (962–922 BC) his kingdom was divided into two, with Israel in the north and Judah in the south. The northern kingdom fell to the Assyrian empire about 700 BC, but this empire came to an end when the city of Nineveh fell to the combined assault of the Medes and Babylonians in 612. Judah followed Israel into servitude when Nebuchadnezzar took and destroyed Jerusalem in 586 and transported a large number of captives to Babylonia. This Medo-Babylonian dominion endured until the Persian Cyrus overthrew the ruler of the Medes in 550 and captured Babylon in 538. He allowed the Jews captive there to return to their homeland. Nevertheless, their country remained under foreign rule. The Persian empire fell to Alexander the Great some 200 years later, and after his death in 323 his empire was divided, with the Seleucids ruling Syria and the Ptolemies Egypt. Palestine lay between the two and was held by the Ptolemies for more than a century; but the Seleucids had wrested it from them by the beginning of the first century BC. From 63 BC the Roman empire expanded into the area.

The Jews believed that God had given them laws and had at the same time bound himself to bestow his benefits upon them, provided they observed these laws. Since neither individuals nor the nation as a whole seemed to receive the benefits in the proportion expected, it was assumed that they would be forthcoming at some future time. Thus looking forward to a happier future formed the core of the Jews' religious ideas from very early times.

The original idea was that the nation would have a better future.[1] The older prophets hoped that it would be morally purified, that its enemies would be destroyed, that it would be governed by a just, wise, and powerful king of the house of David. Later, the future hope was extended from the nation to the world, and with this enlargement there is combined a far more decided reference to the individual. This change was doubtless caused by the breaking down of the tribal barriers and the absorption of the nation in a large empire (first the Greek and then the Roman). In the older days religion could still be a national, not an individual matter. The tribe could expect its God to succour it in matters which concerned the well-being of all, such as the growth of its crops or its fortunes in war. But when the nation ceased to exist as an independent unit, the deity could no longer be a tribal appurtenance, and, as the God and ruler of all mankind, he would be regarded as favouring not a particular tribe, but rather particular individuals. As individuals were dying all the time, and as the virtuous were no less mortal than the wicked, the hope of a blessed future could no longer remain in the form of an expectation of earthly bliss, from which the dead would have been excluded. It had to become a belief in individual resurrection after death. While the belief related only to Israel as a nation there was no need for it to be supramundane. The nation would always be there to benefit from its fulfilment. But once the expectation had been transferred from the nation to the individual, it was necessary to provide for the virtuous dead.

Another consequence of the absorption of the nation in a large empire was the birth of the ideas that the whole existing world would be destroyed by a miraculous act and that God would inaugurate his kingdom with a universal judgement of the living and dead. These ideas are expressed in the Jewish apocalypses which succeeded the prophetic literature. 'Apocalypse' means 'revelation', and apocalypses purport to be supernatural revelations imparted by men of God. The prophets had promised the nation delivery from political and moral ills, and had prophesied fighting and great affliction before this would occur, but nothing in the way of supernatural catastrophe. The apocalypses, however, foretell a deliverance preceded by the stars falling from heaven and the whole natural order passing away.

It is not difficult to see how this apocalyptic type of writing sprang from the changed world situation of the Jews. When the prophets were active, the world they knew consisted of God's people, a number of small neighbours (Edom, Moab, Phoenicia) and the two great powers of Egypt and Assyria at opposite ends of the geographical horizon. The Jews could measure their strength with the small kingdoms, and even the two large ones were so countered by one another that Israel could turn to the one for protection against the other. But with the rise of Alexander the Great's Empire, which extended from Greece to Persia, and later with the even more extensive Roman dominion, the Jews found themselves facing a situation where political independence was out of the question. The old hope of national prosperity had to fade, and it was not surprising that they should begin to think that only a cosmic act of God would have the power to break the vast empires oppressing them. However, even at the beginning of our era, the old hope of a glorious future for the nation was still alive, so that the ideas of these later times were a mixture of conflicting expectations. Old ideas survived alongside newer ones, as always.

What part did the idea of the Messiah play in this development? The Hebrew word means 'anointed' and was used to designate the early Israelite kings, who were anointed with oil. Saul, the first of them, is called "the Lord's anointed" (1 Samuel 24:6). Thus the term did not, at this stage, signify a future redeemer, but denoted the reigning king. However, the inadequacies of these kings caused the Jews to look forward to a future which would bring them more worthy monarchs. Isaiah's "Immanuel" prophecy, for instance (cf. p. 68 above) could be taken to refer to "an ideal kingly child of the Davidic house, . . . soon to be born, who will be what the true Anointed should be, the representative or embodiment of the presence of God with His people".[2] A century later, Jeremiah likewise promises, speaking in the name of Yahweh, that "I will raise unto David a righteous Branch, and he shall reign as king and deal wisely, and shall execute judgement and justice in the land" (23:5).

Early literature was subject to later re-interpretation. In the Psalms, the phrase 'thy anointed' is used to denote the reigning king, or the Davidic king as such without reference to a particular person, but not meaning a deliverer to come in the future. The second Psalm, for instance, complains that the rulers of the earth "take counsel together against the Lord and his anointed". Commentators agree that this was written in response to some specific historical situation: a king who, as "God's anointed" represented Yahweh, was threatened by other potentates. What the actual occasion was it is not possible to say: something such as the conflict between David and the Philistines (2 Samuel 5:17ff) or the attack on him by Syrians and others (2 Samuel 10:6ff). After the kingship had been brought to an end by Nebuchadnezzar's destruction of Jerusalem and the transportation of the nation into captivity at Babylon, pious Jews could not believe that such references in the Psalms were simply to a historical situation that was over and done with; and so they looked again for an anointed king to whom the words of the sacred hymns should apply with a force never realized in the imperfect kingship of the past, and the Psalms came to be viewed as prophetic. We have seen above (p. 138) that, in the Christian Scriptures, this passage from Psalm 2 is understood as a prophecy of Jesus's arraignment by Pilate and Herod Antipas (Acts 4:25–27).

In sum, then, the term 'Messiah' originally meant any anointed person, but came in time to mean a particular individual who was expected. Among early Christians there was a further development. The Septuagint and the Greek New Testament both render the term as 'Christos', and this came to mean not only the title of a particular person, but also his name. Many early Christians read their Old Testament in Greek, and so when they read in Psalm 2 of "the Lord and his anointed" — in the Greek, 'the Lord and his Christ' — they understood this as a reference to Jesus, named Christ. In some New Testament passages 'Christ' is still a title (e.g. "God hath made him both Lord and Christ", Acts 2:36), but mostly it is a proper name, even in early epistles: Paul writes of "the grace of Christ" and "the gospel of Christ" (Galatians 1:6–7), and the author of the letter to the Hebrews tells that "Christ" became "a high priest of the good things to come" (Hebrews 9:11).

With the rise of the apocalyptic literature it became possible to regard the Messiah as a supernatural being. If only a supernatural act, involving the destruction of the whole natural order, could liberate the Jews from the empires oppressing them, then no human leader would be strong enough to rectify things. But older ideas survived, so that in New Testament times some looked for a human Messiah to free the nation from Roman rule, while others awaited a supernatural personage.

ii. THE BOOK OF DANIEL

Ezekiel said about 580 BC that Israel was about to experience its last trials, ushering in an era of unclouded prosperity. He describes the mustering of the forces of Gog, their attack and their overthrow, which will serve as a lesson to the nations who will subsequently no longer molest Israel (Chapters 38–39). The final chapters give a detailed plan of the new temple and stress the importance of the priests.

In another work of this period, the book of Jeremiah, it is stated that after 70 years the people should be restored from Babylonian captivity to their own land and there be ruled justly by a Davidic king (23:5–6; 25:11ff; 29:10). Later, Zechariah asks (1:12) why, although the 70 years have passed, Yahweh's anger still rests on Judah and Jerusalem; and the Lord answers that all will be well when the temple is rebuilt. (According to Ezra 6:15, this was completed in 516 BC.)

The book of Daniel explains that Israel is nevertheless still oppressed because it has sinned abominably. The angel Gabriel tells Daniel that, when Jeremiah had said that 70 years must pass before there is an end to the desolations of Jerusalem, what was really meant was 70 weeks of years (Daniel 9:2, 24), i.e. each seven years are to count as one week, so that in all 490 years will be required. The author's prayer in this chapter 9 shows that he wrote at a time of great affliction: "for under the whole heaven hath not been done as hath been done upon Jerusalem" (verse 12). He begs the Lord to turn his anger away from the city and let his face shine upon "thy sanctuary that is desolate" (verse 17).

The first six chapters of the book bring (probably pre-existing) stories of Jewish exiles (including Daniel himself) in Babylon in the sixth century BC who stood firm under pressure to give up their faith. Although the book is set in this period, all critical scholars now agree that it is a product of the Maccabaean rebellion against the Seleucid ruler of Syria, Antiochus IV, some 400 years later, and that its purpose was to encourage the Jews he was persecuting and strengthen their resolve to resist his attempts to hellenize their country.

Antiochus ruled Syria from 175 BC. He assumed the title 'Theos Epiphanes' ('God Manifest'—his enemies nicknamed him 'Epimanes', 'the Madman'), and tried to subdue Egypt. On a first campaign he was successful, and on his way back to Syria he put down a rebellion in Jerusalem, massacring the people and plundering the temple. When he returned to Egypt in a second campaign, he was required by envoys from Rome to withdraw at once, and when he did so he was again confronted with trouble in Jerusalem. He determined to hellenize Judaea completely, forbade under penalty of death the observance of the sabbath and the practice of the rite of circumcision. In the temple he had a pagan altar, probably in honour of Zeus, set up on the altar of burnt offering (hence Daniel's reference to "the sanctuary that is desolate"). The Jews reacted with the Maccabaean revolt. Syrian forces were driven from the temple, and in 164 the sanctuary was rededicated. Antiochus died in 163 during a campaign against the Parthians.[3]

The language of the book shows that it is post-exilic. Chapter 2 (from verse 4a) to chapter 7 is in a late dialect of Aramaic, while the rest is in late Hebrew. As Porteous notes in his valuable commentary, "the presence of Greek words points to an age after the conquests of Alexander."[4] And the book is not alluded to by other writers until the mid-second century.[5] Its developed angelology (important angelic beings — Gabriel and Michael — are given personal names) also stamps it as late, as does its doctrine of resurrection — a doctrine conspicuously absent from the older parts, indeed practically from the whole of the Old Testament. The only real Old Testament parallel to the resurrection promised at Daniel 12:2 is in a late apocalypse included in the book of Isaiah (26:19), which may or may not be of earlier date. Historians of Israel have noted that, since under Antiochus righteous men were brutally done to death, "the belief that God would vindicate his justice beyond the grave became an absolute necessity for the majority of Jews".[6] That the book of Daniel was placed not among the prophetic books but in the third and final division of the Jewish canon, the Hagiographa, suggests that it was available only after the prophetic writings, produced between the eighth and the third centuries BC, had been terminally edited, about 200 BC.[7] Probably such a late composition was granted canonical status at all only because it provides a clear basis for the doctrine of resurrection.

The author has detailed knowledge of the history of Alexander's Greek (Macedonian) empire. He describes the events that took place in it in veiled terms that might be expected of a seer foreseeing it all from far in advance, but the details are recognizable from what is stated in histories of the period, such as the first and second books of the Maccabees in the Old Testament Apocrypha. In chapter 11 of Daniel the rivalry between the kings of Egypt and Syria in the third and second centuries is accurately described, and verses 21–39 cover the reign of Antiochus IV in some detail. The author knows, for instance, that he was successful in a first campaign against Egypt, that on his way home "he acted against the holy covenant", and then went again to Egypt, this time without success, since "ships of Kittim" (Roman envoys) came against him; whereupon he had "indignation against the holy covenant". He profaned the Jerusalem temple, took away the continual burnt offering and replaced it with a pagan altar, "the abomination that maketh desolate" (11:30–31. This 'abomination' is referred to repeatedly in the book—at 8:12; 9:27 and 12:11—and these references were, as we shall see, understood by early Christians as prophecies of events still to come in their own day). Daniel is acquainted too with the first Maccabaean victories, but not with the rededication of the sanctuary—for him, as we saw, it is still desolate (9:17)—and so obviously wrote between these two events, ca. 166 BC. His only genuine prophecies concern later events, as when he predicts the death of Antiochus with details which conflict with the well-attested facts. Attempts to reconcile these with what Daniel says on the matter are, says Porteous, "a waste of time" (p. 170).

The author's acquaintance with the Babylonian and Persian periods is sketchy and inaccurate compared with his knowledge of the Greek. At 5:31 a person called "Darius the Mede" is said to succeed to the Babylonian throne, to be succeeded in turn by "Cyrus the Persian" (6:28). But critical scholars agree with H. H. Rowley that Darius the Mede "has no place in history and . . . is a fictitious creation out of confused traditions."[8] As the prophets had foretold that Babylon would fall to the Medes (Isaiah 13:17; 21:2; Jeremiah 51:11 and 28), our author supposed that there had to be a Median kingdom prior to the Persian. In fact, as we saw, there was first a Medo-Babylonian empire, after which Cyrus first overthrew the ruler of the Medes and then established the Medo-Persian empire by capturing Babylon. There was no Median kingdom intermediate between Babylonian and Persian.

In sum, if our author wrote in the sixth century BC, "his mind was illumined with accurate knowledge of future times, while at the same time thoroughly befogged as to the events in which he himself"—if we are to believe his account—"played no mean part" (Rowley, p. 176).

Fundamentalist scholars, while admitting that there are references in the book to Antiochus Epiphanes, still argue that Daniel himself wrote it in the sixth century, or that it was compiled not later than the middle of the fifth. They deny, sometimes with a great show of learning, that his knowledge of these early periods is defective. Harrison claims that he "possessed prophetic gifts" and "foretold nothing that would be outside the powers of a gifted seer". Any more sceptical judgement must be deferred "until more is known about the psychic factors that are involved in foresight and foretelling". As our psychologists are still unable to explain very much about what is involved even in normal experience, the sceptics, on this view, are silenced indefinitely. Part of the price of this achievement, however, is commitment to the view that human choice (or indeed human prayers) can have no influence on the course of history, to which God has decreed a definite and inexorable course in which the individual actors simply play out the parts he has long ago alloted to them. Harrison does admit that "there appears to be a certain element of determinism in the mind of the author to the extent that he was able to think of all things as working out according to a predetermined plan."[9]

Wallace too speaks up for those who find that to accept the book as late and therefore pseudepigraphic is incompatible with "our belief in the nature of Holy Scripture" and would appear "to besmirch the holiness of God, just as factual or historical error seems incompatible with the God 'who never lies' ". And so he suggests (one notes how guarded is his language) that the book is "a genuine word of God from the tradition of Israel's days in Babylon", but was "issued afresh" in "a fresh vision" in the days of Antiochus Epiphanes. He thinks that some of the verses in chapter 11 which are applicable to what is known of the career of that monarch may refer to the Antichrist who is to come before Christ's final reign. Earlier he says that many passages in the Jewish Scriptures have "a double reference" — to a pre-Christian historical situation and to some aspect of Jesus's career, such as his Resurrection or his own prophecies about the end. Wallace's critical standpoint is illuminated by his statement that "no honest man can make a case" against "what has come to us directly from Jerusalem through Jesus Christ", and that only "perversity" can prompt the denial that here is "what is final in the truth about man and God".[10]

According to Harrison, the critical view of Daniel has been sustained merely by academic prejudice: "by the second decade of the twentieth century no scholar of general liberal background who wished to preserve his academic reputation either dared or desired to challenge the current critical trend" (p. 1111) — as if these scholars, clerical one and all, were obstinately determined to hold fast to ideas which have proved so subversive of Christian faith (cf. above, p. 6 for a similar imputation concerning their dating of the gospels). The way in which sensible argument can be suppressed by a consensus of opinion is better illustrated by the earlier history of the book's interpretation. Late in the third century AD the Neoplatonist Porphyry saw that its 'prophecies' degenerate into erroneous guesses concerning the last years of Antiochus Epiphanes, and he attributed it to a Palestinian Jew writing during that monarch's reign. Porphyry's work was condemned to be burned (after Constantine had tried unsuccessfully to suppress it) and survives only as fragments quoted by hostile authors. R. H. Charles notes, in his still valuable commentary on Daniel in the old *Century Bible* series, that Porphyry's theory "was in the opinion of his contemporaries and of subsequent generations so successfully refuted by the counter-treatises of Jerome, Methodius, Eusebius of Caesarea and Apollinaris that it was not fully revived till the nineteenth century".[11]

Apologists who concede the historical inaccuracy of Daniel of course claim that its 'religious value' is not thereby impaired. The author clearly believed that Israel's religion was incomparably superior to pagan religions — he even makes Nebuchadnezzar acknowledge as much (2:47)! — and wanted to encourage complete fidelity to the Jewish law, even at the risk of death. Rowley transmutes this message into more universal terms, saying that the book is of value because it "tells us that every force which elevates itself against God shall be broken, and that they who are humbly loyal to Him, and who find in His fellowship their strength, shall be able to laugh at the lions, for theirs shall be the kingdom" (p. 181). But this supposedly valuable message is simply not true unless the millions innocently slaughtered by forces of evil in this life survive into an after-world to break into laughter there. As Paul Badham concedes: "If one believes that death is the end, then there is simply no way belief in divine justice for the individual can be reconciled with life as we experience it." And so he concludes, with John Hick: "We cannot hope to state a Christian theodicy without taking seriously the doctrine of a life beyond the grave" (pp. 8–9). Thus, to validate one dubious theory, another, equally dubious, has to be premissed. For those who find such a premiss unacceptable, Daniel has a sadder message, illustrating as it does the stubborn adherence of the Jews to their traditional ideas which has throughout the ages brought them so much persecution. Antiochus tried to hellenize Judaea, and, as Porteous concedes, "the narrowness of the reaction to hellenism with its failure to recognise the great contribution that hellenism had to make to the world doubtless in the event condemned Israel to the ghetto" (p. 21).

But it is time to return to the story which Daniel tells. In chapter 2 we learn that Nebuchadnezzar had a dream which Daniel interpreted as a divine revelation concerning subsequent world history: there are to be three further "kingdoms", i.e. empires, after the Babylonian. The traditional Christian view has been that the last of these is the Roman empire; for the text states that, in the days of the fourth and final earthly kingdom, God "shall set up a kingdom which shall never be destroyed" (2:44); and this, for Christians, meant Jesus's establishment of God's kingdom in Roman times. However, allusions later in the book show that the fourth empire is the Greek. Even here, in chapter 2, it is indicated that it is to be a divided one (verse 41), as Alexander's was after his death; and two verses later there is an allusion to marriages between Seleucidae and Ptolemies which did not lead to reconciliation between them.

In chapter 7 Daniel records a dream of his own in which he saw "four great beasts come up from the sea, diverse from one another", representing, so he is told, the four successive empires (verse 17). The fourth beast has ten horns — ten kings arising from the fourth empire (verse 24), and a further little horn "with eyes like the eyes of a man and a mouth speaking great things", i.e. arrogantly (verse 8). This is a king who shall "speak words against the Most High, and shall wear out the saints of the Most High: and he shall think to change the times and the law" (verse 25). On the traditional Christian view, this 'little horn' is "some great anti-Christian persecutor of the true church arising within the Christian era and within the civilization created by the Roman empire" (Wallace, p. 129). Wallace does admit to some difficulty over this, as he concedes that the 'little' horn of Daniel's next chapter undoubtedly refers to Antiochus Epiphanes (p. 130). And the vision of that eighth chapter, in which the little horn figures as the final evil actor, is expressly interpreted by the angel Gabriel as "belonging to the time of the end" (8:17).

According to Daniel's account, 69½ of the 70 weeks of years will have passed when human history reaches the period of the little horn's activity, leaving only half a week (three and a half years) before the final consummation, the inauguration of the rule of the saints of the Most High (7:22, 9:24–27; 12:6–7). The 'saints' means not Israel as a whole, but those Israelites who rejected hellenization and were not "perverted" by Antiochus's "flatteries" (11:32).

As the kingdoms of the world are represented by beasts from the sea, so is the kingdom of the saints represented in the vision by a human form which descends from the clouds of heaven;

> I saw in the night visions, and, behold, there came with the clouds of heaven one like unto a son of man, and he came even to the ancient of days . . . And there was given him dominion and glory, and a kingdom, that all the people, nations and languages should serve him; his dominion is an everlasting dominion (7:13–14).

The apparition in human form is, then, simply a symbolical way of representing the "saints of the Most High". It is they to whom the kingdom is given, as the writer goes on to note when he explains the symbols he has been using.

Daniel thus looks forward to the universal and eternal dominion of the "saints", by which he means not Israel as a whole, but those who refused to compromise their religious beliefs. He thinks that this kingdom will be set up not merely by a judicial sentence of God, but by actual fighting between the saints and the others (2:44), so that the last times are to be characterized by universal strife. Nevertheless, "at that time thy people shall be delivered, every one that shall be found written in the book" (12:1). The next verse expresses the hope of the resurrection of the body: "Many of them that sleep in the dust of the earth shall awake, some to everlasting life and some to shame and everlasting contempt". Here, then, as in earlier Jewish literature, there is hope for a glorious future for the nation, but with the double modification that the future kingdom is conceived as a universal one, and that all the saints who have died will share in it.[12]

Commentators have welcomed Daniel's clear statement of a doctrine of resurrection, while regretting that the author, in making it, "did not rise above the crude demand for strict retribution which runs through the Old Testament like an acrid stream".[13] But the apocalyptic sections of the New Testament are no improvement on the Old in this respect. The author of the New Testament apocalypse (the book of Revelation) sees the souls of Christian martyrs crying out to God for vengeance. They are told to wait a little longer until those who have yet to be martyred are killed (Revelation 6:9–11). The seer is also told by "him that sitteth on the throne" that "the unbelieving" and other offenders, including "idolaters and all liars", will be cast into "the lake that burneth with fire and brimstone, which is the second death" (21:5-8). The position is no better in Matthew, where Jesus delivers an apocalyptic discourse in which he understands Daniel's reference to "the abomination of desolation" not as an allusion to the heathen altar erected in the temple in 168 BC, but as an event still to come (but in the near future) presaging the final tribulation. (Mark 13:14 refers laconically to an unnamed written source, while Matthew (24:15) characteristically gives explicit reference to Scripture and speaks of the abomination "which was spoken of by Daniel the prophet standing in the holy place".) In Matthew's account of the final judgement, in the same apocalyptic discourse, the judge will gather all the nations before him, separate them "as the shepherd separateth the sheep from the goats", and consign the latter "into the eternal fire which is prepared for the devil and his angels" (Matthew 25:31–46). The passage is not included in the other gospels. Matthew seems to derive a certain grim satisfaction from having people cast into "outer darkness" and listening to their "weeping and gnashing of teeth" (8:12, a characteristic Matthaean phrase).

The Roman occupation of Judaea, to which Daniel's veiled references to Greek rule could be referred by early Christian writers, still did not prelude the end of the world. And so many later interpreters have taken his 'prophecies' as references to their own times, understood as the final ones. A recent example is Hal Lindsey's interpretation (in a book that has sold well over a million copies) that the ten horns of Daniel 7:24 refer to a revived Roman empire, namely the then (1970) ten-nation European Economic Community.[14] This is but one illustration of what Porteous has justly called "the deplorable history of the interpretation of this book" (p. 47).

iii. FURTHER JEWISH APOCALYPSES

The book of Enoch (1 Enoch) purports to come from the Patriarch Enoch, the seventh in descent from Adam. In the New Testament epistle of Jude this ascription is accepted and the work is quoted as a reliable authority. We may gather from Tertullian that some people did wonder how it had managed to escape the Flood.

The book is now regarded as a combination of five originally independent parts, four of which belong to the early second century

(200–160 BC), while the so-called Similitudes or Parables (chapters 37–71) are assigned to some time in the first century AD, possibly as late as its final quarter.[15]

In chapters 85–90, from one of the older sections of the book, the author has a dream vision of the history of the world up to the Maccabaean revolt. After that, the gentile nations will assemble for their final attack on Israel, which will be defeated by God's intervention (90:16–19). He will then sit in judgement and will consign both fallen angels and Israelite apostates to the fiery depths. A new 'house' (a new Jerusalem) will replace the old one, and the gentiles will pay homage there to the pious Israelites (verse 30). Then the Messiah will appear and the gentiles will be converted (verses 37–38). Schürer comments: "The transcendental character of the later Messianic idea is manifest here: the new Jerusalem has nothing in common with the old, but is brought miraculously down from heaven". And "the form of the messianic king towers over the ordinary human dimensions."[16]

The later Parables or Similitudes describe the coming judgement, when "the Chosen One" will have sinners utterly destroyed, and will dwell in a transformed Earth in eternal blessing and light (chapter 45). Following Daniel's chapter 7, Enoch sees this Chosen One as a supernatural being whom he calls "the Son of man", who will judge the kings and the mighty (chapter 46). We recall that Daniel had spoken of one coming down from heaven in the form of a man, and that this was, for him, an allegorical way of representing the kingdom of the saints, while the heathen empires that have successively oppressed Israel he represented as beasts which rise up from the sea (cf. above, p. 167). The author of the Similitudes of Enoch has taken the term 'Son of man' for a title of the Messiah. In Daniel the phrase is indefinite — "like a son of man" — but in Enoch it is made to refer to one person, "*the* Son of man". Thus Enoch takes the coming down from heaven quite literally, so that the Messiah is, for him, no mortal, but a pre-existing supernatural being who comes down from on high. Schürer notes that such ideas are fully comprehensible not only from such a misreading of Daniel, but also from other Old Testament premisses: "Statements such as that in Micah 5:1 that the origins of the Messiah are from ages past, from the beginning of days . . . may easily be taken in the sense of pre-existence from eternity". Such interpretation "was encouraged by the whole development which tended to assert that everything truly valuable pre-existed in heaven".[17]

The New Testament has interpreted Daniel in the same way, and like Enoch tells of a Messiah who will come from heaven, calling him "the Son of man". Enoch's picture of the final judgement is strikingly paralleled at Matthew 25:31–46. Enoch says that "the Lord of Spirits seated the Elect One on the throne of his glory"; Matthew reads: "When the Son of man shall come in his glory . . . then shall he sit on the throne of his glory". Both writers go on to describe how the righteous are vindicated while the rest are banished to flame and torment. Both may well have been writing at about the same time, and presenting a *mise en scène* much older than either.[18]

The Messianic hope, as it was at the end of the first century AD, is further documented in the apocalypses of Baruch and Ezra. According to Baruch, the last days will be heralded by general and terrible confusion and fighting. Those who escape this will then face, as successive dangers, earthquake, fire and famine. Survivors will be delivered into the hands of the Messiah who, when made manifest, will assemble the nations, wipe out those who had oppressed Israel, and then sit on the throne of his kingdom for ever.

The Jewish Ezra apocalypse comprises chapters 3–14 of the book entitled 2 Esdras in the Apocrypha. (The previous and the following chapters are later, Christian additions). The seer is grieved that a righteous God should let his people suffer, but is assured by Uriel that the end of this present age is near. He goes on to re-interpret the vision of Daniel's seventh chapter. In Daniel the fourth beast was the Greek empire, but for this apocalypticist, who lived 200 years later under Roman rule, it naturally had to be Roman; and so he states that Daniel's interpretation was not correct, that the fourth kingdom "will be" — like Daniel, he is pretending to prophesy a future which was, for him, already present — "an empire more terrible than any before" (12:10–12); but the Messiah will destroy it and deliver the righteous. In the next chapter, the Messiah figures as a transcendent figure flying with the clouds and destroying his enemies with fire from his mouth — an idea which appears also in 2 Thessalonians 2:8, where Jesus, at his second coming, is expected to "slay the lawless one with the breath of his mouth". The burning desire of the author of Ezra is, says Russell, that "his own people will be saved and the Gentiles destroyed". His book is "a medley of ideas" where "only one thing is certain: the consummation of all things is in the hands of God and the end is near".[19]

iv. THE NEW TESTAMENT APOCALYPSE

The first three gospels include discourses, spoken by Jesus, about the end of the world and the phenomena that will be linked with it. We saw in the previous chapter that the Marcan Jesus tells his Jewish accusers: "Ye shall see the Son of man sitting at the right hand of power and coming with the clouds of heaven" (Mark 14:62). Before his arrest, he had told Peter, James and John that in the last times there will be great tribulation, including persecution of his followers, followed by the darkening of the sun and moon and the stars falling from heaven. After this "the Son of man" will be seen "coming in clouds with great power and glory", and his angels will "gather his elect" from all over the earth. All this is to happen in "this generation" (Mark 13:3–30).

I have commented elsewhere (HEJ, chapter 4) on this so-called 'great apocalyptic discourse' which fills Mark's thirteenth chapter, on Luke's rewriting of it so as to bring out different implications, and on the way Matthew used it and added to it. Here I wish to examine the one wholly apocalyptic book of the New Testament, entitled in the RV 'The Revelation of St. John the Divine'.

Lohse notes that not a few scholars have followed Calvin in making Revelation the only New Testament book on which they have failed to produce a commentary.[20] Their embarrassment is understandable, for, as Caird says, the book "has been the paradise of fanatics and sectarians, each using it to justify his own particular doctrine and so adding to the misgivings of the orthodox".[21] These misgivings result partly from the book's thoroughly repulsive theology of wrath. Sweet concedes in his Pelican commentary that "there is a vindictive harping in chapters 6–20 on the torture and destruction of enemies"—a spirit, he claims, that "is at home in the Old Testament but hardly in the New".[22] This, as we saw (above, p. 167f) is by no means a just distinction, and Sweet himself remarks (p. 22) on the "incendiary language" of such passages as Luke 3:17, where it is said that the coming one will burn up the chaff with unquenchable fire, and Luke 12:49, where Jesus declares that he "came to cast fire on the earth".

The author of Revelation is above all a seer; he saw the visions recorded in his book when he was "in the Spirit" (1:10 and elsewhere), i.e. in a state of ecstasy. The Pauline letters show that this kind of thing was a common phenomenon in the early days of Christianity ("in the spirit" a man can "speak mysteries", 1 Corinthians 14:2) and also that the resulting medley of conflicting or unintelligible revelations could have unsettling effects (cf. above, p. 44). Hence repeated injunctions to put seers to the test so as to detect imposters: "Quench not the Spirit; despise not prophesyings", yet "prove all things" (1 Thessalonians 5:19–21). "Believe not every spirit, but prove the spirits, whether they are of God: because many false prophets are gone out into the world" (1 John 4:1). And Revelation itself mentions "apostles" who, when put to the test, turned out to be liars (2:2).

Revelation begins and ends with assurances that the visions recorded in it concern "the things which must shortly come to pass" (1:1). Jesus will come soon (3:11; 22:20) on the clouds (1:7) at the final judgement. Beasley-Murray observes, justly, that this "conviction of the nearness of the end is by no means exceptional", but "characteristic of all prophets of both Testaments". He adds that, "in face of the perpetual non-occurrence of the promise of the kingdom many are tempted to view the promise as a chimera". He finds, however, that "to take such a stance is virtually to question whether there is any word of God at all in the Bible."[23] As such a "central" doctrine has repeatedly been falsified, this is a query which not unnaturally crosses one's mind.

According to Revelation the final judgement will follow a series of the most ghastly catastrophes involving torment and death for the majority of mankind. Only those will be saved whose names "have been written in the book of life from the foundation of the world" (17:8; cf. 13:8). All others will be "cast into the lake of fire" (20:15). Daniel had reserved salvation for those "written in the book" (see above, p. 167), but the author of Revelation studiously adds the predestinarian qualification. The point he is trying to make is that a seemingly evil world is, and always has been, completely under God's control. The course of history is simply and solely what God has decreed (particularly clear at 17:17). But such a view is not to be reconciled with passages elsewhere in the book which imply that any individual is free to achieve salvation by rejecting false religion and by adhering, even under duress, to the true faith. It is on such passages that Beasley-Murray must be relying when he claims that "to all men of little hope or none . . . , the book of Revelation offers strong consolation" (p. 46).

Like the book of Daniel and other Jewish apocalyptic works,

Revelation was written to reassure the faithful that God did really care for them in a situation where persecution was to be reckoned with. To understand what was involved we must be clear about relations between Church and state in the late first century.

Nero's persecution of Christians in AD 65 was an isolated incident confined to Rome (HEJ, p. 81). Decisive evidence of later imperial persecution does not come until Pliny's letter to Trajan (AD 112), which shows that it was then neither a complete novelty, nor established policy, but had occurred locally and sporadically.

Every Roman subject who was not a Jew was bound to at least nominal conformity to the state religion as much as to its political system; and every Christian, however politically loyal, was likely to refuse if required to show his loyalty by making sacrifice to the state gods. Hence persecution of Christians was bound to occur, almost anywhere in the empire, once the practices of taking an oath by the emperor's genius, of offering libation and incense before his statue, and addressing him as *Dominus* (Lord) had become prevalent. There is general agreement that these practices first grew up in the reign of Domitian (AD 81–96) and were retained by Trajan and later emperors. In Roman law, any religion — except that of the Jews — was illicit or unauthorized outside its country of origin. Christianity "was not a *religio licita*, and if it drew attention to itself, then its members were liable to punishment. Otherwise sleeping dogs would be allowed to lie".[24]

The seven churches of the Roman province of Asia, to which messages are addressed in the opening chapters of Revelation, were all seats of imperial jurisdiction and therefore places where the emperor cult was promoted. One of them is Ephesus, where remains of a temple dedicated to Domitian have been found. Another is Pergamon, with many pagan temples. The author of Revelation calls it "the throne of Satan", and Christianity must have had a hard time there.[25]

Nevertheless, Christianity's situation, as it emerges from statements in Revelation, was not adverse to an extreme. The author "was in the isle that is called Patmos for the word of God and the testimony of Jesus" (1:9). This may mean that he was banished there (but not executed) for preaching the faith, or simply that he went there voluntarily in order to preach it. Short terms of imprisonment are said to be a possibility believers must reckon with (2:10). But martyrdoms have occurred, and a man named Antipas is mentioned at 2:13 as a "faithful witness", killed for his faith. 'Faithful' is used throughout to designate those who choose to die rather than compromise their beliefs, and Jesus himself is called, in this sense, "the faithful witness" (1:5). At 6:9 the souls of martyrs cry out for vengeance and are told (verse 11) that there must be yet more martyrdoms. Christians have been put to death for refusing to worship a picture or image of the emperor made to speak by the skill of pagan priests (13:15). The imperial authority is hated as a "scarlet woman", "drunk with the blood of the martyrs of Jesus" (17:6). The seer looks forward to a time when "the great city", "the mother of the harlots and of the abominations of the earth" (17:5), will have imposed on her the (death) sentence she herself imposed on "saints, apostles and prophets" (18:20). Commentators agree that only Rome can be meant, although the city is given the coded name 'Babylon', the Old Testament paradigm of godlessness. A writer of the first Christian century can mean only Rome when he describes "Babylon" as the great city which has made *all nations* drink "of the wine of the wrath of her fornication" (14:8; 'fornication' is a standard metaphor for idolatry, taken from the Old Testament). The book stresses at every turn the importance of *persevering* in the true faith: cowardly persons are classed with others (unbelievers, idolators, liars, and so forth) who will be damned (21:8), and this is obviously meant as criticism of those who abjure Christianity under duress.

In the given situation Christians were tempted at least to compromise with paganism, to the extent, for instance, of eating things sacrificed to idols (2:14 and 20). Sweet goes so far as to say that Revelation was written principally to combat such complacency; that Rome was not then relentlessly persecuting Christians, who needed to be reminded of her true hateful character at this time when some of them were disposed to "join the world in finding God in Caesar, who is 'Antichrist' " (pp. 11, 20, 26).

That Domitian's reign is a likely date for the book's composition is suggested too by the lack of any residual traces of Pauline ideas in the seven letters it addresses to Christian communities in Asia Minor — an area where Paul had, a generation earlier, founded such communities. Lohse remarks on the absence from these letters of cardinal elements of Pauline thinking, such as a theology of the cross (Passion mysticism: believers have been crucified to the world and the world to them, Galatians 6:14), justification by faith, and assurance of *present* salvation.[26] For the author of Revelation, salvation lies in the future, to be won by those who persevere and "over-come" (21:7). In a recent article, Lohse has reaffirmed the view taken in his commentary that the book was written "in anticipation of intensified dangers from the policy of Domitian".[27] The expectation that the world will soon come to an end (prominent in the earliest Christian literature) seems to have been rekindled by this threat of persecution, as was to happen too in later periods of Church history.

The revelation embodied in the book purports to have been given by God to Jesus (risen and exalted to heaven, not during his earthly existence) who sent his angel (22:16) to "his servant John" who in turn "bare witness" of it (1:1). So God told Jesus, who told his angel, who told John, who tells Christians. The idea is, of course, to suggest not that the message is nth-hand, but that it is validated by all three supernatural authorities named.

Of these authorities, Jesus is given almost equal status to God, and this is one of the indications that the book does not belong to the oldest extant layer of Christian tradition (cf. above, p. 23). The doxology of 5:13 (unto them be "the blessing, and the honour and the glory and the dominion for ever and ever") is addressed to both God and Jesus, a similar doxology at 1:6 to Jesus alone. In the oldest Christian documents such statements are made only with reference to God (e.g. Romans 11:36, Galatians 1:5). If at Revelation 1:8 it is "the Lord God" who says he is "the Alpha and the Omega",[28] at 1:17 it is Jesus who likewise claims to be "the first and the last". Throughout the book, Old Testament predicates of God are applied directly to him; and at 5:12, figured as "the Lamb that hath been slain", who redeemed mankind with his blood, he is worshipped in song (in the same terms as is God at 4:9–11) as "worthy . . . to receive the power, and riches, and wisdom, and might, and honour, and glory, and blessing". Bauckham points out that never, in the Jewish texts, are such hymns as this sung to any except God.[29]

If Jesus is, with God, the giver of revelation, angels are, with John, the author, merely the channels through which it is conveyed. They are "fellow-servants" with him and with his "brethren", and an angel before whom he prostrates himself in worship twice rebukes him for this (19:10 and 22:9). The epistle to the Hebrews likewise stresses (1:3–4) Jesus's superiority to angels; and in his letter to the Colossians Paul seems specifically to combat the view that angelic agencies are necessary to salvation, for he declares that it is in Jesus that "all the fulness" dwells (1:19; cf 2:9: "in him dwelleth all the fulness of God"). All this illustrates very well the way in which early Christian writers were concerned not with any public ministry of Jesus (which they never mention) but with his supernatural status and his relation to other supernatural entities.

If the author of Revelation admits to being but a channel of information, he is nevertheless in no doubt about the importance of his message and warns that, if any one adds to "the words of the prophecy of this book", God will "add unto him the plagues which are written in this book". Likewise, if anyone subtracts from the message, God will "take away his part from the tree of life" (22:18-19).

Who, then, is this John who speaks with such authority? Four other New Testament books (a gospel and three epistles) have titles ascribing them to someone of this name, and the prolonged discussion as to the authorship of all five has been, so a theologian tells us, exceptionally "bewildering, disappointing and unprofitable".[30] Revelation is the only one of the five where the author is named as John within the book itself. The gospel is anonymous (cf. above, pp. 10f), as is also the first epistle. The second and third epistles purport to be written by someone who calls himself "the elder", probably meaning the leader of a Christian community who can speak with some authority. What Moody Smith has called the "real and not insignificant" differences between the gospel and these three epistles make common authorship unlikely.[31] Nor can Revelation have been written by the author of the gospel which, as we saw, knows nothing of any expectations that the world is coming to a speedy and catastrophic end, while this idea dominates Revelation. Also, this latter is written in what has been called extraordinary Greek (quite different from that of the gospel) — a Greek, says Sweet, which follows Hebrew idiom so as to do "frequent violence to grammar and syntax, not out of ignorance but it seems deliberately, to create a 'biblical' effect on the hearer" (p. 16).

The Fathers (beginning however only with Irenaeus, ca. AD 180) naturally ascribed all five works to John the son of Zebedee, one of the twelve disciples in the gospel traditions, as writings regarded as canonical were supposed to be the work of trustworthy witnesses. But the author of Revelation calls himself simply a "servant" (the Greek means 'slave') of Jesus, and never suggests that he had known him during his incarnate life, of which he in any case says nothing. As he has detailed knowledge of the seven churches in Asia Minor to which he writes, he was obviously an active preacher in that area before leaving for Patmos. Hence his authoritative tone towards them derives from his former position there, not from any connection with the pre-AD 70 Palestinian community.

At Revelation 2:2 the author says that certain "apostles" at Ephesus have been put to the test and revealed as liars. 'Apostle' is here used in its original sense of Christian missionaries, not companions of Jesus during his lifetime (cf. above, p. 34). At 21:14 he mentions the "twelve apostles of the Lamb", whose names are on the twelve "foundations" or basement courses of the New Jerusalem which represents the perfected religious community. The pseudo-Pauline epistle to the Ephesians, written about the same time as Revelation (cf. HEJ, pp. 53–55), likewise represents the Church as "built upon the *foundation* of the apostles" (2:20, using the same Greek noun), in that it is based on their preaching.

The New Jerusalem of Revelation is a square of side 12,000 stadia, having a wall 144 cubits high, with twelve gates, twelve angels at them, and the names of the twelve tribes inscribed on them. The author's prime concern is clearly to show the importance of the number twelve in the perfect community. As elsewhere in the book, ancient astrological lore underlies what is said here, although the author will no longer have been aware of the original mythological implications. Sweet mentions such old ideas as "the city of the Gods, suggested by the heavens with the sun and moon and the twelve signs of the Zodiac and the twelve gates through which they were conceived to pass" (p. 302). The year runs its course in twelve months, and Revelation places "the tree of life" in the city, bearing "twelve manner of fruits", one for each month (22:2). In ancient Babylon, divine honours were paid to twenty-four constellations — twelve to the north and twelve to the south of the zodiac — and this is reflected at Revelation 4:4, where we learn of 24 thrones around God's throne in heaven. For all these reasons, says Lohse (p. 23), twelve is the number representing perfection; and the queen of heaven wears a crown of twelve stars (12:1). Twelve apostles are thus appropriate for the ideal community envisaged in chapter 21, however many there may have been in the actually existing communities of the author's day and earlier.

Concerning Jesus's earthly existence, Revelation mentions only his Davidic ancestry (5:5) and his sacrificial death (he "loosed us from our sins by his blood", 1:5). The author does not say who it was who "pierced" him (1:7) in "the great city which spiritually is called Sodom and Egypt" (11:8). Sweet observes that Jerusalem is called Sodom by the prophets (e.g. Isaiah 1:10 and 3:9), but thinks the reference here in Revelation is not to any particular city, but to "the city as the social and political embodiment of human self-sufficiency and rebellion against God" (p. 187). This is not as far-fetched as it might seem, as the author of Revelation is speaking "spiritually" (allegorically), and in the same context he says that the bodies of "two witnesses" killed in the same city were on view for a time to persons "from among the peoples and tribes and tongues and nations" (verse 9). Such an international audience does not suggest Jerusalem, although Rome would be a possibility. Elsewhere in the book, "the great city" certainly refers to Rome. Caird thinks that here, however, "the great city is a myth, which John intends to use to delineate the true nature of Roman imperial power", Rome being "simply the latest embodiment of something that is a recurrent feature of human history" (p. 138). These comments illustrate the difficulty of pinning down historical allusions in the book — a difficulty which has made it a godsend to the zealous, who have found in it references to "important historical events in the time of various Popes, Martin Luther, Napoleon, Kaiser Wilhelm, Mussolini, Hitler and others".[32] Once the circumstances in which it originated had passed away, its whole purport was no longer understood, but it became a source of endless apocalyptic speculation, particularly at times of political upheaval or in tense international situations, when people are very frightened and suggestible. The only thing such speculations have in common is that the final crises specified in the book are taken as references to the period in which the interpreter himself lives.

The author's prime concern, then, is not with the 'historical' Jesus, but with the Jesus who reigns in Heaven, "the ruler of the kings of the earth", "the firstborn of the dead" (1:5), in that his Resurrection heralds a general resurrection and judgement. At 1:13–16 John recalls a vision in which he saw him as "one like unto a son of man", with various supernatural attributes, such as seven stars in his right hand and a two-edged sword in his mouth. The simile concerning the son of man is taken from Daniel 7:13 (quoted above, p. 167). Later (14:14), the same simile is used to introduce him "sitting on the cloud" (this again follows the same passage from Daniel) and holding a sharp sickle with which he "reaps" the Earth (14:16). This is an image for judgement, as elsewhere in the New Testament. ("God is not mocked: for whatsoever a man soweth, that shall he also reap", Galatians 6:7). It is probably inspired (as Sweet notes, p. 232) by the ingathering of the world for judgement as described at Joel 3:12–13:

> I will sit to judge all the nations . . . Put ye in the sickle, for the harvest is ripe, . . . for their wickedness is great.

In the earliest Christian literature, 'son of man' is not used at all with reference to Jesus. Paul never uses it; and when the author of the letter to the Hebrews quotes (2:6) the phrase from Psalm 8, he does so in a context where he is applying the passage that follows in the Psalm to Jesus. But he does not attempt to do this with the phrase 'son of man'. Had he known it as a designation of Jesus, as it is used in the gospels, he could have hardly failed to do so. Revelation follows Daniel in using the phrase merely as a simile ('one like a son of man'), but referring not to the kingdom of saints, as in Daniel, but specifically to Jesus, reigning in heaven. By the time we reach the gospels, the phrase is no longer a simile, but a title: Jesus is *the* Son of man who will come on the clouds (as the Similitudes of Enoch envisage the coming of the Messiah, called by the same title; cf. above, p. 169). There are further passages in the gospels which use this title to mean not the heavenly Jesus who will come as judge, but the Jesus who suffered and died on Earth and then rose. As I have shown in DJE (pp. 114–16), theologians have recognized that the two sets of passages are completely separate, so that each set must derive from traditions independent of those represented in the other. All this constitutes yet another good example of how religious traditions can develop in different directions and then, in later documents, be put alongside each other.

Revelation's figuring the heavenly Jesus as a lamb with seven horns and seven eyes "which are the spirits of God sent forth into all the earth" (5:6) is a manifold reworking of old traditions. Horns are a sign of power (Deuteronomy 33:17) and in Daniel designate kingly power. The seven eyes which inform the lamb of what is happening all over the earth seem to be residues from ancient astrological lore (no longer understood in any astrological sense by John), according to which God's eyes are the sun, the moon and the five planets then known (Lohse, pp. 15, 22, 43). From this old astrological basis, the number seven is used throughout Revelation to indicate complete fulness. Another basis for figuring Jesus as a lamb is that, as elsewhere in the New Testament, he is the lamb sacrificed for the sins of the world, and in Revelation he is said still to bear the marks of slaughter. We recall that in the fourth gospel he is the lamb of God that takes away the world's sins and dies not according to the chronology of the other three gospels, but at the very time when the passover lambs were being sacrificed. All this derives to some extent from the story of the servant of Yahweh in Isaiah 53, who redeems "many" when he is slaughtered like a lamb.

The Lamb is declared worthy to open the book with seven seals held by God, and as he breaks each one (chapter 6) terrible woes ensue: peace is taken from the Earth, men are impelled to slay each other; war, famine and wild beasts kill a quarter of mankind. Then comes an earthquake, with the stars falling from heaven, while all mankind cowers before "the wrath of the Lamb".

Oddly, it is only after all this that angels are instructed (chapter 7) to do no damage on Earth until those who are to be saved have been marked with a seal on their foreheads. Only 144,000, twelve thousand from each of the twelve tribes of Israel are to be sealed and spared. This can hardly be meant literally, as the author regards Jews, for their opposition to Christianity, as "a synagogue of Satan" (2:9). Commentators say the Church is meant, just as elsewhere in the New Testament (e.g. Galatians 6:16) it is said to be the true Israel. Later, the 144,000 are described as "they which were not defiled with women: for they are virgins" (14:3-4). The ascetic ideal is strongly advocated in other documents, both Christian and Jewish (e.g. the Dead Sea Scrolls) of these times; but again the statement may not be meant literally, as in the Old Testament disobedience to God is frequently imaged as sexual indulgence.

After the sealing of the elect, John sees a vast multitude of redeemed ones—not just Jews, but from every nation on earth—arrayed in white robes in heaven (7:9). Shining white is the apparel of heavenly beings generally (cf. above, p. 28), and in Revelation even the souls of martyrs, although they are but souls, are given white garments (6:11). John is told that the multitude in white has "come out of the great tribulation" and that they have "washed their robes and made them white in the blood of the Lamb" (7:14). One would not expect washing in blood to produce white, but the idea is that their faith in the redeeming power of Jesus's death enabled them to stand firm under duress and kept them from evil.

Next the seven angels that stand in the presence of God are given seven trumpets, and at each blast on them further wholesale destruction ensues. A third of the sea becomes blood, and a third of the creatures in it, and the ships on it, are destroyed (8:8). In the next chapter, those who "have not the seal of God on their foreheads" are tormented by demonic locusts, and long for death, but do not find it.

In chapter 11 John is told to "measure the temple of God", but not its outer court, which, with "the holy city" is to be given over to the gentiles for 42 months. The tradition represented here probably derives from a Jewish supposition, during the siege of Jerusalem in AD 70, that the inner sanctuary would be spared. The 42 months (three and a half years) are taken from Daniel 7:25 and 12:7 as a stereotype of a period of tribulation. Revelation has reworked this pre-AD 70 tradition and probably intends the temple to mean the Christian community, which will be embattled but will survive. Such a view of God's temple is represented at divers places in the New Testament and was therefore well-known in early Christian times. True believers are called "a temple of God" (1 Corinthians 3:16; 2 Corinthians 6:16); they constitute "a holy temple in the Lord" (Ephesians 2:21) and "as living stones are built up a spiritual house" (1 Peter 2:5).

Revelation goes on to speak of "two witnesses" who are to have power "to smite the earth with every plague as often as they shall desire" (11:6). Finally they will be killed and left unburied, but after three and a half days will come alive again and ascend to heaven (11:11–12). The two witnesses are further described in terms which have enabled commentators to identify them as Moses and Elijah, expected to return preaching repentance in the last days. This is a variant of the tradition represented in the gospels that Elijah had already returned to Earth during Jesus's life on Earth (cf. above, p. 90). Once again we see what medley of traditions went to the making of early Christianity.

At the blowing of the seventh trumpet, voices in heaven are heard crying that world sovereignty has passed for ever to "our Lord and . . . his Christ" (11:15), and that the time has come for the dead to be judged. There is then a great portent in Heaven: a pregnant woman is seen "arrayed with the sun, and the moon under her feet, and upon her head a crown of twelve stars" (12:1–2). Gunkel thought that this description of the queen of heaven is based on a picture. He mentions an engraving in a Berlin museum of a goddess, possibly Ishtar, clothed in the sun, with the moon and seven stars above her. The twelve signs of the zodiac, he adds, form a circle in the heavens and are for this reason frequently depicted as a crown.[33] If he is right, we have here an instance of the influence of iconography on legend — something on which I commented apropos of the gospel accounts of Jesus's Temptation (above, pp. 105f).

The celestial woman is "delivered of a son, a man child who is to rule all the nations with a rod of iron" (12:5). Jesus is clearly meant. She has other children (12:17), portrayed as true believers, and hence she is mother of the elect community.

While she is in labour, a huge dragon waits to devour her child as soon as it is born, and while he waits in the heavens his tail knocks a third of the stars to earth. But the newborn child is immediately taken up to God's throne. This seems to be the pagan myth of the persecution of Leto and of her newborn child, Apollo, by the dragon, reworked and adapted to Christian purposes, for the dragon is identified with Satan (12:9).[34]

The story of the woman in labour both giving birth to the redeemer and also symbolizing the elect community has a remarkable parallel in one of the Dead Sea Scrolls. The Psalmist of the Qumran Hymn Scroll compares the afflictions he has had with the condition of the woman who is to give birth to "a marvellous counsellor" (a clear allusion to Isaiah 9:6 — "his name shall be called Wonderful, Counsellor . . . "):

> And I was confused like the Woman about to bring forth
> at the time of her first child-bearing . . .
> For the children have reached as far as the billows of Death
>
> And She who is big with the Man of distress is in her pains.
> For she shall give birth to a man-child in the billows of Death,
> and in the bonds of Sheol there shall spring from the
> crucible [i.e. the womb] of the Pregnant one
> a Marvellous Counsellor with his might,
> and he shall deliver every man from the billows
> because of Her who is big with him.

Dupont-Sommer draws attention to the last line, where the mother is explicitly associated with her child's redeeming work, and also to the line which states that he is the "firstborn" of his mother. He infers that "the Woman who is to bring him into the world is the congregation of the just, the Church of the Saints, victim of the persecution of the wicked".[35]

Next in Revelation a beast is seen coming out of the sea and representing a powerful series of rulers (Roman emperors). A second beast, coming from the earth, symbolizes the priests of the emperor cult who are forcing everybody to worship the first beast (13:11-12), on one of whose seven heads is a "death stroke" that was "healed" — an allusion to the emperor Nero. After his suicide in AD 68, it came to be believed that he had not died at all, but had fled to the east and would return at the head of Parthian armies, to regain his throne. As years passed without his return, this legend developed into a belief that he had in the meantime died, but would soon come back to life and reassume power. That Nero is meant is confirmed when the author of Revelation adds that "it was given unto him" (i.e. God allowed him) to persecute Christians, to "make war with the saints and to overcome them" (13:7). And he is said to have the number 666 (13:18). The number of interpretations of this allusion must be almost as great (they include referring it to Mohammed, Luther, and Napoleon), but if the letters of 'Nero Caesar' (Neron Qesar) are taken in the Hebrew alphabet, they add up to 666 (Lohse, p. 82. Both Jews and Greeks formed their numerals from the alphabet, with a = 1, b = 2, and so on). Later there is another allusion to Nero's return: seven "kings" (in the east the emperor was called 'king') are mentioned: five have died, the sixth is reigning, the seventh "not yet come"; and there is an eighth who was also one of the seven (17:9-11). The author, then, writing in Domitian's reign, is expecting Nero to return and resume his persecution.

Those who succumb to emperor worship — no more was necessarily involved than the kind of nominal conformity that goes with standing for a national anthem — are to be most frightfully punished for ever:

> If any man worshippeth the beast and his image . . . he also shall drink of the wine of the wrath of God, which is prepared unmixed in the cup of his anger; and he shall be tormented with fire and brimstone in the presence of the holy angels, and in the presence of the Lamb: and the smoke of their torment goeth up for ever and ever; and they have no rest day and night, they that worship the beast and his image. (14:9-11)

The following chapters detail more supernaturally caused woes. Every living thing in the sea is killed (16:3), presumably to thwart mankind, as fish can hardly be punished for idolatry. Rivers and springs are turned to blood, and the justice of this is said to be that those who have persecuted the elect are thereby given blood to drink (16:5–6). When the sun subsequently scorched men with its flames they (perhaps understandably) cursed the name of the God who had such power to torment them (16:9).

Better news comes in chapter 20. The dragon, alias Satan, is cast into the abyss for a thousand years, while those who "had been beheaded for their testimony to Jesus" and had not worshipped the beast or his image were raised from the dead to reign with Christ for this whole period. After it, Satan is let loose and enlists the help of "Gog and Magog" (20:8). Ezekiel (38:2) had named "Gog of the land of Magog" as a princely enemy of Israel, but in Revelation, as in some Jewish writings of the period, both names have come to represent enemies of the Messiah. They and Satan are destroyed by fire coming down from heaven in a final attack on "the camp of the saints" and "the beloved city". Then the remaining dead (those who had not been raised at the "first resurrection" a thousand years earlier) are raised for judgement, and any who "was not found written in the book of life was cast into the lake of fire" (20:15).

This idea that the Messiah would reign for some hundreds of years before the final judgement is paralleled in Jewish apocalypses (in, for instance, 4 Ezra: see DJE, p. 113) and represents a combination of the older Messianic idea of a glorious king with the later doctrine of a supernatural figure who will come down from on high as judge. As Christianity came to view Jesus both as king Messiah and as supernatural son of man, he could be made to fulfil both functions. The 'chiliasm' of Revelation (the thousand-year reign of Christ before the final consummation) together with what has been called its "extremely confused religious outlook that peculiarly mixes Jewish, Christian, and mythological elements"[36] (that is to say, elements from older mythologies) does not appeal to many educated Christians of today, but well illustrates how the religion of one day is largely a reshuffling of ideas of a yesterday.

At the end of Revelation the unrighteous and the filthy are told to persist in their ways, and the righteous and the holy to "do righteousness still" (22:11). This injunction is placed immediately after an assurance that "the time is at hand" and is followed immediately by the like assurance: "Behold, I come quickly"; and so the meaning of the injunction can only be: the end is so near that there is no point in anyone trying to change his behaviour; all that matters is that the faithful shall hold firm to their faith (as has been reiterated throughout this book). Sanders calls this "retreat from the ethical dimension" the "basic evil" of the whole book, and an evil which today is experiencing a revival:

> When persons today consciously and deliberately reject all obligation to help to seek to overcome the social, international, and individual problems of our time and insist that such problems are not the concern of the individual because Jesus is coming soon, we have the ultimate retreat from ethical responsibility. To the degree that the Apocalypse itself contributes to such views today, its existence and its place in the canon are, in the fullest sense of the word, evil.[37]

Not that, in Sanders's view — and he is a Christian theologian writing for a Christian publisher — the rest of the New Testament is all that much more helpful in providing acceptable ethical guidelines, as so much of it was written from the belief that the final judgement, vindicating only those within the Church, is at hand, or at any rate not too far removed in time.[38]

Finally, I revert to a matter on which I touched at the beginning of this section. There are repeated references in Revelation to Christian "prophets". The "prophets and saints" (18:24) slain by "Babylon" (=Rome) must refer to the deaths of Christian prophets and believers. At 22:9 the angel calls himself a "fellow-servant" with John, "and with thy brethren the prophets, and with them which keep the words of this book". Hill points out that a distinction is here made between 'prophets' and ordinary believers.[39] "The testimony of Jesus", we are told at 19:10, "is the spirit of prophecy"; that is, the prophet is moved by Jesus to pronounce the teachings of Jesus — sometimes using the first person to do so, as at 3:20: "Behold, I stand at the door and knock: if any man hear my voice and open the door, I will come in to him . . . " These teachings come from the risen Jesus, exalted to heaven, not from the 'historical' Jesus. The Pauline letters reflect a similar situation where the risen one speaks to the communities through the voices of Christian prophets (cf. above, pp. 129f). In time it was natural for Christians to suppose that what the heavenly Jesus had taught must also have been taught by him during his incarnate life. And it is easy to see that, in this way, discourses, such as the apocalyptic teaching of Mark 13, came to be attributed to him. Although it is widely admitted that elements in what according to the gospels was his biography were constructed in this way, scholars persist in regarding the Jesus of the gospels as nevertheless underlying the Jesus of the book of Revelation. Caird, for instance, makes the grotesque claim that "the Christology, and therefore the theology" of this book "is firmly anchored in the Jesus of history" (p. 290).

Conclusion

Throughout this book I have been able to draw on the views of serious Christian students of the new Testament whose work shows that it provides little basis for defensible religious belief. They have now themselves begun saying as much. A signal example is John Bowden's *Jesus: The Unanswered Questions* (London: SCM, 1988). Bowden is a Christian minister and director of the religious house that has published his book. It constitutes a very outspoken challenge, to which he has been warming at least since 1975, when he complained that the clerical New Testament critic is expected "to remain faithful on the one hand to the canons of academic discipline in which he writes and on the other to a calling in the context of the church which goes beyond the demands of the scholarly world." He added that "the only successful popularizers appear to have been those who have combined an attractively readable style with a message which has minimally affected the *status quo*."[1] His 1988 book combines readableness with a fully documented message (the notes supply excellent guidance for further reading on each of the matters he discusses) which very much affects the *status quo*; and coming from such a source, it is likely to be taken more seriously than if it were from an atheist. I shall devote much of this the conclusion of my own book to stating the case he makes.

The Old Testament, he says, is not properly to be read as prophecy of Jesus. We prize its prophets "primarily because of their stress on social justice". To make them into "foretellers of Jesus" has been "a distortion of their concern" (p. 188). As for the New Testament, there is much even in the earliest of its 27 books to give pause to a thoughtful reader. Bowden refers here to Graham Shaw's *The Cost of Authority*, with its significant sub-title *Manipulation and Freedom in the New Testament* (London: SCM, 1983). Shaw (until recently Chaplain of Exeter College, Oxford) notes, for instance (pp. 44, 181), that Paul begins his letter to the Galatians by twice cursing

Christians who do not agree with him, and that in all his letters "the eschatological phantasies of the early believers are consistently exploited to inculcate an anxiety which only membership of the apostle's privileged community can allay".

Another feature of these earliest documents (though not one which Bowden stresses) is their truly astounding silence about Jesus's incarnate life. None of the letters ascribed to Paul that are now accepted as genuinely written by him make any allusion to Jesus's parents, let alone to the virgin birth. They do not refer to a place of birth or residence (e.g. by calling him 'of Nazareth'). They mention neither John the Baptist (even though Paul stresses the importance of baptism), nor Judas, nor Peter's denial of his master. (They do, of course, mention Peter, but do not imply that he, any more than Paul himself, had known Jesus while he had been alive.) They give us no indication of the time or place of Jesus's earthly existence. They never refer to his trial before a Roman official, nor to Jerusalem as the place of his execution. And one could never gather from these letters that he had been an ethical teacher, even though they are full of ethical admonitions. Paul is also totally silent about Jesus's miracles, even though he believed in the importance of miracles as a means of winning converts. Furthermore, all extant Christian epistles that can plausibly be dated as among the earliest refer to Jesus in essentially the same manner as Paul does. They stress one or more of his supernatural aspects—his existence before his life on Earth, his Resurrection, and his second coming—but say nothing of the teachings or miracles ascribed to him in the gospels, and give no historical setting to the crucifixion, which remains the one episode in his incarnate life that they mention at all.

Can we really be sure that a person described in these terms ever had any earthly existence? It is customary to draw a distinction between the supernatural Pauline 'Christ' and the 'historical Jesus' of the gospels, and the question arises: what is the relation between them? If Jesus lived ca. AD 30 the kind of life portrayed in the gospels, why did so little of the relevant traditions find their way into earlier Christian literature, where he is described almost exclusively in supernatural terms? S. G. Wilson has written an account of the discussion of these issues, and suspects that often "the topic is instinctively avoided because to pursue it too far leads to profound and disturbing questions about the origin and nature of Christianity".[2] He is quite unconvinced by suggestions "that Paul must have known more of Jesus's teaching than he mentions, or that he assumes a common knowledge shared by himself and his readers" (p. 8). And he points out that "Schmithals has argued that, with the exception of the Gospels, Paul's relation to the Jesus tradition was not much different from all other Christian writers up to the time of Justin" (p. 19), i.e. the mid-second century. This, as Wilson notes, is an exaggeration. It would, however, be true to say that only from about AD 90 do we find that here one and there another Christian writer begins to ascribe to Jesus one or more of the aspects of his life and work familiar to us from the first three gospels, and that by about AD 150 all these aspects are being mentioned. Many, then, if not all of these aspects are no part of the original tradition, but later legendary accretions and modifications. Wilson endorses this to the extent of conceding that Bultmann was right to say that "moving back from the Pauline Christ to the historical Jesus is something which . . . we . . . cannot do" (pp. 19–20). And he concludes: "Driven . . . to the view that there is little that we can confidently assert apart from the mere fact of Jesus's life and death, we are forced to fall back on a mythological figure (the Christ of faith, Pauline or otherwise)". This, he allows, "may not be what we would wish to be the case or what we think ought to be the case in terms of traditional Christian beliefs: it is, however, a conclusion which is difficult to avoid" and "has the effect of placing us, for different reasons and perhaps against our wishes, in the same position as Paul" (pp. 20–21).

The position would be easier for the Christian if there were some evidence supporting the gospels outside the New Testament. But, as Bowden notes (p. 34) the information from such sources is so scanty that it "could easily be written on a postcard" and tells us nothing of substantial interest.

Neither Wilson's nor Bowden's scepticism extends to querying Jesus's historicity. Bowden thinks that much of what is said of him in the gospels may be true, although it is hard to be sure about most of the individual items (p. 32). He stresses that, in these gospels, we find one evangelist changing the words of another not in the interests of historical accuracy, but "for primarily theological reasons". He bluntly spells out the meaning of this innocuous-sounding phrase: Matthew and Luke "altered what they found before them in Mark because they wanted to produce works which were more helpful to their Church" (pp. 38, 40).

If we take these gospels in themselves, independently of whether what they say is corroborated elsewhere, we find much that is obviously legendary. Bowden's verdict on their miracle stories (which form a substantial fraction of their total substance) is that they include "a high proportion of pious legend" and that "the degree of historical reminiscence is usually very difficult to establish" (p. 160). There are even "virtual conjuring tricks" (for example Matthew 17:27, the coin in the fish's mouth) which run riot in the apocryphal gospels, where "a favourite instance is the infant Jesus making good his father's mistakes in carpentry" (pp. 162, 241 n.48). Bowden adds that, within the canonical miracle stories, "the degree of the later elaborations is notably higher at those two points where Christian tradition most wants to see miracles: the virgin birth and the resurrection". Many of the miracle stories presuppose a world dominated by demons, and these, with the Devil and with Hell, have been quietly set aside by many theologians (cf. above, p. 108).

The position is little better if we turn to Jesus's teaching in the gospels. First, there is, as Bowden says, "considerable difficulty in discovering just what it was" (p. 112). The sinister assurance to the disciples that the mystery of the kingdom of heaven is given to them alone, the people being judicially blinded (Mark 4:11–12), is recognized as part of the secrecy doctrine which Mark imposed on his material for purposes of his own (see above, pp. 13f) and is not accepted as genuinely from Jesus. The Sermon on the Mount is not given at all in this, the oldest of the four gospels, and it is substantially different in the two which do record it, namely Matthew and Luke, neither of which can be regarded as representing earlier and more authentic traditions than the other. According to Luke, Jesus said: "Blessed are ye poor . . . blessed are ye that hunger" (6:20–21). But Matthew has it that he said "Blessed are the poor in spirit; blessed are they that hunger and thirst after righteousness" (5:3 and 6). Obviously, he said the one or the other (if anything at all), not both, and no one can now decide which. Then we find that all the items in the Sermon are paralleled in Jewish literature, as what Renan called "the current money of the synagogue", independently of Christian tradition. Then again there is the silence of earlier Christian literature. Paul tells his Christian readers to "bless those that persecute you", bids them "judge not", and urges them to "pay taxes". Surely in such instances he might reasonably be expected to have invoked the authority of Jesus, *had he known* that Jesus had taught the very same doctrines. It seems much more likely that certain precepts concerning forgiveness and civil obedience were originally urged independently of Jesus, and only later put into his mouth, and thereby stamped with his supreme authority, than that he really gave such rulings and was not credited with having done so by Paul, nor indeed by other early Christian writers.

Much of Jesus's teaching, as given in the gospels, is set in a framework of controversy and this again may be quite artificial. Cook, who has studied what the gospels say about his relations with opponents, concludes: "Teachings of Jesus not originally uttered within the context of a controversy may have been supplied with such a setting to render his words more vivid and to provide a model for conduct and response by later Christians in their encounters with the Pharisees of their own day".[3] Some sayings betray in their very formulation that they were put into his mouth in order to cope with problems of the evangelists' days, not of his day. Thus at Matthew 18:17 he is represented as instructing the disciples to take complaints about fellow-believers "to the church" — this at a time when there was, for his followers, no church. And his direction that the disciples should go forth as sheep in the midst of wolves and suffer severe persecution (cf. above, p. 85) is surely the creation of a later age in which persecution had actually been suffered. The doom he pronounces on Galilean cities (Chorazin, Bethsaida, and Capernaum are specified: Matthew 11:20–23, paralleled in Luke 10:13–15) where he is represented as having done most of his missionary work was probably ascribed to him because, although he is said to have been acclaimed in Galilee, the author of the tradition on which the evangelists are here drawing knew that, at the time of writing, there was no Christian community in existence there. As for the doom spoken in Mark's thirteenth chapter, Boring notes that no serious scholar regards this great apocalyptic discourse as authentic in its entirety: it is Mark's adaptation of something composed by "someone in the church".[4] Furthermore, this insistent expectation of an imminent end to the present age conditions much of what is given as Jesus's ethical teaching and puts it in a questionable light, for "What", asks Bowden, "becomes of it, since he proved to be mistaken?" (p. 115). Many Christian moralists have now given up claiming that anything acceptable in his ethical teaching was an innovation. Even the late Professor Barclay (the Glasgow theologian and conservative populariser who was often to be heard on the BBC) admitted that pagans had adequate moral maxims, although he claimed that Christianity alone produced the power to carry them out. In fact, however, the history of Christianity shows that Christian practice has lagged behind the best in ethical theorizing as much as pagan practice ever did.

Appeal is still made to Jesus's parables as authentic teaching. Mark has few of them and lacks most of those included in Matthew and Luke. Half the parables in Luke are peculiar to it, and half of those in Matthew have no canonical parallel. John has no parables at all. Eta Linnemann's close study maintains that Matthew's parable of the wise and foolish virgins (25:1-13) first arose in the early Church, and that Luke's parable of the unjust judge (18:1-8) also does not go back to Jesus, but is "a word of the risen and exalted Lord, a word spoken by a prophet to the community of believers in the name and in the spirit of Jesus".[5] (It argues that, if an unjust judge obliges a widow when she pesters him to vindicate her against her adversary, how much more will God, at Jesus's second coming, vindicate his elect who cry out to him day and night.) At Luke 6:39-40 Jesus asks his followers, as a "parable": "Can the blind guide the blind? Shall they not both fall into a pit? The disciple is not above his master." This, says Fitzmyer (p. 630), "touches on a delicate matter that may reflect the situation in the early church in the time of Luke", and is "probably aimed at some form of false teaching in the early Christian community". Trocmé thinks that Luke found many of the parables he records in the preaching of the churches where he gathered his material. They served as "illustrations and examples for a message which emphasised piety, religious emotion and a morality based upon repentance and forgiveness".[6]

One reason why statements like these are now more frequently made by Christians than ever before is the necessity they now face of coming to some sort of *modus vivendi* with other kinds of believers in modern pluralistic societies. "A properly questioning attitude to one's own tradition and to the problems that it raises", says Bowden, "can be an important asset to dialogue aimed at a greater understanding of those of different faiths" (p. 119). That is, if Christians will only realise that they are keeping a glass house of their own, they will be less ready than of yore to throw stones. It is partly because of this necessity to live alongside others that he and others — he mentions John Hick in this connection — think it "now necessary that Christ should be replaced by God at the centre of the religious universe" (p. 173). Not that belief in God is without its "problems" (p. 182).

Bowden's God is an entity that satisfies emotional requirements, "a power at the heart of things who makes for good and who confronts, judges and absorbs what makes for bad" (p. 190). And his grounds for belief in this entity are emotional. "The proper response" to the question whether God exists is not demonstration, but "hope, trust and worship" (p. 194). He would, of course, like to have arguments as well, since "the religious quest has always been about something more than warmth, comfort and security" (p. 31).

Bowden deplores the way in which the churches have tried to keep down doubt with "dogmatic assertion and protest, coupled with a kind of 'not in the street or you will frighten the horses' mentality" (p. 17). But he can see what it is that continues to motivate such an attitude. "In the present climate . . . the institutional churches are fighting for their survival and cannot afford to have 'fifth columnists' in their midst" (pp. 146–47). Nevertheless, suppressing the real problems does not satisfy many of their members. Complaints from these about "the mental gymnastics they have to go through in order to be able to join in, say, the creeds, or some of the hymns and psalms, are legion" (p. 201). On the other hand, people do not want to be told in church that Christian beliefs have insecure foundations. They want positive and reassuring answers to the problems and difficulties. Audiences whom Bowden has addressed on the lines of his book have responded by saying: "That's all very well, but what about those of us who have to preach?" (p. 207). The problem is a real one, as neither he nor any one else can point to something positive that is left after all the demolition. "The question 'What remains of Jesus?' is not one that I can answer here: it is one that I am still working out, as everyone must work out who has been brought under his uncanny spell" (p. 206). This seems to betray that the task consists in trying to justify an emotional attitude. And Bowden is admitting that it is desperately hard. "The simple truth", he insists, "is that the posturing and postulating Emperors of religious certainty and moralizing absolutism have no clothes" (p. xii). "The fact of the matter is that security, certainty and finality are not to be found in this world—from any source, no matter how time-hallowed, no matter what divine authority it claims" (p. 184). Nor will he allow that truths of religion may constitute a separate species. "There cannot be one kind of religious truth and a completely different kind of secular truth" (p. xvi). And there are limits to the reinterpretation of traditional Christian doctrines which are unacceptable if taken literally; for Christian belief cannot consist in believing just anything (p. 67).

Now that such statements are coming from Christians who have taken the trouble to make a thorough study of the evidence, is it not time to look elsewhere than in the Scriptures for guidance in our living, and to stop basing our decisions and choices on ancient fantasies?

NOTES

Introduction

1. A. Schopenhauer, 'Über die Universitätsphilosophie', in *Werke*, edited by J. Frauenstädt, Leipzig: F. Brodhaus, 1877, vol. 5, p. 205.

2. On "Modernism", see the article so entitled in *The Oxford Dictionary of the Christian Church*, edited by F. L. Cross, London, etc.: Oxford University Press, 1957.

3. C. F. Evans, *Explorations in Theology*, vol. 2, London: SCM, 1977, p. 50.

4. H. Thyen, 'Baptism of Repentance for the Remission of Sins', in *The Future of Our Religious Past*, Festschrift for R. Bultmann's 80th birthday, edited by James M. Robinson, English translation (from the German edition of 1964), London: SCM, 1971, p. 140.

5. I have briefly stated the reasons for doubting whether there ever was a historical Jesus in my 'The Historicity of Jesus' in *Jesus in Myth and History*, edited by R. Joseph Hoffman and Gerald A. Larue, Buffalo: Prometheus, 1986, pp. 27–45. A fuller account is in my HEJ and DJE.

Chapter One: The Reliability of the Gospels

1. F. W. Beare, *The Earliest Records of Jesus*, Oxford: Blackwell, 1964, p. 13.

2. Thus E. E. Ellis says in his commentary on the gospel of Luke (in the series New Century Bible, London: Nelson, 1966, p. 63) that the title 'According to Luke' originated "where a Church had two gospels and desired to distinguish them, or, at the latest, when the gospels were a collected unit".

3. R. T. France, *The Evidence For Jesus*, London: Hodder and Stoughton, 1986, p. 122.

4. Concerning the exact relation to each other of the first three gospels (the so-called 'synoptic problem'), Fitzmyer notes: "Extrinsic, historically trustworthy data about the composition of these Gospels are totally lacking, and the complexity of the traditions embedded in them, the evangelists' editorial redaction of them, and their free composition bedevil all attempts to analyze objectively the intrinsic data with critical literary methods" (p. 63). On the relation of the fourth gospel to the other three, see part 2 of D. Moody Smith's *Johannine Christianity*, University of South Carolina Press, 1984; Edinburgh: T. and T. Clark, 1987.

5. C. K. Barrett, *The Gospel According to St. John*, 2nd edn., London: SPCK, 1978, p. 128.

6. On Luke's rewriting of Mark's chapter 13, see my HEJ, chapter 4.

7. H. C. Kee, *Christian Origins in Sociological Perspective*, London:

SCM, 1980, p. 191, n.13. I have discussed Robinson's attempts to "redate" the books of the New Testament in HEJ, particularly in chapter 4.

8. "The Pharisees, and all the Jews, except they wash their hands diligently, eat not, holding the tradition of the elders; and when they come from the marketplace, except they wash themselves, they eat not: and many other things there be, which they have received to hold, washing of cups, and pots and brazen vessels" (Mark 7:3-4). According to Jewish scholars, the Talmud shows that, up to ca. AD 70, the ritual washing of hands before meals was obligatory only on priests, not on laymen, who included Pharisees and scribes (Nineham, p. 193). After the fall of Jerusalem, when the Pharisees became dominant, they tried to make the laity conform to the Priestly laws of the Pentateuch in matters of ritual purity, arguing that Israel is a holy people, a nation of priests to be fenced off from the rest of humanity.

9. To go (as Jesus is said to in Mark 7:31) from the territory of Tyre by way of Sidon to the Sea of Galilee "is like travelling from Cornwall to London via Manchester" (H. Anderson, *The Gospel of Mark*, New Century Bible series, London: Oliphants, 1976, p. 192); or, as H. C. Kee puts it for his American readers, like stopping off in Boston on the way from New York to Philadelphia (*Jesus in History*, 2nd edn., New York, etc: Harcourt Brace, 1977, pp. 142-43). In his *Community of the New Age. Studies in Mark's Gospel*, London: SCM, 1977, pp. 102-03, Kee notes that Mark's "references to movements across the Sea of Galilee are impossible to trace sequentially. Mention of specific locations near the sea are either unknown sites . . . or are patently inaccurate". That place-names in Mark caused perplexity among early readers is shown by the wide range of variants in the textual tradition. Michael J. Cook holds that, "aside from the testimony of Christian tradition", we have no assurance that any of the authors of the first three gospels "had personal acquaintance with the Palestinian scene" (*Mark's Treatment of the Jewish Leaders*, Leiden: E. J. Brill, 1978, p. 2).

10. Concerning the 'us' in the opening verse of Luke's gospel, Fitzmyer notes that it "denotes the people who are now affected by salva-tion-history . . . It includes the 'many writers' as well as 'the original eyewitnesses and ministers of the word' from whom Luke distinguishes himself in verse 2. It undoubtedly includes also Luke and other third-generation Christians, which is the sense of 'us' in verse 2" (p. 293). On all this, see further Haenchen, pp. 1-4, and also Haenchen's essay on the 'we'-passages in Acts in his *Gott und Mensch* (a collection of essays, in-cluding ten on the New Testament), Tübingen: J. C. B. Mohr, 1965, pp. 262-63.

11. I have discussed the 'we' sections in HEJ, chapter 7. Each of them begins with a sea voyage with Paul and in part reads like a diary entry kept by one of the voyagers. Commentators have shown that by the first

century AD it was a convention of Greek literature to relate sea voyages in the first person, whether or not the author was an actual participant in the voyage, in order to make the description more vivid. (See the evidence in V. K. Robbins, 'By Land and Sea: The We-Passages and Ancient Sea Voyages', in *Perspectives on Luke-Acts*, edited by C. H. Talbert, Edinburgh: T. and T. Clark, 1978, p. 228.) Another possibility is that the relevant passages may have been present in some travel diary (not the author's own) from which he drew, and that he retained the 'we', and even inserted it into some passages where it is obviously inappropriate, in order to suggest that the narratives have an eyewitness basis. (On this, see Haenchen's essay, as cited in note 10 above).

12. P. Vielhauer, 'Franz Overbeck und die Neutestamentliche Wissenschaft', reprinted in Vielhauer's *Aufsätze zum Neuen Testament*, Munich: Chr. Kaiser, 1965, p. 246.

13. A. J. Mattill, Jr., 'The Value of Acts as a Source for the Study of Paul' in *Perspectives on Luke-Acts*, as cited in note 11 above, pp. 88, 98.

14. R. E. Brown, *The Community of the Beloved Disciple*, London: G. Chapman, 1979, p. 34n.

15. *Did Jesus Rise from the Dead? The Resurrection Debate Between Gary R. Habermas and Antony G. N. Flew*, edited by Terry L. Miethe, San Francisco etc: Harper and Row, 1987, p. 110. (This book includes comments on the debate by Wolfhart Pannenberg.)

16. F. F. Bruce, *The Acts of the Apostles*, 2nd edn., London: Tyndale Press, 1952, p. 147.

17. R. E. Brown, *op. cit.* in note 14 above, p. 7.

18. Cf. D. Moody Smith, *Johannine Christianity*, as cited in note 4 above, p. 177: "In John, Jesus' teaching has a very narrow focus . . . He teaches about himself and that teaching is distinctly Christian . . . . The content as well as the style of his teaching [in the Johannine discourses] can scarcely be historically authentic". Attempts to demonstrate the contrary "often end up appealing to well-worn hypotheses of a secret or esoteric teaching found only in John".

19. R. E. Brown, *The Gospel According to John* (Anchor Bible Series), 1966; quoted from the reprint of 1971, London: G. Chapman, vol. 1, pp. xxxiv–xxxvi, xciii, c; vol. 2, pp. 969–972.

20. Brown, *op. cit.* in note 14 above, pp. 31, 33–4, 34n.

21. On all this, see Barnabas Lindars's commentary on the gospel of John in the series New Century Bible, London: Oliphants, 1972.

22. *Op. cit.* in note 14 above, p. 7.

23. The apostle Peter (Cephas) with whom Paul quarrelled (Galatians 2:11ff) was a leader of the Christian community which existed at Jerusalem about AD 60, and Paul does not suggest that Peter had been a

companion of the historical Jesus, any more than Paul himself had been. The ascription of the epistle to this person is suspect because its dependence on Pauline ideas is not what one would expect from Paul's account of Peter. That Peter had known Jesus personally is, in my view, a legend introduced at the later stage of developing Christian tradition that is represented in the gospels. If he had in fact been Jesus's companion, he is even less likely to be the author of the epistle, which "shows no evidence at all of familiarity with the earthly Jesus, his life, his teaching and his death, but makes reference only in a general way to the 'sufferings' of Christ" (W. G. Kümmel, *Introduction to the New Testament*, English translation of the 17th revised edn., London: SCM, 1975, p. 424). Furthermore, a Galilean fisherman could not have written what Kümmel calls such "cultivated Greek", with "many rhetorical devices", and with all the Old Testament quotations and allusions deriving from the Greek version of these scriptures, not from the Hebrew original.

24. Francis Watson, 'The Social Function of Mark's Secrecy Theme', *Journal for the Study of the New Testament*, 24 (1985), pp. 52, 58.

25. See Huxley's 'The Value of Witness to the Miraculous' in his *Science and Christian Tradition*, London, 1897, pp. 184–86, and his comments on this essay in his 'Agnosticism and Christianity', p. 329 of the same volume.

26. H. C. Kee, *Community of the New Age*, as cited in note 9 above, p. 36.

27. Craig Blomberg, 'Concluding Reflections' to *Gospel Perspectives*, vol. 6, *The Miracles of Jesus*, edited by Blomberg and David Wenham, Sheffield: JSOT, 1986, p. 446.

28. David L. Edwards, *The Futures of Christianity*, London, etc: Hodder and Stoughton, 1987, p. 27.

29. E. R. Dodds, *Pagan and Christian in an Age of Anxiety*, Cambridge University Press, 1965, pp. 3–4, 124–26.

30. Francis Watson, *Paul, Judaism and the Gentiles*, Cambridge University Press, 1986, pp. 91–93.

31. David R. Catchpole, *The Trial of Jesus. A Study in the Gospels and Jewish Historiography from 1770 to the Present Day*, Leiden: E. J. Brill, 1971, pp. 69–70. The seven Jewish scholars are: E. Joseph, S. Ben-Chorin, Jules Isaac, A. I. Polack, S. Sandmel, H. Martel, and H. J. Schoeps.

32. "Die Stelle ist *als ganze* nachträglich eingesetzt" (Hans Conzelmann, art. 'Jesus Christus', in *Religion in Geschichte und Gegenwart*, 3rd edn., edited by K. Galling, Tübingen: J. C. B. Mohr, 1959, vol. 3, p. 622.

33. Cf. R. J. Hoffmann, *Jesus Outside the Gospels*, Buffalo: Prometheus, 1984, p. 54.

34. L. Herrmann, *Chrestos. Témoignages païens et juifs sur le chris-tianisme du premier siècle*, Brussels: Latomus, 1970, p. 97.

35. Cf. Herrmann (as cited in previous note, p. 95): "Donc tout le passage sur le Christ est interpolé, puisque l'exécution du 'faiseur de miracles' n'a amené aucun 'trouble', ayant été, selon les évangiles eux-mêmes, voulue d'un common accord par le haut clergé et Hérode An-tipas, réclamée par la population, et acceptée par Ponce Pilate à l'occa-sion d'une fête religieuse".

36. Habermas, *op. cit.* in note 15 above, p. 43.

37. Ulrich Wilckens, *Resurrection. Biblical Testimony to the Resurrec-tion. An Historical Examination and Explanation*, translated by A. M. Steward, Edinburgh: St. Andrew's Press, 1977, p. 1.

38. Jesus's subordinate status to God is not denied by the Pauline passages quoted on pp. 6f above, one of which says that, before his in-carnation, he was "in the form of God". This is not equivalent to 'being God', any more than his "taking the form of a servant" (i.e. slave), name-ly human form, at his incarnation implies that he was a slave during his earthly life (cf. F. W. Beare, *A Commentary on the Epistle to the Philip-pians*, 3rd edn., London: A. and C. Black, 1973, pp. 78–79).

39. F. Jacoby, *Fragmente der griechischen Historiker*, vol. 2 B (Leiden: E. J. Brill, 1962), p. 1156, and the companion volume of commentary (with the same date and place of publication), pp. 835–36.

40. H. Conzelmann, loc. cit., in note 32 above. France allows (p. 24) that "we do not know whether Thallus actually mentioned Jesus' crucifix-ion, or whether this was Africanus' interpretation of a period of darkness which Thallus had not specifically linked with Jesus. In addition, since the date of Thallus' writing is unknown, there can be no certainty that, if he *did* refer to Jesus explicitly, this reference may not have been drawn from Christian sources".

Chapter Two: The Resurrection

1. Karl Barth, *The Doctrine of Reconciliation*, vol. 4, part 1 of *Church Dogmatics*, edited by G. W. Bromiley and T. F. Torrance, Edin-burgh: T. and T. Clark, 1956, p. 340.

2. P. W. Schmiedel, art. 'Resurrection and Ascension Narratives'. *En-cyclopaedia Biblica*, ed. T. K. Cheyne, London: A. and C. Black, 1903, paragraphs 8 and 10. John Wenham quotes Schmiedel and also more re-cent eminent theologians to the same effect, and for the conservative side is able to quote only I. H. Marshall as having said in 1977 that the Resur-rection narratives are not necessarily irreconcilable, but that "so far nobody has produced a convincing hypothesis". Wenham's own attempt at harmonization evades the real problems and premises that the gospel writers were "providentially equipped by God to give the church a sound

account" of the Resurrection events. For him, "one thing is certain: Jesus was a concrete, complex and fascinating figure of history, and any method of study which fails to reveal him as such is working on the wrong lines" (*Easter Enigma*, Exeter: Paternoster Press, 1984, pp. 10, 128).

3. P. Badham, *Christian Beliefs About Life after Death*, London: SPCK, 1978, p. 19.

4. D. F. Strauss, *Der alte und der neue Glaube*, Leipzig: G. Hirzel, 1872, p. 72.

5. After the Galilean ministry, "when the days were well-nigh come that he should be received up, he steadfastly set his face to go to Jerusalem" (Luke 9:51, with no equivalent in the other gospels). In the first 15 chapters of Acts, every area missionized is subordinated to Jerusalem in one way or other, and one reason why the author thus exaggerates the city's authority is his desire to show that Christianity had not lightly or readily broken away from its Jewish foundation. For details, see E. Haenchen, *The Acts of the Apostles*, English translation, Oxford: Blackwell, 1971, pp. 100ff, 461. (This book is a work of outstanding scholarship. The 7th, posthumous edition of the German original appeared in 1977, two years after the author's death.)

6. C. H. Dodd, 'The Appearances of the Risen Christ. An Essay in Form-Criticism of the Gospels', in *More New Testament Studies*, Manchester: University Press, 1968, pp. 118, 127.

7. C. H. Dodd, *The Founder of Christianity*, London: Collins, 1971, p. 167.

8. *The Nature of Christian Belief* (A Statement and Exposition by the House of Bishops of the General Synod of the Church of England), London: Church House, 1986, p. 21.

9. Peter Carnley, *The Structure of Resurrection Belief*, Oxford: Clarendon Press, 1987, p. 232. Carnley is Anglican Bishop of Perth, W. Australia.

10. H. Conzelmann, art. 'Auferstehung Christi I' in *Religion in Geschichte und Gegenwart*, 3rd edn., edited by K. Galling, Tübingen: J. C. B. Mohr, vol. 1, p. 699.

11. Lampe notes (pp. 50–51) that Luke's references to the physical reality of the risen Jesus "reflect controversies about the Easter appearances. It was evidently being objected that the appearances may have been hallucinations, or that what the disciples saw was merely a ghost. In answer to this it was being asserted that the presence of the risen Lord was corporeal, tangible and possessed of flesh and bones: this despite the obvious inconsistency with the Pauline tradition and with elements incorporated in Luke's own narrative, namely the sudden appearance within a room".

12. This is rightly stressed by U. Wilckens, 'The Tradition-History of

the Resurrection of Jesus', in *The Significance of the Message of the Resurrection Faith in Jesus Christ*, ed. C. F. D. Moule, London: SCM, 1968, p. 69.

13. Brown notes that "Paul recalls the tradition of the appearances of Jesus to show that, even if he came out of time and last of all, he did see the risen Jesus, just as did the other well-known apostles" (*The Gospel According to John*: Anchor Bible Series, 1966; quoted from the reprint of 1971, London: G. Chapman, vol. 2, p. 971.

14. On the meaning of the term 'apostle', see W. Schneemelcher, 'Apostle and Apostolic', in E. Hennecke, *New Testament Apocrypha*, ed. Schneemelcher, English translation edited by R. McL. Wilson, London: Lutterworth Press, 1965, vol. 2, pp. 25-31.

15. See G. N. M. Tyrell, *Apparitions*, revised edn., London: Duckworth, 1953, pp. 8, 109, 114.

16. A. J. P. Taylor, *English History 1914-1945*, Harmondsworth: Penguin Books, 1970, p. 34.

17. D. Rössler, art. 'Marienerscheinungen' in *op. cit.* in note 10 above, vol. 4, p. 761.

18. Colin Jeffery and Paul Dunn, *Fatima—A Story of Hope*, Woking, Surrey: Gresham Press, n.d., pp. 39-40.

19. Eduard Schweizer, *The Good News According to Mark*, English translation, London: SPCK, 1971, p. 364.

20. See H. Conzelmann's discussion 'On the Analysis of the Confessional Formula in 1 Corinthians 15:3-5', *Interpretation*, 20 (1966), pp. 15-25.

21. On the twelve see my DJE, chapter 5, where I refer to the arguments of W. Schmithals and G. Klein which, as Beare has noted (p. 240), are not to be lightly dismissed. Earlier theologians who denied (or at least doubted) that Jesus selected twelve companions include J. Wellhausen (*Einleitung in die drei ersten Evangelien*, Berlin: G. Reimer, 1905, p. 112) and R. Bultmann (*Theologie des Neuen Testaments*, 6th edn., Tübingen: J. C. B. Mohr, 1968, p. 40).

22. Schneemelcher, *art. cit.* in note 14 above, p. 28; P. Vielhauer, 'Gottesreich und Menschensohn', in *Aufsätze zum Neuen Testament*, Munich: Chr. Kaiser, 1965.

23. Isaiah (6:1ff) was called to God's service by a vision of the Lord. Initiation into the pagan mystery religions involved "a personal meeting with the God", and Isis afforded "comfort through visions" (R. E. Witt, *Isis in the Graeco-Roman World*, London: Thames & Hudson, 1971, pp. 153, 189).

24. J. Hick, *Death and Eternal Life*, London: Macmillan, 1985, pp. 171, 175-77.

25. W. Pannenberg, in *Did Jesus Rise From the Dead? The Resurrec-*

tion Debate, edited by Terry L. Miethe, San Francisco: Harper and Row, 1987, p. 134.

26. P. W. Schmiedel, *art. cit.* in note 2 above, paragraph 24e.

27. M. Goguel, *La foi de la résurrection de Jésus dans le christianisme primitif*, Paris, 1933, pp. 169ff; quoted in English translation by Fuller, p. 26.

28. J. L. Houlden, *Connections. The Integration of Theology and Faith*, London: SCM, 1986, p. 152; cf. Fuller, p. 18: "The apocalyptic hope provides the cultural and linguistic context in which the resurrection of Christ could be proclaimed in the kerygma of the early Christian community".

29. John Bowden, *Jesus. The Unanswered Questions*, London: SCM, 1988, p. 143.

30. J. A. T. Robinson, *The Human Face of God*, London: SCM, 1973, pp. 130–31.

31. G. Shaw, *The Cost of Authority, Manipulation and Freedom in the New Testament*, London: SCM, 1983, p. 167.

Epilogue to Chapter 2

1. R. Bultmann, 'New Testament and Mythology', in *Kerygma and Myth*, edited by H. W. Bartsch, two volumes published as one, London: SPCK, 1972, pp. 19, 39–40, 42.

2. On form criticism and redaction criticism, see above, p. 13.

3. O. Pfleiderer, *The Early Christian Conception of Christ*, London: Williams and Norgate, 1905, pp. 157–58.

4. A. J. Beagley, *The 'Sitz im Leben' of the Apocalpyse with Particular Reference to the Role of the Church's Enemies*, Berlin and New York: De Gruyter, 1987, p. 24; W. Bousset, *Die Religion des Judentums im späthellenistischen Zeitalter*, 4th revised edition, edited by H. Gressmann, Tübingen, 1936, p. 374.

Chapter Three: The Virgin Birth

1. Ernst Haenchen, *Das Johannesevangelium*, Tübingen: J. C. B. Mohr, 1980, p. 128. (An English translation was published by Fortress Press, Philadelphia, in two volumes in 1984. It is not always accurate, and so I give my references to the German original.)

2. For details see JEC, pp. 170–71 and DJE, pp. 92 and 93 n.9. The silence of other early non-canonical writers about the virgin birth cannot be due to chance, for some of them "develop quite detailed speculations about the Lord's origin and earthly form" (Von Campenhausen, p. 19). Even after Ignatius, Justin Martyr, writing about AD 150, still knows of

Christians who regard Jesus as "made man of man" (*Dialogue with Trypho*, 48:2). It is thus obvious that, even then, there was "in the camp of the orthodox . . . still a good deal of latitude with regard to the doctrine of Christ's incarnation" (Von Campenhausen, p. 21).

3. A. E. Harvey, *Jesus and the Constraints of History*, London: Duckworth, 1982, p. 11.

4. Cf. Brown, p. 36: "In Matthew there is no hint of a *coming* to Bethelehem, for Joseph and Mary are in a house at Bethelehem where seemingly Jesus was born (2:11). The only journey that Matthew has to explain is why the family went to Nazareth when they came from Egypt instead of returning to their native Bethlehem (2:22–23)."

5. A. R. S. Kennedy, *Leviticus and Numbers* (The Century Bible), Edinburgh: T. C. & E. C. Jack, n.d., p. 331.

6. C. S. Mann, 'The Historicity of the Birth Narratives', in *Historicity and Chronology in the New Testament* (no. 6 in the series *Theological Collections*, London: SPCK, 1965), p. 48. Mann adds: "Mithridates, Alexander Severus—to name but two—were reported to have had the day of birth celebrated by the advent of a new star."

7. For justification of this rendering of the Greek of Luke 2:2, see Creed, p. 32.

8. I discussed attempts to re-date Quirinius's legateship in JEC, pp. 36–37.

9. The Roman Historian R. Syme, in an article of 1973, quoted by Fitzmyer, pp. 404–05.

10. Brown gives a very full discussion of the evidence as to whether Mary or Elisabeth is the one who speaks the Magnificat. He is quite undogmatic on the matter, but thinks that there are better arguments for its ascription to Mary than to Elisabeth (pp. 334–36).

11. Howard C. Kee, *Miracle in the Early Christian Church*, New Haven and London: Yale University Press, 1983, p. 186n.

12. Morna D. Hooker, 'Beyond the Things that are Written? St. Paul's Use of Scripture', *New Testament Studies*, 27 (1981), p. 295.

13. The only problem in this section of the genealogies is that, instead of Matthew's "Ram" (1:3, taken from the list in 1 Chronicles 2:9), Luke (3:33) has "Arni", and many manuscripts have, additionally, "Admin". Both are otherwise unknown. There is considerable manuscript variation in respect of both names, probably because copyists could not identify these two persons with any in the Old Testament.

14. On all this see Brown, pp. 70, 82–83, and Burger, pp. 94–97.

15. M. D. Johnson, *The Purpose of the Biblical Genealogies*, Cambridge University Press, 1969, p. 164.

16. Ibid., pp. 178, 209.

17. G. Murray, Introduction to his translation of Euripides's *Ion*, London: Allen and Unwin, 1954, p. 8.

18. J. M. Robertson, *Christianity and Mythology*, 2nd edn., London: Watts, 1910, p. 292.

19. Plutarch, *Vit. Numa* 4, quoted by M. S. Enslin, 'The Christian Stories of the Nativity', *Journal of Biblical Literature*, 59 (1940), p. 325.

20. Enslin, as cited in the previous note; and A. E. Abbott, art. 'Gospels', para. 21, in *Encyclopaedia Biblica*, ed. T. K. Cheyne, London: A. & C. Black, 1903.

21. E. Hennecke, *New Testament Apocrypha*, edited by W. Schneemelcher, English translation, London: SCM, 1973, vol. 1, pp. 190–93.

22. Thomas Boslooper, *The Virgin Birth*, London: SCM, 1962, pp. 185, 234–36.

23. O. Cullmann's 'The Origins of Christmas', in Cullmann's *The Early Church*, ed. A. J. B. Higgins, London: SCM, 1956, p. 29. On the integrating force of Christianity in the Empire, see my edition of *J. M. Robertson: Liberal, Rationalist, and Scholar*, London: Pemberton, 1987, pp. 173–75.

24. Art. 'Nativity', para. 4 (by H. Usener), in *Encyclopaedia Biblica*, as cited in note 20 above.

25. M. S. Enslin, as cited in note 19 above, p. 324.

26. See Haenchen's analysis of the prologue to the fourth gospel in *op. cit.* in note 1 above.

27. James P. Mackey, *Modern Theology*, Oxford University Press, 1987, pp. 98–99.

28. Bruce M. Metzger, *The Canon of the New Testament. Its Origin, Development and Significance*, Oxford: Clarendon Press, 1987, pp. 166–67.

29. For details Metzger refers the reader to E. J. Goodspeed's account, *Strange New Gospels*, Chicago: University of Chicago Press, 1931.

Chapter Four: The Prelude to the Public Ministry

1. G. Stanton, 'Form Criticism Revisited', in *What About the New Testament?*, Evans Festschrift, ed. Morna Hooker, SCM, 1975, p. 14. Morna Hooker entitles the second chapter of her book on Mark (cf. p. viii above) 'Like Pearls on a String', and says (p. 19): "The tradition came to Mark piecemeal; each story had been told and retold in the Church community for its own sake, and had no kind of date label attached to it", so that Mark's ordering of events cannot be treated as a reliable chronological outline of Jesus's ministry. "Mark's retelling of the story

certainly does not suggest that he is interested in the chronology of particular incidents: with rare and significant exceptions, he is content to introduce events with a vague 'in those days' or a simple 'and'."

2. On 'Q', see Howard C. Bigg, 'The Present State of the Q Hypothesis', *Vox Evangelica*, 18 (1988), pp. 63–73.

3. Howard C. Kee, *Jesus in History*, 2nd edn., New York, etc: Harcourt Brace, 1977, p. 83.

4. J. A. Fitzmyer, 'The Oxyrhyncus *Logoi* of Jesus and the Coptic Gospel According to Thomas', *Theological Studies*, 20 (1959), p. 508. The Coptic ms dates from about 400 AD, but the date of composition is of course much earlier.

5. Josephus, *The Antiquities of the Jews*, 18:5,2 (=paragraph 116–19), translated by H. St. John Thackeray in the Loeb Classical Library edition.

6. Quoted by Hugh Anderson, *The Gospel of Mark* (in the New Century Bible series), London: Oliphants, 1976, p. 69. On Qumran see Michael A. Knibb, *The Qumran Community*, Cambridge University Press, 1987.

7. H. Thyen, 'Baptism of Repentance for Remission of Sins', in *The Future of our Religious Past*, Festschrift for Bultmann's 80th birthday, translated from the German of 1964, London: SCM, 1971, p. 150.

8. Details in DJE, pp. 102–03, and above, p. 13ff.

9. For details, see HEJ, p. 126; DJE, pp. 90–91.

10. See Vielhauer's article, 'Johannes der Täufer', in *Religion in Geschichte und Gegenwart*, 3rd edn., edited by K. Galling, Tübingen: J. C. B. Mohr, 1959, vol. 3, p. 807.

11. G. Bornkamm, *Jesus von Nazareth*, 3rd edn., Stuttgart: Kohlhammer, 1959, p. 49. For a reasoned defence of the view that John pointed to Jesus as the one who was to come, see J. C. O'Neill, *Messiah*, Cambridge: Cochrane Press, 1980, chapter 1.

12. Justin, *Dialogue with Trypho*, where the orthodox Jewish speaker says: "Christ, if he is come, and is anywhere, is unknown, nor doth he know himself, nor can he be indued with any power till Elias shall come and anoint him and make him manifest to all men" (chapter 8). Cf. chapter 49: "We all expect a Christ to be born that will be a man of man, and that Elias shall anoint him when he is come".

13. Martin S. Enslin, 'John and Jesus', in *Zeitschrift für Neutestamentliche Wissenschaft*, 66 (1975), pp. 5, 9.

14. Vincent Taylor, *The Gospel According to St. Mark*, 2nd edn., London: Macmillan, 1966, p. 163.

15. Ulrich Mauser, *Christ in the Wilderness*, London: SCM, 1963, pp. 100–01.

16. Peter Pokorny, 'The Temptation Stories and their Intention', *New Testament Studies*, 20 (1974), pp. 119, 122.

17. E. Best, *The Temptation and the Passion: the Markan Soteriology*, Cambridge: Cambridge University Press, 1965, p. 15.

18. Pokorny, as cited in note 16 above, pp. 116, 125.

19. On this, see Tim Schramm, *Der Markus-Stoff bei Lukas*, Cambridge: Cambridge University Press, 1971, p. 36.

20. Cf. R. Bultmann, *Die Geschichte der synoptischen Tradition*, 7th edn., Göttingen: Vandenhoeck and Ruprecht, 1970, pp. 272–73.

21. Quoted in J. M. Robertson's *Christianity and Mythology*, 2nd edn., London: Watts, 1910, p. 318.

22. A. J. Toynbee, *A Study of History*, vol. 6, London: Oxford University Press, 1939, pp. 508–518.

23. R. Graves, *The Greek Myths* (1955), London: Cassell, 1958, p. 21.

24. Arnold Meyer, 'Die evangelischen Berichte über die Versuchung Christi', in *Festgabe für Hugo Blümner*, Zürich: Berichthaus, 1914, p. 459.

25. D. F. Strauss: "If Israel is the *Filius dei collectivus*, Jesus appears as the antitype of the nation" (Quoted by E. Fascher, *Jesus und der Satan*, Halle (Saale): Max Niemeyer, 1949, p. 10).

26. Cf. Terence L. Donaldson, *Jesus on the Mountain*, Sheffield: JSOT Press, 1985, p. 92.

27. Bultmann, in the first edn. of his *Geschichte der synoptischen Tradition*, 1921, pp. 151–52; quoted by Fascher, as cited in note 25 above, p. 19.

28. Donaldson, as cited in note 26 above, p. 91.

29. C. H. Dodd, *The Founder of Christianity*, London: Collins, 1971, p. 123.

30. S. M. Gilmour, art. 'Jesus Christ', para. 8 in *Dictionary of the Bible*, 2nd edn., revised by F. C. Grant and H. H. Rowley, Edinburgh: T. and T. Clark, 1963.

31. Cf. G. H. P. Thompson, 'Called—Proved—Obedient. A Study in the Baptism and Temptation Narratives of Matthew and Luke', *Journal of Theological Studies*, 11 (1960), p. 6.

32. J. S. Kloppenberg, 'Symbolic Eschatology and the Apocalypticism of Q', *Harvard Theological Review*, 80 (1987), p. 298.

33. A literal rendering of the Greek of Hebrews 2:18 gives "being tempted in as much as he suffered".

34. Gilmour, as cited in note 30 above.

35. M. E. Marty, 'Hell Disappeared. No One Noticed', *Harvard Theological Review*, 78 (1985), p. 381.

36. G. B. Caird, *Saint Luke* (The Pelican New Testament Commentaries), Harmondsworth, 1963, p. 79.

Chapter Five: The Passion

1. E. Hoskyns and N. Davey, *The Riddle of the New Testament*, London: Faber and Faber, 1958, p. 57.

2. H. C. Kee, *Jesus in History*, 2nd edn., New York, etc.: Harcourt Brace, 1977, p. 141.

3. N. Turner, art. 'Hosanna' in *Dictionary of the Bible*, 2nd edn., revised by F. C. Grant and H. H. Rowley, Edinburgh: T. and T. Clark, 1963.

4. Paul W. Walaskay, *'And So We Came to Rome': The Political Perspective of St. Luke*, Cambridge: Cambridge University Press, 1983, p. 58.

5. Robert Maddox, *The Purpose of Luke-Acts*, Göttingen: Vandenhoeck and Ruprecht, 1982, pp. 96–97.

6. See my DJE, pp. 161, 163–5, 176 n.1.

7. J. K. Elliott, 'The Anointing of Jesus', *The Expository Times*, 85 (1974), pp. 106–07.

8. John Ziesler, 'Luke and the Pharisees', *New Testament Studies*, 25 (1979), p. 150.

9. Jack T. Sanders, *The Jews in Luke-Acts*, London: SCM, 1987, chapter 4 and p. 176.

10. The beggar in Jesus's parable of Lazarus and Dives (Luke 16:19–31) is not the Lazarus who is raised in the fourth gospel. Yet each of these two stories may have been derived from related streams of tradition: for the parable concludes with the statement that those who have Moses and the prophets and disregard them will not be convinced if someone should rise from the dead; and in John the actual raising of Lazarus does not convince some Jews, who report it to the Pharisees, who in turn plot against Jesus's life.

11. Elliott, art. cit. in note 7 above, p. 107.

12. Eta Linnemann, *Studien zur Passionsgeschichte*, Göttingen: Vandenhoeck and Ruprecht, 1970, pp. 46ff.

13. D. Moody Smith, *Johannine Christianity*, Edinburgh: T. and T. Clark, 1987 (University of South Carolina Press, 1984), p. 179.

14. Hugh Anderson, *The Gospel of Mark*, New Century Bible series, London: Oliphants, 1976, p. 315.

15. Barnabas Lindars, *New Testament Apologetic*, London: SCM, 1961, pp. 129–130.

16. Rudolf Bultmann, *Die Geschichte der Synoptischen Tradition*, 8th edn., Göttingen: Vandenhoeck and Ruprecht, 1970, pp. 287–88. Günter

Klein agrees with Bultmann here. See Klein's 'Die Verleugnung des Petrus', in his *Rekonstruktion und Interpretation*, Munich: Chr. Kaiser, 1969, p. 65.

17. See F. W. Beare, *The Earliest Records of Jesus*, Oxford: Blackwell, 1964, p. 228.

18. This is pointed out by Klein *art. cit.* in note 16 above, pp. 54, 59.

19. Beare, *op. cit.* in note 17 above, p. 233. Full details in David R. Catchpole, *The Trial of Jesus. A Study in the Gospels and Jewish Historiography from 1770 to the Present Day*, Leiden: E. J. Brill, 1971.

20. Cf. Bultmann, *op. cit.* in note 16 above, p. 293.

21. Paul Winter, *On the Trial of Jesus*, Berlin: De Gruyter, 1961, pp. 100–01.

22. C. F. Evans, 'The Passion of Christ', Part 1 of Evans's *Explorations in Theology*, vol. 2, London: SCM, 1977, p. 34. Further references to Evans in this chapter will be page references to this volume, not to his book on Resurrection listed on p. viii above.

23. C. K. Barrett, *The Gospel According to St. John*, 2nd edn., London: SPCK, 1978, pp. 532–33.

24. E. Haenchen, *Das Johannesvangelium*, posthumous volume edited by U. Busse, Tübingen: J. C. B. Mohr, 1980, p. 544.

25. C. H. Dodd, *Historical Tradition in the Fourth Gospel*, Cambridge: Cambridge University Press, 1963, p. 96.

26. Cf. E. Haenchen, 'Jesus vor Pilatus', in Haenchen's *Gott und Mensch*, Tübingen: J. C. B. Mohr, 1965, p. 149. Cf. also D. Moody Smith, as cited in note 13 above, p. 202: "By commonly referring to Jesus' interlocutors as 'the Jews', John creates the impression that Jesus does not belong, or no longer belongs, to the Jewish community or world. By the same token, neither do the disciples (John 9:28), nor, indeed does the evangelist himself. Not only John, but Jesus also, speaks from the perspective of a community separate and distinct from Judaism. Jesus, as well as the evangelist, talks like a Christian."

27. E. Haenchen, 'Der Vater, der mich gesandt hat', in *Gott und Mensch*, as cited in previous note, p. 74.

28. Cf. E. Haenchen, 'Historie und Geschichte in den Johanneischen Passionsberichten', in Haenchen's *Die Bibel und Wir*, Tübingen: J. C. B. Mohr, 1968, p. 201.

29. *Ibid.*, p. 203.

30. H. G. Wood, *Did Christ Really Live?*, London: SCM, 1938, pp. 118, 122.

31. Vincent Taylor, *The Gospel According to St. Mark*, 2nd edn., 1966, London: MacMillan, p. 594. Taylor does not accept this view

himself, but names scholars who do. It is accepted by Winter, pp. 109–110.

32. Martin Werner, *The Formation of Christian Dogma*, English translation by S. G. F. Brandon, London: A. and C. Black, 1957, p. 33.

33. Fitzmyer agrees (in the second volume of his commentary on Luke, as cited on p. viii above, p. 1496) that the "they" who "led Jesus away" (Luke 23:26) cannot mean Romans, but "has to refer to those who 'asked for' the release of Barabbas and to whom Pilate handed over Jesus according to 'their will' (verse 25). This must include 'the chief priests, the leaders and the people' of verse 13".

34. Sanders, *op. cit.* in note 9 above, pp. 9, 15. Sanders also argues (p. 11) that the soldiers who mock Jesus during his actual crucifixion (Luke 23:36) are Jewish.

35. G. W. H. Lampe, 'A.D. 70 in Christian Reflection', in *Jesus and the Politics of his Day*, ed. E. Bammel and C. F. D. Moule, Cambridge: Cambridge University Press, 1984, p. 164.

Chapter Six

1. The following account follows the very lucid exposition given in volume 2, pp. 492ff of the recently revised English edition of Schürer's *History* (cf. p. viii above).

2. James Barr, art. 'Messiah' in *Dictionary of the Bible*, 2nd edn., revised by F. C. Grant and H. H. Rowley, Edinburgh: T. and T. Clark, 1963.

3. On Antiochus IV and the Jews, see D. S. Russell, *The Jews from Alexander to Herod*, London: Oxford University Press, chapter 4.

4. Norman Porteous, *Daniel*, 2nd revised edn., London: SCM, 1979, p. 20.

5. Details in Schürer, III, p. 248.

6. John Bright, *History of Israel*, London: SCM, 1962, p. 439, quoted by Paul Badham, *Christian Beliefs About Life After Death*, London: SPCK, pp. 11–12.

7. Details in R. M. Grant's long article 'Prophecy, Prophets' in *Dictionary of the Bible*, as cited in note 2 above. In 1 Maccabees 4:46, 9:27 and 14:41 it is stated that prophets had "ceased to appear". The hope remained that "God would yet raise up a prophet like Moses (cf. Deuteronomy 18:15) or send his prophet Elijah (cf. Malachi 4:5) before the end would come" (D. S. Russell, *The Old Testament Pseudepigrapha*, London: SCM, 1987, p. 9).

8. H. H. Rowley, *Darius the Mede and the Four World Empires in the Book of Daniel*, Cardiff: University of Wales Press, 1935, p. 5.

9. R. K. Harrison, *Introduction to the Old Testament*, Grand Rapids: Erdmans, 1969; London: Tyndale Press, 1970, pp. 1120, 1130-31.

10. Ronald S. Wallace, *The Message of Daniel* (in the series *The Bible Speaks Today*), Leicester (England) and Downers Grove (Illinois): Inter-Varsity Press, 1979, pp. 19, 22, 109, 166, 192 (This book was originally published under the title *The Lord is King*).

11. R. H. Charles, *The Book of Daniel*, Edinburgh and London: T. C. and E. C. Jack, n.d., p. xliv.

12. Cf. Schürer, II, p. 498.

13. E. W. Heaton's 'Torch' Commentary on Daniel, London: SCM, 1956, quoted for its "real wisdom" by Porteous, as cited in note 4 above, p. 171.

14. Hal Lindsey, *The Late Great Planet Earth*, Grand Rapids: Zondervan, 1970. Details in James Barr's excellent survey *Fundamentalism*, 2nd edn., London: SCM, 1981, pp. 206-07, 356.

15. See Schürer, III, p. 254-56 and Russell, as cited in note 7 above, p. 28.

16. Schürer, II, p. 503, 505.

17. *Ibid.*, p. 522. The appropriate reference is Micah 5:2 rather than 5:1.

18. Cf. D. R. Catchpole, 'The Poor on Earth and the Son of Man in Heaven. A Re-Appraisal of Matthew 25:31-46', *Bulletin of the John Rylands Library*, 61 (1979), p. 379: "In this instance we . . . appear to be dealing with a *scheme* which is much older than both 1 Enoch and Matthew".

19. Russell, *op. cit.* in note 7 above, pp. 110-11.

20. D. E. Lohse, 'Wie Christlich ist die Offenbarung des Johannes?', *New Testament Studies*, 34 (1988), p. 322.

21. G. B. Caird, *A Commentary on the Revelation of St. John the Divine*, London: A. and C. Black, 1966, p. 2.

22. John Sweet, *Revelation*, London: SCM, 1979, pp. 49-50.

23. G. B. Beasley-Murray, *The Book of Revelation* (in the series *New Century Bible*), London: Oliphants, 1974, p. 47.

24. W. H. C. Frend, *Martyrdom and Persecution in the Early Church*, Oxford: Blackwell, 1965, p. 220.

25. See Eduard Lohse, *Die Offenbarung des Johannes* (vol. 11 of the series *Das neue Testament Deutsch*), Göttingen: Vandenhoeck and Ruprecht, 1971, pp. 20, 24, 28. Page references to Lohse in my text will be to this commentary, not to his more recent article cited in note 20 above.

26. Lohse, as cited in previous note, p. 36; cf. p. 88, where he points out that, according to Paul, Christ has already, by his death, "delivered us out of this present evil world" (Galatians 1:4). "If any man is in Christ, he is a new creature: the old things are passed away" (2 Corinthians 5:17).

27. Lohse, art. cit. in note 20 above, p. 335.

28. In Revelation the title "the Lord" mainly follows Old Testament usage and so designates God, although there are a few passages where it refers to Jesus. (Details in Lohse, as cited in note 25 above, pp. 44–45).

29. Richard Bauckham, 'The Worship of Jesus in Apocalyptic Christianity', New Testament Studies, 27 (1981), pp. 330–31.

30. Elisabeth Schüssler Fiorenza, 'The Quest for the Johannine School. The Apocalypse and the Fourth Gospel', New Testament Studies, 23 (1977), p. 403, endorsing the verdict of M. Kiddle, The Revelation of John, London: Hodder and Stoughton, 1940, p. xxxiii.

31. D. Moody Smith, Johannine Christianity, Edinburgh: T. and T. Clark, 1987 (University of South Carolina Press, 1984), p. 17.

32. H. H. Rowley, art. 'Revelation, book of', in Dictionary of The Bible, as cited in note 2 above.

33. H. Gunkel, Schöpfung und Chaos, Göttingen, 1895, p. 386.

34. John M. Court, (Myth and History in the Book of Revelation, London: SPCK, 1979, p. 17) mentions the Apollo legend and other pagan parallels, and quotes a commentator of 1914 who went so far as to say that "the visions of Revelation were not the genuine results of spiritual experience, but were merely a literary elaboration of pagan data".

35. A. Dupont-Sommer, The Essene Writings from Qumran, English translation by G. Vermes, Oxford: Blackwell, 1961, p. 208 and notes.

36. Walter Bauer, Orthodoxy and Heresy in Earliest Christianity, English translation (from the German original of 1934), London: SCM, 1972 (Fortress Press 1971), pp. 77–78.

37. Jack T. Sanders, Ethics in the New Testament, London: SCM, 1975, p. 115.

38. Sanders finds that "the ethical positions of the New Testament are the children of their own times and places, alien and foreign to this day and age. Amidst the ethical dilemmas which confront us, we are now at least relieved of the need or temptation to begin with Jesus, or the early church, or the New Testament, if we wish to develop coherent ethical positions" (vol. cit. in previous note, p. 130). A good discussion of Christian ethics in the Bible and in history, is given (from a non-theological standpoint) by Margaret Knight in her Honest to Man: Christian Ethics Re-Examined, London: Elek/Pemberton, 1974. In my introduction to the

present volume I mention the 1988 symposium published by Prometheus, where the contributors write from varying standpoints.

39. David Hill, 'Prophecies and Prophets in the Revelation of St. John', *New Testament Studies*, 18 (1972), p. 410.

Conclusion

1. John Bowden, 'The New Testament Critic and his Audience', in *What About the New Testament?* (Essays in honour of C. Evans), edited by Morna Hooker and C. Hickling, London: SCM, 1975, pp. 2-3, 7.

2. S. G. Wilson, 'From Jesus to Paul: The Contours and Consequences of a Debate', in *From Jesus to Paul* (Studies in Honour of F. W. Beare), edited by P. Richardson and J. C. Hurd, Waterloo (Ontario): W. Laurier University Press, 1984, p. 3.

3. Michael J. Cook, *Mark's Treatment of the Jewish Leaders* (Supplements to *Novum Testamentum*, no 51), Leiden: E. J. Brill, 1978, p. 79.

4. M. E. Boring, *Sayings of the Risen Jesus. Christian Prophecy in the Synoptic Tradition*, Cambridge: Cambridge University Press, 1982, p. 187.

5. Eta Linnemann, *Gleichnisse Jesu*, 6th edn., Göttingen: Vandenhoeck and Ruprecht, 1975, pp. 128, 133. She does regard some of the gospel parables as based on what Jesus had said.

6. Etienne Trocmé, *Jesus and his Contemporaries*, English translation (from the French original of 1972), London: SCM, 1973, p. 86.

INDEX OF NEW TESTAMENT REFERENCES

GENERAL INDEX

NT = the New Testament
OT = the Old Testament

Page numbers in brackets following references to notes indicate pages where an author is quoted (or his views alluded to) but not named. Thus Evans 195n3 (3) means that this author is alluded to on p. 3, where superscript 3 directs the reader to the note on p. 195 where Evans is named and details of his work are given.

Von Campenhausen, *See* Campenhausen, von

Walaskay, Paul W., 115
Wallace, Ronald S., 164, 166
Watson, Francis, 14–15, 20
Weiss, Johannes, 120–21
Wellhausen, Julius, 201n21
Wenham, John, 199n2
Werner, Martin, 152–53
White, as colour of heavenly apparel,
    28, 180
Wilckens, Ulrich, 23
Wilderness, theological significance of
    89, 94, 100
Wilson, S. G., 188–89
Wink, Walter, ix, 95
Winter, Paul, 21, 140, 144, 148
Wisdom, Jewish ideas of, 40
Witchcraft, evidence concerning, 34–35
Witt, R. E., 201n23
Wood, H. G., 147, 150

Zacharias, father of John the Baptist,
    64–66
Zechariah, book of, 90, 113, 128, 161
Zerubbabel, 73, 75, 77
Ziesler, John, 121–22
Zodiac (*See also* Astrology), 177,
    181–82

DATE DUE

AG _ 9 '94			
9/3/96			
OCT 13 '97			
JUN 0 4 1999			
9/12/99	WITHDRAWN		
DE 12 05			
AP 5 '06			